DEFOE: THE CRITICAL HERITAGE

THE CRITICAL HERITAGE SERIES

GENERAL EDITOR: B. C. SOUTHAM, M.A., B.LITT.(OXON.)

Formerly Department of English, Westfield College, University of London

For a list of books in the series see the back end paper

DEFOE

THE CRITICAL HERITAGE

Edited by
PAT ROGERS

Department of English,
King's College, University of London

ROUTLEDGE & KEGAN PAUL : LONDON AND BOSTON

First published 1972
by Routledge & Kegan Paul Ltd
Broadway House, 68–74 Carter Lane,
London EC4V 5EL and
9 Park Street,
Boston, Mass. 02108, U.S.A.

ISBN 0 7100 7259 7

Printed in Great Britain by
C. Tinling & Co. Ltd., London and Prescot

for Ian Watt

General Editor's Preface

The reception given to a writer by his contemporaries and near-contemporaries is evidence of considerable value to the student of literature. On one side we learn a great deal about the state of criticism at large and in particular about the development of critical attitudes towards a single writer; at the same time, through private comments in letters, journals or marginalia, we gain an insight upon the tastes and literary thought of individual readers of the period. Evidence of this kind helps us to understand the writer's historical situation, the nature of his immediate reading-public, and his response to these pressures.

The separate volumes in the *Critical Heritage Series* present a record of this early criticism. Clearly, for many of the highly productive and lengthily reviewed nineteenth- and twentieth-century writers, there exists an enormous body of material; and in these cases the volume editors have made a selection of the most important views, significant for their intrinsic critical worth or for their representative quality – perhaps even registering incomprehension!

For earlier writers, notably pre-eighteenth century, the materials are much scarcer and the historical period has been extended, sometimes far beyond the writer's lifetime, in order to show the inception and growth of critical views which were initially slow to appear.

In each volume the documents are headed by an Introduction, discussing the material assembled and relating the early stages of the author's reception to what we have come to identify as the critical tradition. The volumes will make available much material which would otherwise be difficult of access and it is hoped that the modern reader will be thereby helped towards an informed understanding of the ways in which literature has been read and judged.

B.C.S.

Contents

CONTENTS

CONTENTS

Preface

Defoe's reputation has described a strange trajectory, and the form of this book reflects that fact. The span of years covered is longer than is the case with most volumes in this series. After a number of bitter personal attacks in his lifetime, Defoe's name disappeared from serious criticism for three-quarters of a century. Hence the arrangement of materials in the text which follows. I have passed rapidly over the eighteenth century, not through any act of editorial judgment; the truth is that there is very little about which one could form an opinion, favourable or otherwise. It is not that Defoe's successors wrote badly about his art; they were not really aware that he was an artist.

Similarly, this collection makes unusually heavy demands on the biographers of Defoe. For reasons explained in the Introduction, men such as Chalmers, Wilson and Lee have played a leading part in the growing recognition of Defoe as a serious creative writer. With Pope or Swift, there was never much dispute about the main events or the major works. In the case of their contemporary Defoe, it was several generations before the first-order problems in biography and bibliography were sorted out. Apart from the contribution made by the lives themselves, these works provoked most of the interesting criticism between 1775 and 1875, the central period covered here. So this volume retains the impress of history, with its sudden flurries of activity after each new biography. But since the critical heritage has been spasmodic, it is only just that this record should follow the same erratic course.

Stock, Essex

Acknowledgments

I wish to express my thanks to the following for permission to reprint copyright material: Sir Basil Blackwell, and Blackwell & Mott Ltd, for No. 2 (a) and (b); Methuen & Co. Ltd for No. 14; the Clarendon Press, Oxford, for Nos 2(f) and 8; Chapman & Hall Ltd for No. 20; Professor T. M. Raysor for No. 13.

I have received great help in the preparation of this volume from my wife, Pauline Rogers. I am greatly indebted to her, not least on account of her superior skill as a photocopying engineer.

I am grateful to Mr David Foxon of Wadham College, Oxford, for his help in locating certain pamphlets listed in the Appendix.

Introduction

I

The shock of recognition is always painful; and it is a natural human impulse to postpone it as long as possible. So we find that major authors often have to wait a number of years before their talent is fully appreciated. But Defoe is surely unique in the delays he experienced before being permitted to arrive as a serious artist. It is not that he had to be rescued from total oblivion, as with Traherne: or even that, like Donne, he was to be raised from a minor cult of the few to an intimate favourite of the broad reading public. No: Defoe was already famous, and he was acknowledged all along to have written one extraordinary masterpiece. For well over a century, however, *Robinson Crusoe* was seen as a freakish *tour de force* – a single-shot triumph by a writer otherwise mediocre in achievement. There was Single-Novel Defoe, to go with Single-Poem Smart and Single-Speech Hamilton. He was not really an obscure figure, but his fame was scarcely that of a creative writer as such.

The process charted in this volume is the one by which Defoe's reputation, very gradually, was brought into some sort of relation with his practice as an imaginative artist. In his own lifetime, as we shall see, Defoe was chiefly regarded – understandably enough – as a polemicist and party writer. He first gained admission to the literary manuals on account of his rough and scabrous verse satires. His inclusion in *The Dunciad* seems to have occasioned little dismay at the time, and after his death there were few signs that the bulk of his work, in fiction or in other forms, would survive. His name was kept alive by quasi-biographic factors: his troubled life-history, his standing as a patriot, his connections with leading statesmen of his time. Throughout the eighteenth century, only a handful of his enormous range of books enjoyed any kind of esteem. Apart from *Crusoe*, there were *The Family Instructor*; the widely popular ghost story, *The Apparition of Mrs. Veal*; in some quarters, *The Complete English Tradesman*; and the *Tour thro' Great Britain*, which reached a ninth edition in 1779. Successive versions through the middle of the century, for some of which Samuel Richardson was responsible, left less and less of the original text of the *Tour*. But from the point of view of Defoe's reputation, it was of more importance that the 'gentleman' credited with the work was identified as Defoe on the title-page of the seventh (1769) and subsequent editions.

It is a commonplace that eighteenth-century criticism of fiction lagged badly behind other areas of literary discussion. At least, however, Fielding, Richardson and Smollett produced their works in a climate reasonably hospitable to the novel. The periodical reviews were already in business, and devoted considerable space to new fiction. But Defoe died in the year which saw the foundation of the *Gentleman's Magazine*. The only books reviewed in his lifetime were the solemn tomes abstracted in the *Journal des Scavans* and similar publications.[1] Even supposing, then, that contemporaries had been able to forget Defoe's contentious literary past, and had wanted to give serious attention to his novels, there really was no suitable outlet in the 1720s. Defoe had opened up new frontiers of writing, and like other pioneers he had to do without service stations along his route. Moreover, unlike Fielding, he betrayed little awareness of his own innovations. He set out no fictional aesthetic of his own. It is all too predictable, then, that when the art of the novel came to be taken seriously, it was too late as far as Defoe was concerned. With a completely new find – some nameless name lost to posterity – a rescue operation might have been mounted. But for Defoe, solid, comfortable, patriotic Defoe, so tidily placed and so familiar as a curiosity of literature – for him it was hopeless. It took all of a hundred and fifty years to reclaim him as a serious creative property.

It might seem from all this that the history of Defoe's reputation must be a gloomy affair to contemplate, a record of lost chances, critical ineptitude and biographic obsession. In fact the process is far less dispiriting than that, and it is one which should interest many others apart from the student of the history of taste. First, the blockages which precluded Defoe's recognition were intimately connected with the moral and artistic prejudices of the age. In the second place, the gradual reassessment of Defoe is all the more instructive because it was made against the grain. Nothing is more characteristic of this tendency (or of this collection) than Leslie Stephen's deeply typical embarrassment – Defoe ought not to be a good novelist, by all the agreed canons, and yet there is this mysterious power . . . The tortuous rationalisations to which a critic in this situation is driven provide the most eloquent testimony of an author's stature. The writer who disturbs the critic and blurs his categories is the one who will last: filing cards in disarray are a strong presumptive sign of high merit, for the lesser talent always submits meekly to having holes punched in the expected places. And third, of course, the earlier critics often surprise us with their insights, even when their general position seems to us primitive or unconsidered. They approach a book like *Roxana* from an angle so unlike our own that they are likely to see much we overlook.

Beyond all this, however, there is an overriding interest. Defoe was a culture hero even when few of his books were read and fewer still admired. He has always had a peculiar personal magnetism, and he did not need to enjoy critical respect to live in the public imagination. His books may have been seldom employed in the working out of a sophisticated rhetoric of fiction: but he still would not lie down. In a sense he was bigger than anything he had written: he figures in a mid-nineteenth-century work called *Eccentric Personages*, though in truth he was as middle-class, as normally sexed, as incompetent in business, as irresolutely ambitious, as any average suburbanite today. As far as personal habits go, alongside Swift he was the acme of orthodoxy. Yet somehow his impact has extended beyond the ordinary boundaries. *Robinson Crusoe* is perhaps the only great creative work to have served regularly as the basis of a pantomime. The British Museum has a copy of one early version, performed at Alexandra Theatre, Liverpool, as a Grand Comic Christmas Pantomime in 1878-9. There is something so Victorian in this, so redolent of Vincent Crummles and Mrs Jarley, that one can scarcely persuade oneself that the libretto derives from a Puritan journalist who had been familiar with William of Orange. The 'book' of this play was larded with *Serious Reflections* as a continuation volume. It is almost as if one had found out that *Peter Pan* was based on *Grace Abounding*. Not surprisingly, all this (there was an operatic drama made of *Crusoe*, too[2]) proved a massive distraction to the critics. They were still trying to cope with an author famous, if not for the wrong things, at least for extraneous reasons. It was only in the twentieth century that greater detachment became possible, so that the panto-mimic *kitsch* no longer got in the way of serious analysis of the novels. Up till then, in the period covered in this volume, we have a fascinating but rather confusing spectacle: that of criticism struggling to accommodate a writer of obvious power, yet alien in his background and assumptions, and disconcertingly basic in his methods. Defoe was intuitively felt to be a great novelist long before the equipment existed to show why he was one.

II

But even here we must pause. Defoe the great novelist is an invention of the nineteenth century. In his own day, as I have said, he was thought of as a controversialist. A scribbler with more talent than most, perhaps – as Pope allowed – but essentially not different in kind from the other pamphleteers and hacks of his time. The only things that markedly distinguished Defoe, to the contemporary gaze, were his fecundity and his talent for making enemies. It is true that if a polemicist does not have opponents he must invent them. All the same, Defoe is notable rather for the *quantity* of hostile material directed against him in his lifetime, than for any particular quality this material may possess. He was a popular target of newswriters and pamphleteers for thirty years; and this notoriety (however justified, or however contrived) was one of the most potent factors affecting Defoe's development as a writer.

There is an important consideration here. In recent times, the literary quarrel has tended to go out of fashion, in this country at least. And even when we have an occasional flurry of words – between H. G. Wells and Henry James, say – the interest of the affair is generally accidental, extrinsic, not *fully* literary. In the Augustan age it was different. The Pope-Curll battle was not something that went on outside literature: it was an artistic episode in its own right. *The Dunciad* is at once an object of art and an event: so that Pope could write, 'The life of a wit is a warfare upon earth'. And this means that Defoe's contests with Tutchin or Leslie are not mere advertisements for himself, as with Hemingway challenging Mr Tolstoi or Mailer taking on the mandarins. They are the stuff of his writing life – they reach into the tone and texture of everything he wrote. People today find it surprising that the best-known contemporary response to *Robinson Crusoe* took the form of a personal attack by a dunce, Charles Gildon (No. 3). I doubt if Defoe was surprised.

Another relevant issue here is the anonymity which, formally anyway, cloaked most of Defoe's works. He first became celebrated as 'the Author of the *True-born Englishman*'. At least half a dozen title-pages so designate him. But he was also 'the Author of the *Hymn to the Pillory*', 'the Author of the *Shortest Way with the Dissenters*', and other variants. Rarely was Defoe's own name attached to his works – and few of these among his better-known productions. Clearly there could be no Byronic cult of a man whose very identity was concealed, as far as the actual letterpress went: if there had been a cult of personality, it

4

was the bookseller alone who stood blazoned at the head of the work. Of course, men and women of the age usually had a shrewd idea of which books Defoe had written and which he hadn't. But they could not always be certain; and this fact lends an air of secrecy and almost subversion to Defoe's career. The bibliographical tangles which remain to this day, with their elaborate problems of attribution and publishing history, reflect an authentic piece of Augustan life, as creative artists knew it.

Evidently, then, Defoe could not have been a cult figure in his own day: could not have attained the role of writer as glamour-boy. Nevertheless, his popularity was very real. From the time of the *Essay upon Projects* (1697), he was known as a capable and successful man of letters. It was *The True-Born Englishman* (1701), running into ten editions within the year and selling, according to Defoe, 80,000 copies in pirated versions, which truly made his name.[3] *The Mock-Mourners* (1702) was scarcely less of a triumph, with seven editions in a few months.[4] Other successes were *Reformation of Manners* (1702), and *A New Test of the Church of England's Loyalty* (1702), which exists in several states. However, an even greater peak of fame arrived with *The Shortest Way with the Dissenters* (1702), which at once made Defoe into a fugitive from the law and into a national figure. It may be a dubious distinction to find oneself the subject of a Government proclamation: but for a writer to be posted up as 'Wanted' is a testimony he may reasonably value. Defoe was often in gaol; he got there, not by brawling and murdering (as did Richard Savage), but by committing words to paper which challenged and disturbed. Again, we see that his troubled history is not a thing apart from his literary career – it is all one and the same. Moreover, Defoe's public disgrace became the occasion for a startling bit of publicity, whereby *A Hymn to the Pillory* (1703) was sold in the streets as its author actually stood in the scaffold. In this work, the 'hi'roglyphick State machin' serves as a symbol of official repression. Defoe's controversial energies have assimilated the facts of his troubled life, and turned them into literature. The whole episode is an emblem of his writing career. Whether they knew it or not, the Secretary of State and the hated snooper 'Robin Hog', messenger of the press, were making a significant contribution to the process of reception. The critical heritage, for Defoe, begins with attempts at suppression. Censorship is only a mutant form of criticism.

The Shortest Way provoked a huge body of comment and reaction in print, too. So famous was Defoe by now that in April 1703 there appeared a pirate *Collection of the Writings of the Author of the True-Born English-Man*. Three months later, an authorised version appeared as *A True Collection*, containing twenty-two of Defoe's most popular tracts and poems. Two years later, a second volume was added. In the event these were to be the last attempts at a 'collected works' until Scott's time, though there were more or less disguised reprints in 1710, 1713 and 1721. One result of this, of course, is that the bulk of Defoe's work, including his fiction, never found its way into anything like a standard edition. His novels were once-for-all offerings to the public. They were never organised into an *œuvre*, as James reshaped his literary past with the New York edition. And even the *True Collection* was, literally, anonymous.

From 1704 Defoe's time was heavily occupied by his newspaper, at first weekly and then bi-weekly, called the *Review*. It lasted until 1713, was garnished with various supplements, attained a separate (though simultaneous) Edinburgh edition, and all in all prospered mightily. The circulation may not have been exceptionally high – it has been calculated from stamp-duty returns that in 1704 the sale was no more than 400 copies – but its currency was plainly greater than the audit figure reveals.[5] We know that a single copy would be read by many readers in a coffee-house: and there were many such places in the vicinity of the City, whose concerns are never far from the *Review*'s attention. Moreover, in an era when reading aloud was more common, particularly within the family, one can rarely be sure that one buyer is equivalent to one unit of audience reached. There is plenty of evidence from contemporary comment that the *Review* had a wide and continuous impact. It remains a surprisingly little-known side of Defoe's work, and one can only suppose that its bulk and general air of permanence have put off those who expect periodicals to be flimsy and ephemeral.

For the next portion of his life, Defoe was directly involved in politics. First he was Robert Harley's political informant, not to say spy; then he served the Lord Treasurer, Godolphin, in Scotland – this at the time of the Union; and then he acted as a kind of staff pamphleteer again for Harley, now Earl of Oxford and Prime Minister. In saying this I do not wish to imply that Defoe sacrificed his independence or sullied his honour, though he did leave a convenient handle for opponents who wanted to say as much. The point is simply that Defoe tended to write as a defender, rather than as a critic or subversive, as formerly. Boldly he defended Oxford even after the Minister's fall and the accession of George I. Moreover, Defoe was forced into a life of subterfuge which may have increased a tendency to double-bluff and what might be called over-irony (as with over-kill) in his writing. His secret service activity obliged him to correspond with his masters as Claude Guilot or Alexander Goldsmith; and this too may have had its repercussions. For a curious feature of his last period is an increasing fondness for pseudonyms, with 'Andrew Moreton' the special favourite. It is true that Defoe all along liked to pose as 'a Gentleman' or 'an Officer' or 'a converted Thief'. But it was only in his final decade that he regularly chose to write under a specific assumed name. Perhaps this can be connected with the deception by which Captain Carleton entered the realms of literary mythology, and that which provoked a series of Victorian students to seek out the original cavalier of the *Memoirs*. A good deal of recent criticism has fixed on the element of impersonation in Defoe's novels. It is not far-fetched to speculate that his preference for the seemingly autobiographic mode may go back to his experience as an undercover agent. More than most authors, Defoe had *lived*.

After the Hanoverian accession, he was at first an object of a good deal of suspicion, besides something of an invalid. Yet he contrived to gain employment by the Ministry, doctoring opposition journals: fifth-column work again. Even stranger, he happened on the side to invent the English novel. The first part of *Robinson Crusoe* appeared on 25 April 1719. It is now known that there were six – not, as once supposed, four – printings within four months, and that three printers were employed on later editions – clear evidence of a rapid sale. From the ledger of one of these printers, it emerges that a run of a thousand copies per edition is likely, a highish but not exceptional quantity.[6] The sale of the novel in this period, then, may not have been much more than 5,000; and bibliographers are inclined to accept on this basis the view of Ian Watt, that the novel was 'not, strictly speaking, a popular literary form'.[7] In any event, though, *Crusoe* was a definite commercial success, and an unquestioned event on the literary scene. Its relatively modest sale, by later standards, by no means indicates a muted response at the time.

Now Defoe began his remarkable series of creative works in the early 1720s. By this I mean not just the novels and imaginative documentaries, such as *A Journal of the Plague Year*, but also such books as the *Tour thro' Great Britain* and his criminal lives. We know less about the fortunes of these works, but the circumstantial evidence of piracy confirms the success of *Moll Flanders*. *Colonel Jack* had three editions within a year, and it is clear that the *Tour* did well, as it continued to do in one guise or another for sixty-odd years. The *General History of the Pirates* (1724–8) was another best-seller. However, it was treatises of practical advice or moral suasion which seem to have pleased most. *The Complete English Tradesman* went through a bewildering series of changes between 1725 and 1728. There can be little doubt that success, rather than failure, occasioned such tampering with the text. *Conjugal Lewdness*, surprisingly, had a less compulsive market, and was reissued with the title *A Treatise Concerning the Use and Abuse of the Marriage Bed*. Perhaps Defoe had miscalculated for once. Meanwhile, *The Family Instructor*, part i, had reached an eighth edition, and it was joined by *Religious Courtship* as a steady seller in the 1720s.

Defoe died in 1731. The story of his works thereafter, as far as the bare facts of publication go, is soon told. A handful of works continued to appear in print with great regularity: *Crusoe*, *Religious Courtship* and *The Family Instructor* at the head, with editions running well into double figures by the end of the century. *Moll Flanders* and *Roxana* came out from time to time, not always in a wholly recognisable guise. The *Tour* received the ministrations of Samuel Richardson and others, though it was not till 1769 that Defoe's name was associated with the production – an association by now growing ever more marginal. It is symptomatic that when the bookseller Lowndes bought one thirty-second share in the rights of the *Tour*, as he did in 1760, he had to pay five guineas. The price for one ninety-sixth share in 1772 was a guinea and a half. The total rights might be estimated at roughly £150. But Lowndes got one eighth share in *Roxana* and *Moll Flanders*, in 1770, for one guinea. He had thrown in the entire rights of *The Life of Prince Eugene* and *The Life of David Price*.[8] Such company did these books then keep.

Towards the end of the century, a wider range of works began to be reprinted. The *History of the Union* was brought out by George Chalmers, who also issued *Robinson Crusoe* with the *Farther Adventures* still intact for once. By this time, the spate of adaptations and abridgments of *Crusoe* had started – there are now sixteen columns of them in the British Museum catalogue. The book was on the way to becoming a children's classic; but Defoe as a writer for adults made slow progress. The Ballantyne edition of the novels and miscellaneous works, with the aid of Scott, was a major advance; but the truth is that biographies contributed more than the texts themselves at this period. Walter Wilson's life, in 1830, was a specially important event, and to it we owe much of the most interesting early Victorian comment, as will appear presently. The Talboys edition, long the most complete, came out in 1840. William Hazlitt jun. edited a three-volume *Works* in 1840–3, with a memoir largely pillaged from Wilson; whilst a collection for Bohn's British Classics proved somewhat abortive, seven volumes appearing from 1854 to 1867. *Crusoe* came out with great frequency, but the other novels only intermittently. Lee's *Life* in 1869 reprinted many of Defoe's journalistic offerings for the first time, whilst Henry Morley's *Life and Chief Earlier Works* (1889) is still the most convenient text for some items, including *The Consolidator*. George Saintsbury edited selections from the 'minor' novels in 1892, whilst the admirable G. A. Aitken produced a most serviceable edition of *Romances and Narratives* in sixteen volumes. The most important twentieth-century contribution has been the Shakespeare Head edition in 1927–8, though this was largely confined to the novels. Meanwhile the first collected edition in the proper sense is projected by the Southern Illinois University Press. It will reprint many of Defoe's works for the first time and – equally important – will provide a reliable critical edition for numerous others. With a writer so prolific as Defoe this is an invaluable service. The absence of such an aid has, beyond doubt, impeded understanding of Defoe, and made the history of his reputation less profitable than it could have been.

III

CONTEMPORARY CRITICISM: 1701 TO 1730

Defoe's contemporary reputation, as I have suggested, was largely determined by his controversial writings. It was works such as *The True-Born Englishman, The Shortest Way with the Dissenters* and *Jure Divino* which received most attention. Later on, just before and after the Hanoverian accession, his pamphlets on behalf of the chief minister, Harley, provoked almost as much hostile reaction. There was a late flurry occasioned by *Every-body's Business, is No-body's Business* (1725); but nothing ever quite erased the image of 'the true-born Huguenot', two-faced and unreliable, which was built up in the early years of the century. A large body of critical comment appeared in the periodical press, with such organs as Charles Leslie's *Rehearsal* and the *Observator* of John Tutchin (a man strangely like Defoe in background and temperament) keeping up a constant fire.

The range of criticism is very wide. Much of it seems to us purely 'personal' in character. For example, there are repeated allusions to Defoe's past: 'I think it had been better for him he kept to his Burning of *Bricks*, or Selling of *Stockings*, as the best way to keep him from dying in his Shoes,' writes one pamphleteer in 1703 (Appendix, no. 032). Commonly one finds mention of Defoe's bankruptcy, his spell in the pillory, his City connections and the like. So a critic of the *Shortest Way* writes, 'whether you seek for Mr *Fo* the *Hosier*, or Mr *Fo* the Preacher; 'tis all one' (Appendix, no. 036). The same writer alludes to '*Conventicle Foe*'. Two years earlier, another pamphleteer, probably William Pittis, used Defoe's troubled history to make a comment on his quality as a writer: 'he may more properly be stil'd a *Bankrupt*, than a Dealer in that sort of Commodity [Honesty]' (Appendix, no. 014). This pamphlet makes curious references to Defoe's flying 'from the *Scourges* of *Ireland*'; and a similar innuendo appears elsewhere (Appendix, no. 015):

> I fear that in his Time it was his lot,
> Over *Hibernian* Bogs on Foot to trot.

Such thrusts appear of dubious relevance. However, the brushes with authority that brought Defoe into gaol and the pillory were fair game – by the polemical conventions of the day, at least. Hence references to Defoe as a '*Newgate Saint*' and to his courtroom experiences (Appendix, no. 031); to the 'Wooden Ruff' fitted for his neck (Appendix, no. 065); to the 'rotten Eggs like *March* Hail' showering on his person in the pillory (Appendix, no. 033); and to a likely fate in store for Defoe (Appendix, no. 0310):

> The Manner of Death your Case wont alter,
> Be it on your *Bed* or in a *Halter*.

'*De Foe* hath little Credit to lose,' observes a Scottish critic (Appendix, no. 091); and there were even stories suggesting Defoe had been guilty of petty deceits such as horse-stealing (Appendix, no. 111). Occasionally the abuse is still more unfocused, with Defoe portrayed as 'a loathsome Thing, shap'd like a Toad' (Appendix, no. 0110). At its lowest this becomes mere character-assassination: 'He is a Man of great Rashness and Imprudence, a mean mercenary Prostitute, a State Mountebank, an Hackney Tool, a scandalous Pen, a foul Mouthed Mongrel, an Author who writes for Bread, and lives by Defamation, &c.' (quoted in Appendix, no. 081). This of course was the common coinage of pamphlet battles at this time; and it was an idiom Defoe himself had learnt to employ when there was need.

However, there was not a complete dearth of literary comment as such. The most frequent criticism was that of wordiness. This is strange, in view of Defoe's modern reputation for writing in a terse and taut fashion. But his opponents found in his work 'a Heap of Words to no Purpose' (Appendix, no. 018), a 'Fardle of Falsities' and an 'indigested Heap of malicious Suggestions' (Appendix, no. 013), 'a Bundle of Tautology, and a Heap of Thoughts not rightly digested' (Appendix, no. 022). Later pamphleteers alluded to 'a heap of Words without Ideas' (Appendix, no. 148) and 'a confus'd heap of Words' (Appendix, no. 146) – see also No. 1g. This criticism was often linked to another, namely Defoe's lack of skill in framing an argument. 'If Mr. *D.F.* shal give a Reply to this Paper,' observes one author (Appendix, no. 072), 'the only Favour I desire of him, is to go first to the University, and learn the Art of clos Reasoning: for I must sincerely declare ... he overmatcheth all Men I ever knew (*excepting* S[ir] R[oger] L['Estrange]) in running down solid Argument with a Croud of Words that are nothing to the purpose.' His forte was 'Words without Arguments' (Appendix, no. 116). On other occasions Defoe is rebuked for his tendency to 'hyperbolize in ... Romantick Commendations' (Appendix, no. 091); and, unjustly as it happened, for plagiarism (Appendix, no. 052). This latter pamphlet has a nice line in broad invective, with references to 'the most unserene Daniel Foe ... Clergy-Flogger in Ordinary to his Highness Prince of Darkness.' More common is the charge of ignorance, as in Joseph Browne's contemptuous remark, 'it wou'd be more difficult to teach him to be a Critick, or to understand how to write correctly' (Appendix, no. 057). It is a regular strategy to align Defoe with forgotten scribblers such as Tutchin and Stephens (Appendix, no. 041); and also to accuse 'this mean mercenary prostitute' (Appendix, no. 053) of excelling only in detraction (Appendix, no. 0110). A favourite epithet is 'amphibious', and this easily shades into the comment that '*De Foe* is very vacillant and often changes sides' (Appendix, no. 072). Defoe is branded as a scandalmonger and a purveyor of 'indecent Language' (Appendix, no. 043).

Of course, much of this heat was generated by extraneous factors. The flaws are discovered because of political spite in the first instance. We are much nearer the nub of things when we find it stated that Defoe wrote *The Shortest Way* 'on purpose to set the Nation in a Flame, and to engage us in an intestine War, that the *French* King may have an opportunity to force the Pretender upon us' (Appendix, no. 034: see No. 1b); or when it is contended that 'the *Design* of his *Writing* is levell'd at the *Establish'd Church*,' or that Defoe 'runs his Reader infallibly into *Commonwealth Systems*' (Appendix, no. 051). Nevertheless, it is still the case that the actual terms of the criticism are often stylistic or structural; Defoe simply was not considered a particularly good writer by many of his contemporaries. The excerpts selected in No. 1 are representative from this point of view, as from others. It was the habit of controversialists to play to their opponents' weaknesses: and clearly there was a widespread view that Defoe's literary competence was distinctly open to attack.

The best-known of the contemporary onslaughts was that of Charles Gildon, following the publication of *Robinson Crusoe* (No. 3). It should be apparent from what has been said that Gildon was merely projecting into the fictional realm the techniques and idiom forged in earlier controversy. (It is perfectly possible that Gildon had himself contributed to these disputes, since he was himself in trouble over political journalism in 1705.) Through the 1720s there was a continuous buzz of hostile comment maintained – John Oldmixon sneered at *Crusoe* in two critical books published in 1728.[9] However, it was the viewpoint of the Scriblerian party which came to dominate at the end of Defoe's life (No. 2), with *Peri Bathous* and *The Dunciad* soon followed by *An Author to be Lett* and the sneers of the *Grub-street Journal*. The mild commendations of Giles Jacob (No. 4) counted for still less in that Jacob himself figured as a prominent Dunce. Meanwhile, a more favourable judgment was expressed by Benjamin Franklin, in the *New-England Courant*, 13 August 1722. Later, in his autobiography, Franklin acknowledged the profound influence on his mind left by the *Essay upon Projects*.[10] This is one of the few concrete indications that Defoe was as congenial to the colonial mentality as one would have supposed.

1731 TO 1780

It is normal for a writer to suffer some loss of esteem in the years following his death. But Defoe practically disappeared from the literary map. For half a century the bulk of his work became a *terra incognita*, in which fanciful conjectures could be supplied like the fabulous creatures filling the blanks of early maps. The most famous allusion to Defoe continued to be that in *The Dunciad*, retained in all versions of the poem up to Pope's death. For the rest, though *Crusoe* and the domestic manuals must have retained a wide hold on the public taste, their appeal was subterranean: Defoe's name hardly ever comes up in serious literary discourse in the 1730s and 1740s. The *Tour* went through several editions, garnished with Samuel Richardson's 'improvements', but the identity neither of the original author nor of the reviser was known at this stage. This state of affairs went on undisturbed past the middle of the century. The interest of Defoe's political and historical writings was thought to have ebbed with their topicality. The 'secondary' novels were occasionally reprinted, but under rather shabby auspices – they belonged to a *demi-monde* of the world of letters, little frequented by polite readers. Defoe figures in Cibber's *Lives* as a poet (No. 5), but he was not thought worthy of inclusion in the first edition of *Biographia Britannica* (1747–66).[11]

One development which came too late to help Defoe was the rise of the literary review – 'the beginning of a new tribunal or literary Star Chamber,' as Leslie Stephen puts it, when 'the professional critic has appeared who will make it his regular business to give an account of all new books.'[12] Defoe could neither benefit nor suffer from this new 'tribunal', as did all writers from Richardson and Fielding on. Nor was his name often invoked as a comparison when the increasingly popular novel form came under discussion. His subjects must have seemed *outré* to the sentimentalists, whilst his treatment was felt to be pedestrian by a generation taught by Fielding to approach the 'romance' with a high degree of expectation and self-consciousness.

Nor did the next considerable novelist, Tobias Smollett, mend matters. His widely circulated *History of England* (1757–8), continuing Hume's work, curtly alluded to 'the production of one Daniel de Foe, a scurrilous party-writer in very little estimation' – this of the *History of the Kentish Petition*, scarcely Defoe's most representative work. But at least Smollett admitted Defoe to the ranks of 'the most remarkable political writers' of his age, along with Swift, Steele, Addison, Bolingbroke and others less conspicuous. This is in contrast to Goldsmith, whose own *History of England* (1764) manages to discuss the leading authors of the early eighteenth century without citing Defoe – although Rowe, Garth, Parnell and others do figure. Since this work had immense popularity – there were twenty-five English editions by 1823 – the omission of Defoe's name must have played its part in his slow acceptance as a creative talent of the first order. A better-known book still was the European best-seller, *The Vicar of Wakefield* (1766). In this there was a glancing allusion to Crusoe's long-boat (ch. XVI), which showed that the myth was alive even if its progenitor was forgotten. The creation survived, the agent was lost from view. More interesting is Olivia's comment to her father (ch. VII): 'I have read a great deal of controversy. I have read the controversy between Thwackum and Square; the controversy between Robinson Crusoe and Friday the savage, and I am now employed in reading the controversy in *Religious Courtship.*' The Vicar's reaction is to instruct his daughter to 'go help [her] mother to make the gooseberry-pye'; despite this flippant rejoinder, it is something to find Fielding and Defoe implicitly aligned, which the formal criticism of the day would not have attempted to do.

Rousseau's standing in England was such that his support (No. 6) may have been counter-productive; and Johnson's warm commendations of Defoe (No. 8) were not known until Boswell and Mrs Thrale published their recollections some time later. The eighth edition of the *Tour* (1778) was greeted in the *Monthly* mainly on account of its 'additions and improvements',[13] and up to this time there were few signs that official taste, as represented by the journals, had come to a healthier appreciation of Defoe's claims as an imaginative writer.

1780 TO 1830

It was this period which, after a slow start, witnessed the gradual acceptance of Defoe as a major literary figure. It is true that, until Lamb, there was little interest in the novels other than *Robinson Crusoe*. But at least we find an increasing willingness to accord Defoe respect for reasons apart from his patriotism, his Protestantism or his personal fortitude – though inevitably these things retain some hold in most accounts of Defoe. By 1830, even if much work remained to be done, there were the beginnings of a valid artistic appreciation.

In the 1780s the most interesting references continue to appear in the journals, notably the *Gentleman's Magazine* and the *Monthly Review*. Reprints of *Memoirs of a Cavalier* and the *Tour* occasioned favourable, if not especially penetrating, comment (No. 7b, c). It is a sign of the widespread ignorance still prevailing that a writer could be so tentative as to say, 'I think *Robinson Crusoe* is allowed to have been the work of Defoe – but I know . . . no[t] what other books he wrote' (No. 7d). Conjectures were often wild; the story that Robert Harley, first Earl of Oxford, was the true author of *Crusoe* (a tenacious myth) cropped up in the *Gentleman's Magazine* 1788. Again, a writer in the same organ next year remarked that the *Tour* was originally written 'I have heard say in his *closet*'. The rider was added that the book 'may claim the assistance of the admirers of that very ingenious author [Defoe]'.

How wide this circle of admirers was, it is hard to be sure. George Chalmers's repeated efforts to bring Defoe before the public testify to his own missionary zeal, rather than an existing demand. However, it seems likely that Chalmers's biography (No. 11), his editions of *Crusoe* and *The History of the Union*, and his general advocacy did much to revivify Defoe for the educated reader. His services as a bibliographer were of high value in making possible for the first time intelligent appreciation of the sweep of Defoe's writing. Moreover, as was often the case then, his biography was the direct begetter of whatever periodical criticism found its way into print. Generally the results are unimpressive: witness a two-part article in the *Universal Magazine of Knowledge and Pleasure* 1793. These 'Memoirs of the Life and Writings of DANIEL DE FOE', garnished as they are 'with a fine Portrait of that celebrated Author', represent an unashamed crib from Chalmers. Long passages are quoted verbatim; and few independent judgments are ventured. As significant as anything, perhaps, is the fact that the article is divided about the year 1706 – Defoe's earlier career continuing to arrogate a prominence which the twentieth century rarely chooses to accord it. The essay is one of naked popularisation; and the best one can say is that Defoe had now reached a stage where he was considered worth exploiting. For the rest, Chalmers's work occasioned a thoughtful review by John Noorthouck (No. 7g), although Defoe emerges a little sentimentally from this notice.

Otherwise the most important contributions in this decade are those of Beattie and Blair (Nos 9, 10). The difference here is that both critics try to assimilate Defoe to a wider tradition of the novel (or more strictly, the romance). They are not afraid to cite parallels, French as well as English; and they each see *Crusoe* as an individual and innovative book which can yet be fitted into an overall pattern of historical development. This was a significant step forward. It meant that Defoe's best-known work could still be regarded as unique, *sui generis*, without any deprecating implication that it was merely an unaccountable sport. From this time on, it became easier to put *Crusoe* into some sort of perspective, as a *tour de force* certainly, but one not absolutely beyond the power of criticism to analyse or categorise. Beattie, in particular, deserves well of students because of his useful alignment of the book with contemporary works such as *Gulliver* and *John Bull*.

As time went on, the comparison with Swift became something of a commonplace. The best known instance is probably afforded by Scott (see headnote to No. 12), but there were other examples. The earliest among these was John Dunlop, in his *History of Fiction* (1814). Shortly afterwards William Monck Mason, in his *History* of St Patrick's Cathedral, developed the comparison to the advantage of Swift. According to Mason, 'the events related by Defoe were mere ordinary occurrences,' as opposed to the fantastic experiences of Gulliver – consequently, to achieve verisimilitude was a simpler matter for Defoe.[14] It is a dubious argument; and it required the unproved assumption that the two writers were striving for the same *kind* of realism anyway. Like most nineteenth-century critics, Mason was loath to concede any function beyond that of straight reportage to Defoe's narration.

In the first decade of the century, there is nothing more stimulating than a minor set-to in the *Gentleman's Magazine* 1809–10 regarding the 'authenticity' of *A Journal of the Plague Year*. A contributor signing himself 'Londoniensis' had expressed surprise that a writer should have referred to the *Journal* as a 'genuine piece of history'. More in anger than in sorrow, seemingly, E. W. Brayley leapt into the fray: 'for despite of his unqualified assertion of its being *"well known* that De Foe's History is as much a *work of imagination as his Robinson Crusoe*, except as to the circumstance of there having been a plague in the year 1665"; I must take the liberty of stating my conviction that all portions respecting that fatal calamity . . . are both *essentially* and *literally* true.' Of course, Brayley had some right on his side, but his uncritical warmth leads him into overstatement. These were matters that were not to be fully explored till Watson Nicholson brought out his book on the *Historical Sources of Defoe's Journal of the Plague Year* (1919): and even then the precise imaginative status of the work was hardly settled.

The *Journal* continued to excite interest. A few years later, one Professor John Wilson, now among the illustrious obscure, brought out a poem famous in its day, entitled *City of the Plague*. This was noticed in the *Edinburgh Review* 1816. The praise allotted to Defoe may look to be only a token compliment, but it is less hedged about with qualification than the commendations thirty years earlier: 'Most of our readers are probably familiar with De Foe's history of that great calamity – a work in which fabulous incidents and circumstances are combined with authentic narratives, with an art and verisimilitude which no other writer has ever been able to communicate to fiction.'[15] The area of Defoe's supremacy is carefully restricted: but within that area his prime position is by now almost unchallenged.

However, it was the major Romantic critics who, towards the end of this period, established a whole new basis of assessment. I exclude here Wordsworth, for his contribution (No. 19) was made later and was not known for many years. We may omit De Quincey, too, in so far as his remarks occur in passing, and date from 1841. However, it might be added that De Quincey was exposed to Defoe around 1803. He reports in his autobiography a dispute with his uncle, just before he went up to Oxford, concerning the merits of *Memoirs of a Cavalier*. The young man felt that this gave 'in some places an unfair, and everywhere a most superficial account' of the Civil Wars. So far as I can judge he never retracted this opinion. However, a more positive notice prevails in the observations of his contemporaries, Scott, Coleridge, Lamb and Hazlitt.

Walter Scott had two great advantages as a critic of Defoe. First, he knew the eighteenth century well, not just from an antiquarian standpoint, but in his very bones. Second, he was not a member of the English upper classes; to be Scottish was to be removed from certain unquestioned assumptions and sympathies. As time went on, he acquired a third, uncovenanted advantage. His own money troubles must have equipped him to understand Defoe's lifelong preoccupation with personal and financial security. However, that factor had barely supervened when he committed to print his views on Defoe (No. 12). As always, Scott reveals himself a perceptive, shrewd and observant critic. His comments on Defoe's use of coincidence, of the supernatural, and of deliberately plain language, are all strikingly original as well as forceful. Again, Scott was the first critic to consider the *nature* of Defoe's literary impersonations, as opposed to the mere identity assumed. He makes another departure in attending with such care to the plot of *Robinson Crusoe*; no one previously had noted such characteristic features of Defoe's narrative method as the summary dismissal of Xury from the book (see p. 76). All in all, Scott may be seen as the first critic sufficiently literal-minded and sufficiently alive to technical matters to be able to cope with Defoe.

Coleridge's observations (No. 13) are also detailed, and they happen to have become more famous. Indeed, the most celebrated juncture in the story of Defoe's reputation is that recorded on p. 82, when Coleridge greets Defoe across the years as a writer of Shakespearian grandeur and simplicity. Unfortunately, as we now know, the crucial semicolon was really a comma in the early edition.[16] But if this is something of a mare's-nest, so trivial a consideration cannot wipe away Coleridge's authentic and deeply sensitive response to *Crusoe*. His recognition that 'our imagination is kept in full play, excited to the highest, yet all the while we are touching or touched by a common flesh and blood' is a healthy corrective, after the dreary series of 'realist' accounts of Defoe. Moreover, Coleridge's willingness to give Defoe the credit for the effects he achieved – to see in him a conscious, almost classical artist, judging, selecting, arranging emphasis and shifting balance – this was a completely new way of approaching the novel. Coleridge is the greatest critic represented in the body of this volume; and even his marginalia show him to be such.

Hazlitt's contribution (No. 17) is a little disappointing. This may be a result of its occasion, a notice of Wilson's biography. Certainly Hazlitt seems obsessed to a surprising degree by non-literary considerations; and even when he turns to the novels, in the passage quoted in the text, he cannot leave alone the supposed paradox of 'moral' author, 'immoral' writings. It is not that the essay is wholly misguided, still less dull; but by Hazlitt's standards it wears a rather puzzleheaded, dutiful appearance. Defoe's qualities as a writer were evidently not those which would call out Hazlitt's greatest gifts as a critic – his zest and his love of colour; his admiration for spirit and energy; his sane and generous humanity. Hard as he tries, Hazlitt cannot get at the centre of Defoe's art, or quite locate a magic he obscurely knows is there. With Lamb (No. 14) it is different. His contribution, short as it is, had an immense influence on English taste. Many of the Victorians came to look on the young Colonel Jack through Lamb's eyes, as a Dickensian waif; and a number of subsequent writers echo his comments on Defoe's power to evoke solitude. By present-day standards Lamb may appear gushing, if not fulsome. But he was the first critic to make a serious claim for books such as *Captain Singleton*, and indeed the first to appreciate the link between *Crusoe* and the other novels, as they treat of endurance and survival in a hostile environment. No doubt Defoe would have come into his own, sooner or later. But it was the heartfelt advocacy of men such as Lamb which speeded the process. By this generation, Defoe was sometimes seen as a Romantic born before his time. He was enlisted as an ally against restrictive and cerebral classicism; as a spontaneous chronicler of the human heart; as a champion of liberty and as one oppressed by an authoritarian society. These claims were often dubious – as Ian Watt says, Defoe is 'surely the most unromantic of writers'[17] – but that is unimportant beside their genuine effect of liberating opinion and articulating first-hand response. From now on Defoe was acceptable, if not always accepted.

1830 TO 1880

The *Memoirs* of Defoe brought out by Walter Wilson in 1830, in three copious volumes, mark an important stage in the critical reception (No. 16). This is not altogether a matter of the merit in Wilson's book, informative as it is. What this biography did was to bring Defoe into the mainstream of intellectual discussion. Hazlitt's review has already been mentioned, and there were many others in 1830–1. Wilson had written with the confessed aim of rehabilitating Defoe, not just as a writer but as an Englishman. By this he meant 'Protestant' as well as patriot. His work is diffuse largely because he can never resist describing at length the religious controversies of the day, with a marked bias against the High Church party. Wilson did in fact uncover a wide range of new findings concerning Defoe, but this was overlaid in the contemporary mind by his doctrinal position.

This is most evident in the notice by the *British Critic and Quarterly Theological Review* 1830 (No. 18). Both Wilson and Defoe himself are taken to task for their theological aberrations; and the triumph of *Crusoe* is seen as even more inexplicable than usual, coming from such a hopeless backslider as Defoe. Defoe's pamphleteering enemy, Charles Leslie, is described as 'a name never to be mentioned without honour by any true son of the Church of England' – an assessment which seems to rank deist-hunting higher than literary skill. In the same year a more intelligent notice appeared in the *Westminster Review*. This has been attributed to William Hazlitt the younger, but since he was still in his teens at this time the ascription is highly implausible.[18] Like most reviewers, the *Westminster's* critic thought less highly of the 'secondary' novels than did Wilson. None the less, he acknowledged Defoe's skill in characterisation and even a touch of 'sublimity' in *Robinson Crusoe*. The analysis throughout displays more careful and judicious reading than Defoe had generally received up to this time.

In the early Victorian period there were few important discussions of any substance. Dickens's friend, John Forster, provided one exception to this statement, in the form of an essay in the *Edinburgh Review* 1845, later reprinted separately (No. 22). For the most part, however, this is a phase chiefly notable for tributes in a casual vein. 'Casual' is perhaps not the right word for Landor's stately verses (No. 20), which seem designed for an imaginary epitaph. But they are occasional work; and in this respect they can be aligned with the tributes of Wordsworth (No. 19), De Quincey (No. 21) – more astringent than most – and

Borrow (No. 23). Most of these writers conceive of Defoe as a nursery classic, and though they give *Crusoe* unstinted praise there is to modern eyes some condescension in their approach. This applies even to Ruskin's well-known description of his reading *Crusoe* and the *Pilgrim's Progress* on Sundays as a child, 'my mother having it deeply in her heart to make an evangelical clergyman of me.' In the end, says Ruskin, he 'got all the noble imaginative teaching of Defoe and Bunyan,' without following the course prescribed for him.[19]

Meanwhile the pace of appreciation (if one can call it that) quickened perceptibly after the middle of the century. In 1851 the *Eclectic Review* was still at the point of reviewing Wilson's life. This it did sensibly enough for the most part, stressing the endearing qualities of *Crusoe* along with its absence of style. Indicative of the changing climate is the remark, 'He was hated, and persecuted, and wronged in every way by his contemporaries; but posterity have [*sic*] done him justice, and there are few hearts now that refuse respect, if not reverence, to his name.' Less temperate, if more individual, was a strange biography put together by a Yorkshireman called William Chadwick in 1859. Defoe is seen as a champion of free trade amongst other things, and annexed to every Victorian cause that occurs to the writer. He is called 'this poor neglected genius', 'both good and great', 'not only statesman but philanthropist'. Defoe's burial place is 'that sacred spot of departed patriotism'. Like most of the early biographers, Chadwick spends an inordinate time on the first decade of the eighteenth century – it takes 430 pages to reach 1714, only thirty more to dispatch the years of Defoe's major achievement. As a writer Chadwick has his engaging moments ('I have been a tile-maker myself, and about as successful as De Foe'), and he is full-blooded if nothing else: 'Bravo! De Foe! Never had Britain a subject more devoted, more loyal, and more religiously thankful for the glorious revolution of 1688 than thee. It was a moment after thine own heart, Daniel!'[20] All the same, it is a work more revealing as a sign of the times than valuable for serious criticism. Its purpose is to congratulate Defoe on having anticipated Victorianism in so many directions.

The same sentiments are apparent in Mark Pattison's comment, published in *Fraser's Magazine* 1860, to the effect that Defoe was 'in many things before his age'. Similarly the *Dublin University Magazine* 1856 found that Defoe's 'moral constitution, like his wit, was beyond his era' (No. 25). Characteristic of this phase in taste, though it actually dates from 1869 and draws on Lee's biography of that year, is an essay called 'A Gentleman of the Press'. This came out in Dickens's journal *All the Year Round*, and it follows the usual intimate, simple, homely style of the magazine. Defoe 'may be described as a brave, simple, honest, industrious, far-seeing man of genius, of the noble souls . . . who have helped to build up the liberties c. England.' He 'sinned a little, but suffered much, and left behind him a name as a statesman, a patriot, a philosopher, and a novelist, that shall last as long as the English language.' If only, one is meant to feel, he had not fallen on the dusty soil of Augustanism. Incidentally, Dickens himself thought relatively ill of Defoe, though he did express in an early letter to Forster a high admiration of *The Political History of the Devil*, a book thought by some to have influenced *Oliver Twist* – which Dickens was then composing.[21]

By this time Defoe criticism may be said to have come of age. The crucial juncture was the appearance of an essay in the *National Review* 1856 (No. 24). There are reasons for believing that the author may have been Walter Bagehot. Whether or not that is so, the article remains as good a short study of the novelist as can be found. For the first time the mechanics of Defoe's art are fully explored; the distinctive feel and atmosphere of his books are evoked; and the characteristics of his imaginative world are presented with cogency and force. The *National Review* essay set a standard to which few nineteenth-century critics aspired; and it can still provoke and challenge a student of Defoe. At such moments the history of the 'critical heritage' spills over into live and urgent issues – a process which volumes like the present one can usefully forward.

After 1860 came something of a deluge. Disregarding the interesting but exotic (literally and culturally) pieces by Taine and Marx (Nos 26, 27), a series of remarkable studies began to appear in England. Leslie Stephen's essay (No. 28) was for long the best-known single account of Defoe, and traces of its influence are still not unknown in under-graduate examination papers. Adroit and skilfully managed as its argument is, one may feel that Stephen was not altogether in sympathy with his subject, and that his comments do not get so close to the heart of the matter as the *National* critic's. However, Stephen did much to bring public attention to Defoe. So, in another way, did William Lee, whose *Life and Recently Discovered Writings* came out a year later. In fact only the first volume is Lee's own work; the second and third contain excerpts from Defoe's periodical writings, attributed a little recklessly on occasion. Lee continued the process set in motion by

Chalmers, and took the score of Defoe items up to 250. His critical comments, as represented here (No. 29), are workmanlike and sometimes perceptive. Once again, a spurt in activity followed the publication of a major biography. One of Lee's main findings had concerned the part played by Defoe in Mist's *Weekly Journal* and his alleged employment as a sort of ministerial counter-censor and double agent. This led to a veritable crisis of conscience among the critics, tough- and tender-minded alike. The episode looms large in subsequent notices, among them those in *Blackwood's* 1869, *British Quarterly Review* 1869, *Edinburgh Review* 1870 and *Cornhill Magazine* 1871 (Nos 30–3).

For this or other reasons, Defoe passed the peak of his renown by the 1870s. The reservations implicit in some comments on Lee ('Mr Lee discovered Defoe's guilt, he condoned it'[22]) were expressed more widely as the decade proceeded. In some sense, then, William Minto's volume for the English Men of Letters series (No. 34) marked a turning point on its appearance in 1879. The more extreme claims for Defoe were by now rejected – they had been tied up with hostility to 'Augustan' culture and to various political or religious issues. On the other hand, there was no danger that Defoe's reputation would be allowed to fall to the low level current in 1800. Minto had to mediate between these over- and under-estimates, and this he performed with excellent judgment. Finally, his assessment of Defoe's merit is a little lower than that of (say) the *National Review* twenty years earlier. But he is alive to Defoe's skills, and contributes an especially telling paragraph on *Crusoe*: 'Whatever it was that made the germ idea . . . take root in Defoe's mind, he worked it out as an artist.' Equally valuable is his demonstration that the 'episodic' nature of the book is functional and effective, rather than clumsy and inartistic. Minto makes a fitting conclusion to this volume; his book provides a convenient summary of the state of criticism after something like a hundred years of serious attention to Defoe.

The remaining twenty years of the century call for little comment. Defoe's star was in the descendant, if anything, and though he had his champions (notably R. L. Stevenson, a great admirer of *Colonel Jack* amongst other books[23]) he was not likely to benefit from the Aesthetic Movement.

THE RECEPTION ABROAD

Defoe's influence abroad was confined to a single aspect of his work; but in that area it was immense. Only *Crusoe* made any sort of impact in Europe, yet this novel by itself attracted a huge body of imitation and outright plagiarism. Defoe had, arguably, founded the English novel. Posthumously he inspired an entire sub-branch of continental literature. This was the *Robinsonade* (the form both in French and German). Basically the genre is distinguished by its use of the desert-island setting, although other forms of solitary voyage are sometimes admitted. The flood began almost straight away: '*Robinson Crusoe* was hardly allowed to dry before it was imitated ... [throughout Europe] writers of fiction ... soon tried to deflect some of its popularity toward their own writings.'[24] Ulrich was able to list the following items (up to 1895): 196 English editions (this includes abridgments); 110 translations; 115 revisions; and 277 imitations. Of this latter group some of the better-known were English: these include Peter Longue-ville's *The Hermit*, also called after its hero *Quall* (1727), and Robert Paltock's *Peter Wilkins* (1751), a work popular well into the nineteenth century. But the vogue was principally a continental one. Among the imitations, that by Joachim Hendrick Campe achieved the greatest success. *Robinson der Jüngere*, first published in Hamburg in 1779–80, had run into 117 editions by 1894. The chief departure lay in the fact that the hero was shipwrecked with no utensils of any kind to assist him. Campe's book, like Paltock's, is a work of some independent interest. But the majority of their competitors were undistinguished, and they carried over little of Defoe's attributes apart from the basic concern with isolation. The truth is that the *Robinsonade* is a genre beloved of antiquarians rather than literary students as such. It belongs to the world of scholarly curios, not the living history of the novel.

However, there is abundant evidence to justify Kippenberg's phrase, 'Defoes allbekanntes Werk', said to have exerted 'as extraordinary an influence on world literature as any book, either before or since'. Signs of this influence appear in the very titles, from *Der französische Robinson* (and so with every other nationality) in the 1720s to La Bédollière's *Dernier Robinson* (1860) and Montgomery Gibbs's *Six Hundred Robinson Crusoes* (1877). Moreover, the name was often applied to very different works for purely commercial reasons. Le Sage's *Gil Blas* became, amazingly, *Der spanische Robinson* (1726), which is no more appropriate than calling *Guy Mannering*, say, the Scottish *Gulliver*. Even Fenimore Cooper's *Crater* (1847) was turned into *Le Robinson Americain* (1851–4). Clearly the label had long ceased to convey anything precise.

Meanwhile more respectable translations continued to pour out. Ulrich lists 49 French versions, beginning in 1720; 21 German (1720 onwards); 5 Dutch (1720–2); as well as Italian, Swedish, Hebrew, Armenian, Danish, Turkish, Hungarian, Bengali, Polish, Arabic, Estonian, Maltese, Coptic, Welsh, Persian and other translations. The strangest of all, perhaps, is a *Robinson Crusoe* in Ancient Greek (1840). This may be the place to mention another deathless title, Mary Godolphin's *Robinson Crusoe in Words of one Syllable* (1867). More resistant than most countries was Spain, where the first translation I have found listed dates from 1836. All this, of course, in addition to a variety of more or less rational abridgments. Sometimes the link is disguised a little, as in the *Voyage de Robertson aux Terres australes* (1866). Such was the curious fate of Defoe's masterpiece. Flattering as such a weight of imitation is to the novelist's memory, it cannot be altogether an adequate compensation for the lack of serious critical discussion or of adult response to the full range of the *œuvre*.

The earliest sustained consideration of Defoe to be found in any foreign source is that of Philarete Chasles, in *Revue de Paris* 1833. This is a two-part biographic study, mostly derived from Chalmers and Wilson; it portrays Defoe as loyalist and martyr. 'Yes, the author of *Robinson Crusoe*, your childhood friend, creator of this novel, more historic than history, and as well known as the Bible – was in the pillory!' And later: 'He died without glory, after having done more for the progress of humanity than Rousseau or Locke, as it would be easy to prove.' Defoe's bankruptcy is likewise seen as incurred 'without guilt, without bad faith, perhaps even without imprudence!' Defoe was simply duped by crooked associates. These are views modern research would scarcely support; but they are the kind of whitewashing operations that were necessary in Defoe's case before objective assessment of his art was possible. As for the novels, Chasles asserts that their character is to be un-novelistic ('*pas romanesques*'). This is in line with contemporary British criticism. Defoe's 'natural', artless manner of writing is set against the artificiality of other eighteenth-century writers. A similar emphasis is found in Taine (No. 26); Defoe's imagination is 'not [that] of an artist'.

As Wilson had obviously set Chasles to work, so William Lee was to inspire an article in *Revue des deux Mondes* 1870. This was 'Un publiciste du dix-huitième siècle', by H. Blerzy. The poems are taken more seriously than usual; there are some useful observations on the place of criminal biography in Defoe's work; and both the *Review* and *Captain Singleton* are accorded sympathetic treatment. The essay is sensible and lucid, though without any particular literary insight. It indicates that in France as in this country a better-balanced view of Defoe's achievement was now attainable: but the triumphs of French 'realistic' fiction had apparently not yet opened the way to a worthwhile exploration of his artistry.[25]

In the twentieth century, as one would expect, Defoe has received greater benefit from the alignments that can be made between his work and those of the nineteenth-century naturalists. His recent admirers have included distinguished novelists such as François Mauriac and Cesare Pavese; whilst continental scholars such as R. G. Stamm, E. G. Jacob and L. L. Schücking have contributed much to our understanding of Defoe. Today, *Robinson Crusoe* remains a 'world-book', as the Germans describe it; and *Moll Flanders* is equally an international classic.

IV

Defoe's reputation in later days has traced a course not unlike Pamela's career. After long neglect, the Victorian revaluation had the air almost of virtue rewarded. In the twentieth century, there has been the due sequel – Defoe in his exalted condition. This has meant three things: Defoe's overall standing has gone up; the range of his achievement has been more widely appreciated; and certain works have enjoyed a marked increase in critical appreciation. The most striking benefits have accrued to what used to be called 'the secondary novels', pre-eminently *Moll Flanders*. But almost every corner of Defoe's work has been more fully explored than hitherto.

This is not to say that the new concentration of interest has in every case caused, or been caused by, an advance in the literary stock-market. Indeed, as Ian Watt has pointed out, the casebook on *Moll Flanders* is now bulging as a direct result of two studies which 'in different ways . . . challenged the more extreme claims made for Defoe as a novelist by the previous generation of critics.'[26] Much the same is true in respect of other areas of the canon. None the less, if the rise of Defoe studies is not to be equated precisely with a rise in his reputation, the two processes have certainly overlapped to a considerable extent. There is a sense in which to explain so much is to justify everything, artistically. Today, 'Defoe is read, studied, argued over, enjoyed. If the Establishment was beyond him in his own day, he has certainly made it now.'[27]

For some time after Minto's book, *Robinson Crusoe* continued to arrogate most of the attention. Some worthwhile biographical and bibliographical findings were made by G. A. Aitken, W. P. Trent and others, whilst in the 1890s K. D. Bülbring published two new works from manuscript – *The Compleat English Gentleman* forming an important addition to the canon. Trent's chapter 'Defoe – the Newspaper and the Novel' in the *Cambridge History of English Literature* (1913) was valuable and sometimes perceptive. Nothing is more characteristic of the new century than this chance collocation of judgments: 'It is . . . as a realistic picture of low life in the large that *Moll Flanders* is supreme, just as the book of the next month, *Religious Courtship*, is the unapproachable classic of middle class smugness and piety.' So swiftly does the critic dismiss what was long placed amongst Defoe's major gifts to literature and to humanity. Trent went so far as to say that one could without rashness call 1722, the year of *Moll*, of *Religious Courtship*, of *Due Preparations for the Plague* and *A Journal of the Plague Year*, of *The History of Peter the Great*, and of *Colonel Jack*, 'the greatest *annus mirabilis* in the career of any English writer.'[28] This is a startling claim, even to an admirer of Defoe – one is apt to be plagued by nagging recollections of the productive early years of Scott and Dickens – but it illustrates the point Defoe had now reached.

Probably the most influential single item, however, was an essay by Virginia Woolf in the first *Common Reader* (1925), followed by another on *Crusoe* in the second series (1932). The effect these essays had lies not no much in the explicit contentions made on Defoe's behalf as in the sense of engagement, the awareness of a challenge lying behind Defoe's pedestrian-looking prose – the recognition, in a word, that Defoe repaid adult and sensitive reading. Mrs Woolf even managed to make it seem like a duty – 'For the book itself [*Crusoe*] remains. However we may wind and wriggle, loiter and dally in our approach to books, a lonely battle waits us at the end. . . . It is a masterpiece largely because Defoe has throughout kept consistently to his own sense of perspective. For this reason he thwarts us and flouts us at every turn. . . . We read; and we are rudely contradicted on every page. There are no sunsets and no sunrises; there is no solitude and no soul.' One can see that it need not be a very long step to an existentialist Defoe, an absurd Crusoe, a dark period of The Last Novels. Actually, that is not how Mrs Woolf's argument proceeds; but she had opened the way to criticism of a more inward and more self-conscious kind than that which had prevailed hitherto. James Joyce's high praise of Defoe, written in 1911, was unknown for many years.

The most important work of the twenties and thirties still lay in the exploration of Defoe's life and ideas. His characteristic themes were well described by Paul Dottin, James Sutherland, Rudolph Stamm, A. W. Secord and others. There is a surprisingly good article on 'The Religion of Robinson Crusoe' by James Moffatt in 1919; whilst G. D. H. Cole and Edmund Blunden brought out well the social and economic components of the *Tour*. But though Defoe was early taken up by the Marxists, and enlisted in some fairly unlikely causes ('in the Twenties, Defoe seemed a useful ally in the rebellion against both Victorian prudery and the studied formal perfection of the Flaubertian and Jamesian novel'[29]), his artistry was rarely analysed in concrete detail. In a recent study, one critic has described what he regards as 'architectonic' elements in the structure of *Crusoe*: suspense and surprise, parallelism and contrast, juxtaposition and confrontation.[30] Whether or not one agrees with this particular reading – or even the 'organising theme', irony, recurring images, a 'desire-fear ambivalence' predictably discovered – it is apparent that the account is close to the text, sensitive to directly literary effects, alive to the novel *as* novel. One does not have to feel that Defoe is a very poetic novelist to accept that poetics and rhetoric are the clues to his art, rather than theology, economics or sociology. Only very recently have such beliefs penetrated Defoe criticism.

The post-war years have seen such a body of work on *Moll* and *Crusoe*, in particular, that only selective discussion is possible. On the former, Mark Schorer wrote a suggestive and in some ways hostile essay in 1950; subsequently Robert Alter, Maximillian Novak, R. A. Donovan, Arnold Kettle and Denis Donoghue have contributed short but incisive readings, for the most part rather more affirmative in spirit. However, the most influential studies have appeared in two general studies of the eighteenth-century novel: A. D. McKillop's *The Early Masters of English Fiction* (1956) and Ian Watt's *The Rise of the Novel* (1957). The latter has proved an especially fruitful source of controversy, and whilst many would feel that Watt underrates Defoe's artistic control in *Moll Flanders*, there has been no convincing rebuttal of his position. The defence of *Moll* against Watt is a routine exercise in American critical journals, but his study remains, with McKillop's, the nearest we have to a definitive reading of Defoe.

Work specifically based on *Robinson Crusoe* includes chapters in three valuable books by Novak, G. A. Starr and J. Paul Hunter. An essay by Watt on '*Robinson Crusoe* as a Myth' has exerted wide influence, though his acceptance of the political economist's annexation of *Crusoe* has not gone without criticism.[31] Diana Spearman's interesting but sometimes crookedly-argued *Novel and Society* (1966) makes the telling observation that 'no one in his senses would choose the story of a man cast alone on an uninhabited island to illustrate a theory which only applies to the exchange of goods and services',[32] one of a number of excellent points Mrs Spearman has regarding *Crusoe*. More academic and orthodox is William H. Halewood's essay, 'Religion and Invention in *Robinson Crusoe*' (1964),[33] but this too contains a healthy emphasis on the book as 'a work of conscious invention' rather than a kind of Jungian by-product of Defoe's overtaxed imagination.

It would be perverse not to recognise that this spate of work has produced criticism of unprecedented quality – unmatched in earlier years for its subtlety, concrete observation, range of knowledge and sense of critical relevance. None the less, the situation is still patchy. There is still no general introduction to Defoe's novels, along the lines (say) of House's *The Dickens World* or Quintana's *Swift: An Introduction*. The student is ill-served in other directions. There is no proper critical edition yet of *Crusoe* or *Moll*. The invaluable facsimile text of the *Review* published in 1938 is sadly hard of access. Moreover, major portions of the *œuvre* remain almost uncharted. There is little by way of rhetorical analysis of Defoe's political pamphlets, although works such as *The Shortest Way with the Dissenters* are as amenable to this approach as anything by Swift. Similarly, admirable works of imaginative reconstruction such as *A Journal of the Plague Year* and *Memoirs of a Cavalier* await a due understanding of their literary genetics: the latter is almost a forgotten book. *The History of the Union*, a singularly adroit and well-managed piece of special pleading couched as objective annals, also deserves fuller study: 'history as art' was rarely more cunningly set off by skills of narrative and argument. Finally, the *Tour* is unaccountably neglected. Perhaps Defoe's most characteristic achievement, it blends first-hand observation, curious antiquarian lore, gossip and superstition, economic data and Georgic fancy, legend and pastoral. It is partly a guidebook, partly a reporter's jottings, partly a hymn to England, and quite extensively a well-concealed plagiarism of Camden. In all these respects (not least the cribbing) it is wholly typical of its author. When we can do full justice to this strange cento – its literalness and its poetry, its deceits and its plundering from reality – we shall probably be near to a mature assessment of Defoe's work as a whole. We shall have come to terms with Defoe in all his complexity (as the nineteenth century could not quite do) and all his simplicity (as the twentieth century has not yet done). We shall take him for what he is – a fabricator of genius, inside or outside his art.

NOTES

1 A French translation of the *Political History of the Devil* was noticed in the *Bibliothèque Raisonée* in 1729; but this was a rare exception.

2 This is apart from an opera, one of ninety-odd by the prolific Offenbach, a creative spirit almost as fecund as Defoe himself. This seems to go unperformed nowadays.

3 There were at least twenty-five editions by 1750: see Foxon, D62–92 (Bibliography, section III).

4 See Foxon, D40–52.

5 Cf. the article by C. E. Burch in *Philological Quarterly*, 1937, listed in the Bibliography.

6 K. I. D. Maslen, 'Edition Quantities for *Robinson Crusoe*, 1719', *The Library*, xxiv (1969), 145–50.

7 Ian Watt, *The Rise of the Novel* (Harmondsworth, 1963), p. 43.

8 British Museum, Add. MS. 38370, ff. 39, 168, 200.

9 *An Essay on Criticism*, p. 88; *The Arts of Logick and Rhetorick*, p. 27.

10 *The Papers of Benjamin Franklin*, ed. L. W. Larabee (New Haven, 1959), vol. i, pp. 32–6; *Benjamin Franklin's Autobiographical Writings*, ed. C. Van Doren (1946), p. 223. For copies of *Reformation of Manners* in the Carter family library, see L. B. Wright, *The First Gentleman of Virginia* (San Marino, 1940), p. 283. For *The Complete English Tradesman* in a Pennsylvania private library, see F. B. Tolles, *Meeting House and Counting House* (New York, 1963), p. 186.

11 Defoe was included in the second edition (1778–93), when the leading contributors were dissenting ministers Andrew Kippis (1725–95) and Joseph Towers (1737–99). Towers's article is not of great interest, but Kippis's supplement (vol. v, pp. 74–5) does merit quotation. 'By some persons,' he says, Defoe 'has been spoken of with contempt; and others have only regarded him as a ready miscellaneous author. But the world is at last become sensible of his great and various Talents. The world is at last become sensible that he was a very uncommon man: and that, as a novelist, a polemick, a commercial writer, and a historian, he is entitled to a high degree of applause. His poetry, though celebrated in its day, constitutes the smallest part of his praises.' Clearly it was Chalmers who inspired this judgment. Kippis also hints that Richardson may have learnt his craft in characterisation and in dialogue from Defoe – a suggestion not to be developed until much later.

12 Leslie Stephen, *English Literature and Society in the Eighteenth Century* (1904), p. 88.

13 *Monthly Review*, lxxxix (November 1778), 396. The *Annual Register* for 1771 (xiv, 65) had mentioned the execution of John Joseph Defoe, 'said to be grandson to the celebrated Daniel Defoe, who wrote the *True-born Englishman*, *Robinson Crusoe*, *Col. Jack*, and other ingenious pieces'.

14 See *Swift: The Critical Heritage*, ed. Kathleen Williams (1970), pp. 300, 307, 339–40.

15 For praise in similar terms, see Archbishop Whately's comments in 1821, quoted in *Jane Austen: The Critical Heritage*, ed. B. C. Southam (1968), p. 96.

16 See Watt, *The Rise of the Novel*, p. 124.

17 Ian Watt, 'The Recent Critical Fortunes of *Moll Flanders*', *Eighteenth Century Studies*, i (1967), 110.

18 Burch, 'British Criticism of Defoe as a Novelist 1719–1860', 185–6, gets in a terrible tangle over this article. It is the second article to which Burch gives this reference which actually appeared in the *Westminster*.

19 Quoted from *Fors Clavigera*, letter of 7 September 1871; the same passage was recast as part of the opening paragraph in *Praeterita*. See *The Works of John Ruskin*, ed. E. T. Cook and A. Wedderburn (1903–12), vol. xxvii, p. 167; vol. xxxv, p. 13.

20 William Chadwick, *The Life and Times of Daniel De Foe* (1859), pp. 56, 66, 463–4.

21 Quoted by John Forster, *The Life of Charles Dickens* (1911), vol. i, p. 84.

22 Quoted from the *Saturday Review* by Burch, 'Defoe's British Reputation 1869–94', 414. I have not seen this article.

23 See Burch, 'Defoe's British Reputation 1869–94', 422.

24 Gove, p. 122. (This section is based on the authorities listed in the Bibliography, section II). One imitation, by a certain Ambrose Evans, appeared within days of *Crusoe*.

25 W. E. Mann, p. 133n., mentions a report that Alphonse Daudet had expressed a high admiration for *Crusoe*; but states that he had been unable to locate the reference. So have I.

26 Watt, 'The Recent Critical Fortunes of *Moll Flanders*', 109.

27 *Twentieth Century Interpretations of Moll Flanders*, ed. R. C. Elliott (Englewood Cliffs, 1970), p. 1.

28 W. P. Trent, 'Defoe', *CHEL*, vol. ix, p. 22.

29 Watt, 'The Recent Critical Fortunes of *Moll Flanders*', 110.

30 *Twentieth Century Interpretations of Robinson Crusoe*, ed. F. H. Ellis (Englewood Cliffs, 1969), pp. 9–15.

31 Watt, 'Robinson Crusoe as Myth', *Essays in Criticism*, i (1951), 95–119.

32 Spearman, op. cit., p. 166.

33 Halewood, 'Religion and Invention in *Robinson Crusoe*', *Essays in Criticism*, xiv (1964), 339–51.

In most cases the text is that of the original publication of a given book or article. In a few instances, where an author reprinted a periodical contribution later in book form, and appears to have taken some care with the text, the second version has been preferred. Thus, John Forster (No. 22) is quoted not from the *Edinburgh Review*, but from the revised and expanded essay which appeared in *Daniel Defoe and Charles Churchill*. Where there was no publication in an author's lifetime, as with Coleridge's marginalia, I have used modern scholarly editions. The text is always reproduced literatim, except that obvious misprints have been corrected and the long s modernised. Any omissions are indicated by leader dots. Defoe's name is spelt as in the source quoted. Titles of books by Defoe have been italicised where the original is in roman type.

1. Contemporary comments on Defoe

1703–18

This is a selection of representative comments from a huge volume of references made in Defoe's lifetime (see Introduction, pp. 9–12, and Appendix I). The extracts chosen illustrate the polemical climate in which Defoe passed the greater part of his writing career. Works such as *The True-Born Englishman*, *The Shortest Way with the Dissenters* and *The Secret History of the White Staff* excited a particularly vehement response. After 1714, though certain books (such as the popular *Crusoe*, for which see No. 3) provoked a strong reaction, there were in general fewer rejoinders published.

Apart from (c) and (e), all passages come from anonymous works. Extract (c) is from *The Life and Errors* of John Dunton (1659–1733), eccentric author and publisher; the text is from the edition by J. B. Nichols (1818), vol. i, pp. 180–1, collated with the first edition of 1705. Passage (e) brings together remarks from two pamphlets by John Clark, minister of the Free Church in Glasgow: *A Paper concerning Daniel De Foe* (1708), p. 7, and *A Just Reprimand to Daniel de Foe* (1709), p. 3. The pamphlet cited in (f) was attributed by Walter Wilson to John Oldmixon (1673–1742), miscellaneous writer and an untiring critic of Defoe. M. E. Novak accepts this ascription in the *New Cambridge Bibliography of English Literature* (1971), vol. ii, col. 907. Extract (g) comes from a work assigned by me to Oldmixon on external and internal evidence. These comments are of special interest in that Oldmixon knew Defoe several years before the latter became famous as a writer – the only instance throughout the entire critical heritage where this can be safely asserted. Passage (b) is typical of many accusations that Defoe was in the pay of the Jacobites or even of the French: see Introduction, p. 11. Passage (d) comes from one of the broadside ballads attacking Defoe, and (h) represents the extensive comment found in newspapers of the day.

(a) From *The True-Born Hugonot, &c. A Satyr* (1703):

> Hymns let him write, when he should Mercy pray,
> And Satyrize the State, *The Shortest Way*;
> Invectives against Monarchy indite,
> To make his Impudence surpass his Spight.
> In Publick View he shall again appear,
> Nor shall his City *Friends* protect him here . . .
> A true Malignant, Arrogant and Sour,
> And ever Snarling at Establish'd Power . . .
> That *others* Lands has for his *own* Convey'd,
> And *Bought* and *Sold* Estates, for which he never paid. (pp. 4–19.)

(b) From *Reflections upon a late Scandalous and Malicious Pamphlet Entitul'd, The Shortest Way with the Dissenters* (1703):

It were endless to animadvert upon all the extravagant Passages of this envenom'd Libel, which is writ on purpose to set the Nation in a Flame, and to engage us in an intestine War, that the *French* King may have an opportunity to force the Pretender upon us. (p. 22.)

(c) From Dunton's *Life and Errors* (see headnote):

Mr. *Daniel De Foe* is a man of good parts, and very clear sense: His conversation is brisk and ingenious enough. The World is well satisfied that he's enterprizing and *bold*; but, alas! had his prudence only weighed a few grains more, he'd certainly have writ his *Shortest Way* a little more at length. There have been some men in all ages, who have taken that of Juvenal for their motto:[1]

> *Aude aliquid brevibus Gyaris et carcere dignum*
> *Si vis esse aliquis*

Had he writ no more than his *True-Born Englishman*, and spared some particular Characters that are too vicious for the very Originals, he had certainly deserved applause; but it is hard to leave off when not only the itch and the inclination, but the necessity of writing, lies so heavy upon a man. Should I defend his good-nature and his honesty, and the world would not believe me, 'twould be labour in vain. Mr. Foe writ for me the *Character of Dr. Annesley*, and a *Pindarick in honour of the Athenian Society*, which was prefixed to the History of it. And he might have asked me the question, before he inserted either of them in the

---

[1] Juvenal, *Sat.* i, 73–4: 'You must dare to commit some crime worthy of prison or exile, if you want to be somebody.'

Collection of his Works, in regard he writes so bitterly against the same injustice in others.

(d) From *An Equivalent for De Foe* (?Edinburgh, 1706):

> Let banter cease, and Poetasters yield,
> Since fam'd *De Foe* is master of the Field
> What none can comprehend, he understands,
> And what's not understood, his Fame commands
> This mighty Bard, more mighty in Invention,
> And most of all in humble Condescension,
> Has Left the Pleasures of *Parnassus*-hill,
> And Stoops so low as here to draw his Quil
> 'Mongst us rude *Scots*. . . .

(e) From pamphlets by J. Clark (see headnote):

I doubt not if I had been at pains to gather Informations anent Mr. *De Foe*'s Morals and Politicks from *England*, and other Places of his Residence and Conversation, but I might be able to present the Publick with a ridiculous foul Portrait of this *Thrasonick Zoilus*, unto which I should append this agreeable Motto:

> *Est mihi Penna loquax Bacchus & Alma Caeres.*

> To get my Bread no other way I ken,
> But by the Clatters of my Tongue and Pen.

I cannot pass to notice Mr. *De Foes Paralogistick* way of Tacking together Sentences, spoken at different and distant Periodes by this *Legerdemain* the more plausible to set off his Misrepresentations of me. . . .

(f) From *Remarks on a Scandalous Libel, Entitil'd A Letter . . . Relating to the Bill of Commerce* (1713; for the likely authorship, see headnote):

There are but Two Wretches upon Earth that cou'd write so Villainous a Libel as *the Pretended Letter from a Member of Parliament*. Both of 'em are already branded with Infamy by the Law. One[1] of 'em never had any Principles or Morals, the other has had Principles indeed, but never had any Morals; these Principles he has basely Sold for a Precarious Subsistance, and while he pretends to *Liberty* and *Fanaticism*, he Labours with equal Industry and Impudence in the Service of Popery and *France*.

[1] Jonathan Swift.

How in the Name of Wonder shou'd this Creature know any thing of Trade, unless it was by *Inspiration*? Whom has he conversed with for these Twenty Years past, that shou'd inform him of the Commerce and Wealth of the World, when during all that Period he has been the Abhorrence of the fair Merchant, and herded with none but Owlers, Bankrupts, Projectors, State-Quacks, Lighter-Men and Bailiffs? He had as good e'en throw off the Vizard and own himself a *Jacobite* or a Hireling, for there is no Man so dull but to see he will write any thing, do any thing, *Pro* or *Con*, according to the *Cue* that's given him. Among all the wretched Events that have contributed to make Fools of us, nothing is more to be lamented than Peoples suffering themselves to be amus'd and impos'd upon by a Parcel of Ignorant Mercenary Scriblers, Fellows they wou'd scorn to Converse with in Person, yet in their *Scriptions* they are their Guides and Governors; Inconsistency and Contradiction, which were formerly so Scandalous in Argument, is now become the very Foundation of it; this Man only asserts, and that he calls *Proving*; if detected and expos'd, he asserts again and that he calls *answering*. For my Part, tho' I have no more value for his Masters than I have for him, tho' I think their Merit to be much upon a Level, yet I have so much Respect for their *Denomination*, that I pity 'em for being reduc'd to the Necessity of employing so foul and so prostituted a Pen, but indeed the Cause is such, that no Pen that is not prostituted and foul, will have to do with it. By the Cause, I understand nothing but the *Pretender* and *France*; for the former, he has writ and been chastis'd for it, for the latter, he is writing, and I doubt not, will one time or other, have another sort of Chastisement. Nonsense one wou'd think is a harmless thing, but when 'tis accompany'd with Assurance, and is laid in a Fools way, it does Mischief: A Fool cannot comprehend how a Man can be so Impudent and yet write Nonsense. Boldness he has heard is a sign of Truth, and not being able to distinguish between Boldness and Impudence, between Truth and Falshood, he mistakes the one for the other, and the Mercenary *Mercator*, for what he pretends to be, a Philosopher, a Wit, a Merchant, when in Fact he has nothing but Words and a Forehead to bring to Market. This his Chapmen know, but they know also that Reason and Merit are not of their side, and that such Wares as he sells 'em are at present most in demand with 'em, and most for their Purpose. (pp. 1–3.)

. . . Is this a Matter to be banded about by a *Clerk* to a *Brick Kiln*, under the Protection of a *Foot-man*? Is it a Subject to be trifled with by a

Wordy *Declaimer*? He has Two or Three Months been arguing against downright Fact; not a Line without a Lye in it; the Phrase is not a Jot too strong in this Case. Whatever has had an Appearance of Argument, has been answer'd over and over again, yet his Papers are brought up and sent away by the Carriers in Bundles, *Carriage Paid*, to Poyson or Blind the Poor Country, and make 'em believe a Bottle of *French* Wine is better than a Bale of *English* Wooll and they will Thrive and grow Rich when they make Bonfires of their Looms and hoe for nothing but what we shall have from *France*. (p. 5.)

(g) From *A Detection of the Sophistry and Falsities of . . . the Secret History of the White Staff* (1714), part i, pp. 7–8 (for the authorship, see headnote):

. . . Accordingly five or six Days ago out comes the *Secret History of the White Staff*, written by *Defoe*, as is to be seen by his abundance of Words, his false Thoughts, and false *English*. The Man[1] who set him to work paid him a Pension during all the time of his *Management*, tho he had help'd to set him in the Pillory seven or eight Years before. He gave him for this Work, so necessary to his own Preservation, as many Parcels and Hints of Memoirs, as he thought convenient, which the honest Author of the *Shortest Way with the Dissenters*, of *Jure Divino*, of the *Review*, of *What if the Pretender should come?* and an hundred other such *Scriptions*, was hir'd to put into his sweet way of Writing, to amuse People, if he could not convince them.

(h) From 'The loyal Litany', Read's *Weekly Journal*, 20 September 1718:

> From a vile* *Presbyterian*, with a *Jacobite* Face,
> Who writes on both Sides with an insipid Grace,
> Yet demurely on *Sundays* in the Meeting takes Place;
> *Libera nos.*

[1] Robert Harley, first Earl of Oxford (1661–1724), statesman. In fact Harley had no part in Defoe's punishment.

* *Daniel Foe.*

2. Pope, Swift and the Scriblerians on Defoe

1709–31

The first two extracts are by Swift: (a) from *A Letter Concerning the Sacramental Test* (1709), and (b) from the *Examiner*, no. 15 (16 November 1710). In both cases Swift is comparing Defoe's *Review* with the rival *Observator* newspaper. Quotations from *The Prose Works of Jonathan Swift*, ed. H. Davis (Oxford, 1939–67), vol. ii, p. 113; vol. iii, p. 13. Passage (c) is from John Gay's *The Present State of Wit* (1711), a relaxed look at the current journalistic scene. Text from the Augustan Reprint Society edition by D. F. Bond, (Ann Arbor, 1947), p. 1. Passages (d) and (e) are from *The Dunciad Variorum* of 1729, with subsequent notes where relevant. Passage (f) comes from Pope's conversation as reported by Joseph Spence in *Observations, Anecdotes, and Characters of Books and Men*, ed. J. M. Osborn (Oxford, 1966), vol. i, p. 213. The following extract (g) is from *An Author to be Lett* (1729), probably by the dissolute poet Richard Savage (?1697–1742) with the certain connivance and likely assistance of Pope himself. Quotation from p. 4. Extract (h) is taken from the pro-Pope organ, *Grub-street Journal*, no. 69 (29 April 1731).

(a) Swift, *A Letter Concerning the Sacramental Test:*

One of these Authors (the Fellow that was *pilloryed, I have forgot his Name) is indeed so grave, sententious, dogmatical a Rogue, that there is no enduring him.

(b) Swift, in the *Examiner*:

... two stupid illiterate Scribblers, both of them *Fanaticks* by Profession: I mean the *Review* and *Observator*.... The mock authoritative Manner of the one [Defoe], and the insipid Mirth of the other, however insupportable to reasonable Ears, being of a Levil with great Numbers among the lowest Part of Mankind ...

* Daniel Defoe [marginal note in 1735 ed. of Swift's *Works*].

38

(c) Gay's *The Present State of Wit:*

As to our Weekly Papers, the Poor REVIEW is quite exhausted, and grown so very contemptible, that tho' he has provoked all his Brothers of the Quill round, none of them will enter into a Controversy with him. This Fellow, who had excellent Parts, but wanted a small Foundation of Learning, is a lively instance of those Wits, who, as an Ingenious Author says, will endure but one Skimming.

(d) *The Dunciad Variorum,* I. 93 ff.:

> Much to the mindful Queen the feast recalls,
> What City-Swans once sung within the walls;
> Much she revolves their arts, their ancient praise,
> And sure succession down from Heywood's days.
> She saw with joy the line immortal run,
> Each sire imprest and glaring in his son . . .
> She saw old Pryn in restless Daniel shine,★
> And Eusden eke out Blackmore's endless line;
> She saw slow Philips creep like Tate's poor page,
> And all the Mighty Mad in Dennis rage.

(e) *The Dunciad Variorum,* II. 133 ff.:

> With that she gave him . . .
> A shaggy Tap'stry, worthy to be spread
> On Codrus' old, or Dunton's modern bed;
> Instructive work! whose wry-mouth'd portraiture
> Display'd the fates her confessors endure.
> Earless on high, stood unabash'd Defoe,
> And Tutchin flagrant from the scourge, below:
> There Ridpath, Roper cudgell'd might ye view;
> The very worsted still look'd black and blue.[1]

★ 101. Old Prynn in restless Daniel.] *William Prynn* and *Daniel de Foe* were writers of Verses, as well as of Politicks; as appears by the Poem of the latter *De jure Divino,* and others. . . . Both these Authors had a resemblance in their fates as well as writings, having been a-like sentenc'd to the Pillory.

[1] Pope's satiric intent is manifest in his deliberate alignment of Defoe's name with those of such recognised dunces as Thomas Heywood (d. 1650?), Prynne (1600–69), Laurence Eusden (1688–1730), Richard Blackmore (1655?–1729), Ambrose Philips (1675?–1749), Nahum Tate (1652–1715), John Dennis (1657–1734), John Tutchin (1661?–1707) and Dunton (for whom see No. 1 above). George Ridpath (d. 1725) and Abel Roper (1665–1726) were journalists. In *Peri Bathous* (1727), ch. IX, Pope had written 'Who sees not that *De- F-* was the Poetical Son of [George] Withers . . .'

(f) Pope on Defoe:

The first part of *Robinson Crusoe*, good. DeFoe wrote many things, and none bad, though none excellent. There's something good in all he has writ.

(g) *An Author to be Lett*:

I am very deeply read in all Pieces of Scandal, Obscenity, and Profaneness, particularly in the Writings of Mrs. *Haywood, Henley, W-lst-d, Morley, Br-v-l, Foxton, Cooke, D'Foe, Norton, Woolston, Dennis*, and the Author of the *Rival Modes*.[1]

(h) *Grub-street Journal*:

On Monday in the evening died, at his lodgings in Rope-makers alley, in Moorfields, the famous Mr. DANIEL DE FOE, in a very advanced age. [Daily] COURANT. – It is no small comfort to me, that my brother died in a (good) old age, in a place made famous by the decease of several of our members;[2] having kept himself out of the dangerous *alleys* of those high-flying *rope-makers*, who would fain have sent him long ago, to his *long* home, by *the shortest way with the Dissenters*. . . .

The members [of the Grub Street society] were so much afflicted at the news of the death of that ancient ornament of our Society, Mr. DANIEL DE FOE, that they were incapable of attending to the Papers which were read to them. Upon which our President adjourned the consideration of them till the next meeting. . . . [Quotes an epigram] imagined to be the last work of the great Author deceased, and evidence of his perseverance in his principles to the last.

[1] Another list of *echt* dunces. *The Rival Modes* (1727) was a play by James Moore Smythe. 'Norton' was Defoe's unsatisfactory son Benjamin Norton Defoe. It is relevant to observe that the note to *The Dunciad* quoted in passage (d) originally began, 'The first edition had it, *She saw in* Norton *all his father shine;* a great mistake! for *Daniel de Foe* had parts, but Norton de Foe was a wretched writer. . . .' The incomplete names are those of Leonard Welsted and John Durant Breval.

[2] Ropemakers Alley lay just off the historic Grub Street. The implication is that Defoe was fortunate to survive to a ripe age, since his political opponents had been threatening him with the gallows for thirty years.

3. A satire on *Robinson Crusoe*

1719

Extracts from *The Life and Strange Surprizing Adventures of Mr.
D . . . De F . . ., of London, Hosier.* This has become by far the best
known of the contemporary attacks on Defoe, although it was
merely one of the long series of pamphlets using irony, parody and
innuendo (as well as direct abuse) to blacken Defoe. It was edited
by Paul Dottin in 1923. The author, Charles Gildon (1665–1724),
was a miscellaneous writer with a special interest in drama. By the
end of his life he was blind and destitute, but he was not to be
spared his well-merited niche in *The Dunciad.* As critic, compiler
and scandalous biographer, he was one of the most representative
figures in Grub Street; and his irritation against Defoe was no
doubt intensified by the thought that the hugely-successful
Robinson Crusoe had been turned out by one he must long have
regarded as a fellow-scribbler. The pamphlet is built round two
sections: an imaginary dialogue between Defoe, Crusoe and
Friday; and 'remarks' on Crusoe's life.

(a) Extract from the supposed dialogue:

D[anie]l. Hum, hum . . . well, and what are your complaints of me?

Cru[soe]. Why, that you have made me a strange whimsical, inconsistent Being, in three Weeks losing all the Religion of a Pious Education; and when you bring me again to a Sense of the Want of Religion,
you make me quit that upon every Whimsy; you make me extravagantly Zealous, and as extravagantly Remiss; you make me an Enemy
to all *English* Sailors, and a Panegyrist upon all other Sailors that come
in your way: Thus, all the *English* Seamen laugh'd me out of Religion,
but the *Spanish* and *Portuguese* Sailors were honest religious Fellows;
you make me a Protestant in *London*, and a Papist in *Brasil*; and then
again, a Protestant in my own Island, and when I get thence, the only
Thing that deters me from returning to *Brasil*, is meerly, because I did
not like to die a Papist; for you say, *that* Popery *may be a good Religion*

to live in, but not to die in; as if that Religion could be good to live in, which was not good to die in; for, Father *D . . . l*, whatever you may think, no Man is sure of living one Minute. But tho' you keep me thus by Force a Sort of Protestant, yet, you all along make me very fond of Popish Priests and the Popish Religion; nor can I forgive you the making me such a Whimsical Dog, to ramble over three Parts of the World after I was sixty five. Therefore, I say, *Friday*, prepare to shoot.

Fri[day]. No shoot yet Master, me have something to say, he much Injure me too.

D[anie]l. Injure you too, how the Devil have I injur'd you?

Fri[day]. Have injure me, to make me such Blockhead, so much contradiction, as to be able to speak *English tolerably well* in a Month or two, and not to speak it better in twelve Years after; to make me go out to be kill'd by the Savages, only to be a Spokesman to them, tho' I did not know, whether they understood one Word of my Language; for you must know, Father *D . . . n*, that almost ev'ry Nation of us *Indians* speak a different Language. Now Master shall me shoot?

Cru[soe]. No *Friday*, not yet, for here will be several more of his Children with Complaints against him; here will be the *French Priest*, *Will Atkins*, the Priest in *China*, his Nephews Ship's Crew, and . . .

D[anie]l. Hold, hold, dear Son *Crusoe*, hold, let me satisfy you first before any more come upon me. You are my Hero, I have made you, out of nothing, fam'd from *Tuttle-Street*[1] to *Limehouse-hole*; there is not an old Woman that can go to the Price of it, but buys thy *Life and Adventures*, and leaves it as a Legacy, with the *Pilgrims Progress*, the *Practice of Piety*, and *God's Revenge against Murther*, to her Posterity. . . . Then know, my dear Child, that you are a greater Favorite to me than you imagine; you are the true Allegorick Image of thy tender Father *D . . . l*; I drew thee from the consideration of my own Mind; I have been all my Life that Rambling, Inconsistent Creature, which I have made thee.

I set out under the Banner of *Kidderminster*, and was long a noisy, if not zealous Champion for that Cause; and tho' I had not that *Free-school* and *House Learning* which I have given you, yet being endow'd with a wonderful Loquaciousness and a pretty handsome Assurance, being out of my Time, I talk'd myself into a pretty large Credit, by which I might, perhaps, have thriv'd in my Way very well, but, like you at *Brasil* my Head run upon Whimsies, and I quitted a Certainty for new

[1] A poor quarter of Westminster, near Tothill Fields, in the vicinity of modern Victoria Street.

Adventures: First, I set up for Scribbling of Verses, and dabbling in other Sort of Authorizing, both Religious and Prophane. I have no Call to tell you, whether this Itch of Scribbling, or some other Project of *Lime Kilns* or the like, oblig'd me to quit a certain Court near the *Royal-Exchange*, and to play at Hide and Seek; but this did not much trouble me, for it put me on a Sort of diving more agreeable to my Inclinations, forcing me to ramble from Place to Place Incognito; and, indeed, I thought myself something like the great Monarchs of the East, for I took care to be more seldom seen by my Acquaintance, than they by their Subjects. My old Walk from my Court to the Change was too short for my rambling Spirit, it look'd like a Seaman's Walk betwixt Decks; and for that, and some other Reasons which shall be nameless, I pursu'd the Course which I told you.

Well, all my Projects failing, I e'en took up with the Vocation of an Author, which tho' it promis'd but little in the common Way, I took care to make it more Beneficial to me; the principal Method of doing that, was to appear zealous for some Party, and in the Party I was soon determin'd by my Education, and scribbled on in a violent Manner; till, by making myself a constant Pensioner to all the Rich and Zealous of my Party, I pickt up a good handsome Penny, with little Expence to myself of Time or Labour; for any Thing that is boldly Writ, will go down with either Party; but at last, by a plaguy Irony, I got myself into the damnable *Nutcrackers*; however, that but encreas'd my Market, and brought my Pension in, at least, five fold. I writ on, till some of the wise Heads of the contrary Party thought me worth retaining in their Service; and, I confess, their Bribes were very powerful. I manag'd Matters so well a great while, that both Sides kept me in Pay; but that would not do, my old Friends found that I had in reality forsaken them, and that I trim'd my Boat so ill, that they plainly saw to which Side it inclin'd; and, therefore, a certain Captain not far from *Thames Street*, who had been my Steward or Collector in chief, comes to me, and like the Witch of *Endor*, cried, *God has left thee*, Saul; that is, the Money would be no more given me by the Party, who had every one discover'd that I was enter'd into another Cause. I did all I could to satisfy him and answer his Objections, but all to no purpose, *Buenos Nocoius* was the Word, good Night *Nicholas*, they would be no longer bubbled; so I set out entirely for St. *Germans*[1] or any other Port to which my Proprietors should direct me; but here again, like you, my Son *Crusoe*, in burning the Idol in *Tartary*, I went a little too far, and by another Irony, instead

[1] The court of the Jacobite pretender. 'Bubbled': tricked.

43

of the *Nutcrackers*,[1] I had brought myself to the *Tripos* at *Paddington*, but that my good Friend that set me to work got me a Pardon, and so, safe was the Word; and I have never forsaken him for that good Office—and his Money, my dear Son *Crusoe*, for it is that which always sets me to Work; and which ever Side the most Money is to be got, that Side is sure of *D . . . l*. 'Tis true, I made a pretty good Penny among the Whigs, tho' nothing to what I have since done among the Tories: Let me see, I think, I made by Subscription for my *Jure Divino* about some five hundred Pounds, and yet I writ it in about three Weeks or a Month, six or seven hundred Verses a Day coming constantly out of this Prolifick Head; as for the Sense and Poetry of them, e'en let my Subscribers look to that; they had a *Book*, and a *Book* in *Folio*, and I had their Money, and so all Parties were contented. But what's this to the Tory Writers, where for a Translation one shall get you three or four thousand Pounds subscrib'd; and for an Original, seven or eight Thousand; the Tories therefore for my Money; not that I value the Tories more than I do the Whigs; but nothing for the Whigs will sell, and every Thing for the Tories does. You seem to take it amiss, that I made you speak against the *English* Seamen, but that was only according to my own Nature, for I always hated the *English*, and took a Pleasure in depreciating and villifying of them, witness my *True Born Englishman*, and my changing my Name to make it sound like *French*; for my Father's Name was plain F . . e, but I have adorn'd it with a *de*, so that I am now, Mr. *D . . . l De F . . e.* (pp. viii–xiv.)

(b) Extract from the 'reflections':

I am far from being an Enemy to the Writers of Fables, since I know very well that this Manner of Writing is not only very Ancient, but very useful, I might say sacred, since it has been made use of by the inspir'd Writers themselves; but then to render any Fable worthy of being receiv'd into the Number of those which are truly valuable, it must naturally produce in its Event some useful Moral, either express'd or understood; but this of *Robinson Crusoe*, you plainly inculcate, is design'd against a publick good. I think there can be no Man so ignorant as not to know that our Navigation produces both our Safety, and our Riches, and that whoever therefore shall endeavour to discourage this, is so far a profest Enemy of his Country's Prosperity and Safety; but the Author of *Robinson Crusoe*, not only in the Beginning, but in

---

[1] A slang phrase for the pillory. The 'Tripos' refers to the three-legged stool used by condemned criminals at Tyburn ('Paddington').

many Places of the Book, employs all the Force of his little Rhetoric to dissuade and deter all People from going to Sea, especially all Mothers of Children who may be capable of that Service, from venturing them to so much Hazard and so much Wickedness, as he represents the Seafaring Life liable to. But whatever Mr. F—e may think of the Matter, I dare believe that there are few Men who consider justly, that would think the Profession of a *Yorkshire* Attorney more innocent and beneficial to Mankind than that of a Seaman, or would judge that *Robinson Crusoe* was so very criminal in rejecting the former, and chusing the latter, as to provoke the Divine Providence to raise two Storms, and in the last of them to destroy so many Ships and Men, purely to deter him from that Course of Life, to which at last he was to owe so ample a Reward of all his Labours and Fatigues, as the End of this very Book plainly tells us he met with. (pp. 2–4.)

c) From the 'reflections':

So that upon the whole, we find that *Robinson Crusoe*, even when he pretends to repent, is for throwing the Guilt of his Sin upon others, who, as far as we can possibly discover, did not at all deserve the Charge; and I dare believe, that he was in reality the only Person among them, who ever liv'd so many Years without saying his Prayers, or acknowledging God and his Providence, and is likely therefore rather to have been the Corrupter, than the Corrupted. But it seems he is not yet come so forward towards a true Repentance, as to take the whole Guilt on himself, which in reality no Body else had any Share in. He says, indeed, his Repentance was hinder'd by his Conversation with none but such as were worse than himself, and where he never heard mention of any thing that was good. But, dear D—n, this seems another gross Fib of your Friend *Robinson*, as I hope I have sufficiently prov'd in what I have said upon this Head. I have been longer than I design'd upon these Remarks, and therefore shall only transiently touch upon some few Occurrences of your Book: And tho' Nonsense be too frequent thro' the whole to merit a particular Remark as often as it occurs, I can't pass over this in Page 164: *And now I saw how easy it was for the Providence of God to make the most miserable Condition, Mankind could be in, worse.* How, Friend D—n! Worse than the worst, I thought, that beyond the superlative Degree there was nothing; I am sure that *Robinson's* School Learning could not teach him this, perhaps he had it from his *House* Learning, with all the other false Grammar, which is to be found almost in every Page, particularly the *Nominative Case* perpetually put for the *Accusative*. But this is not worth stopping at. (pp. 22–3.)

(d) From the 'reflections':

To avoid a Lethargy therefore, I shall not dwell upon it, and its perpetual Succession of Absurdities, but only touch upon some few, which may serve for Samples of the whole. I cannot, however, omit taking particular Notice of the Editor's Preface, because it is not only written by the same Hand, but also very singular in its Kind: you begin with a Boast of the Success of your Book, and which you say deserves that Success by its Merits, that is, *The surprizing Variety of the Subject, and the agreeable Manner of the Performance*. It's well you tell us so yourself, the judicious Reader else must have been puzzel'd to find out the Mystery of its Success. For first, as to the Variety of the Subject, it will be a hard Matter to make that good, since it's spread out into at least five and twenty Sheets, clog'd with Moral Reflections, as you are pleas'd to call them, every where insipid and awkward, and in many Places of no manner of Relation to the Occasion on which they are deliver'd, besides being much larger than necessary, and frequently impious and prophane; and always canting are the Reflections which you are pleas'd to call religious and useful, and *the brightest Ornaments of your Book*, tho' in reality they were put in by you to swell the Bulk of your Treatise up to a five Shilling Book; whereas, the Want of Variety in your Subject, would never have made it reach to half the Price; nay, as it is, you have been forc'd to give us the same Reflections over and over again, as well as repeat the same Fact afterwards in a Journal, which you had told us before in a plain Narration. So *agreeable is the Manner of your Performance!* which is render'd more so by the excessive Sterility of your Expression, being forc'd perpetually to say the same Things in the very self same Words four or five times over in one Page, which puts me in Mind of what *Hudibras* says,[1]

> *Would it not make one strange*
> *That some Mens Fancies should ne'er change,*
> *But always make them do and say*
> *The self same Thing, the self same Way?*

Another agreeable Thing in the Performance is, that every Page is full of *Solecisms* or false Grammar. However, this may be, for ought I know, a very agreeable Performance to most of your Buyers.

[1] From Samuel Butler's *Hudibras*, II. i. 9–12.

Your next Triumph is, that the Reproaches of your Book as a Romance, and as being guilty of bad Geography, Contradictions, and the like, *have prov'd Abortive* (I suppose you mean ineffectual) *and as impotent as malicious*; but here, as well as in other Places, you are guilty of a great Abuse of Words: For first, they have not been impotent, since all but the very *Canaille* are satisfied by them of the Worthlessness of the Performance; nor can the exposing the Weakness and Folly of any assuming and ignorant Scribbler be properly call'd malicious; they who malign eminent Worth, may, indeed deserve such a Name; but what hath been said of, or done against such an incoherent Piece as *Robinson Crusoe*, can at worst been only call'd Indignation; and that was what the eminent Satirist was not asham'd to own, as the Motive and Support of his Verses.[1]

Si Natura negat facit Indignatio versum. (pp. 30–2.)

[1] Juvenal, *Sat.* i, 79: 'Even if I am without natural inspiration, my verse will be sustained by indignation.'

4. A biographic entry

1723

The entry, 'Mr. Daniel De Foe', in [Giles Jacob], *The Poetical Register: or the Lives and Characters of all the English Poets. With an Account of their Writings* (1723), vol. ii, p. 293. This work was made up of two volumes, first published separately in 1719–20.

Giles Jacob (1686–1744) is remembered as one of the victims of *The Dunciad*. A miscellaneous compiler, he wrote some limp *Memoirs of Addison* (1724), but his major area of work lay in legal textbooks, abridgments and dictionaries. *The Poetical Register* claims to make extensive use of first-hand material supplied by living authors. Whatever the truth of this, it is a valuable tool for the study of Augustan writers.

This Author was formerly a Hosier, but since he has been one of the most enterprizing Pamphleteers this Age has produc'd; some Parts of his Life his Inclinations have led him to Poetry, which has thrown into the World two Pieces very much admir'd by some Persons, *viz.*

I. *The True-Born Englishman*. This is a biting Satire, and sold many Impressions; but his Descriptions are generally very low.

II. *Jure Divino*, a Poem of considerable Bulk in Folio.

5. The mid-century view

1753

From the article, 'Daniel De Foe', in *The Lives of the Poets* (1753). The work is attributed on the title-page to 'Mr. [Theophilus] Cibber' (1703–58), son of the famous Colley Cibber, and like his father an actor-manager – though an even more eccentric and trouble-prone figure. However, it is now believed that the text was substantially the work of Robert Shiels (d. 1753), a friend of Dr Johnson.

Cibber, if it is he, devotes twelve pages (vol. iv, pp. 313–25, of which pp. 322–5 appear below) to Defoe. He finds a fair amount to say of Defoe's verse, although recognising that 'poetry was far from being the talent of Defoe. He wrote with more perspicuity and strength in prose, and he seems to have understood, as well as any man, the civil constitution of the country, which indeed was his chief study' (pp. 315–16) – a slightly odd sequence of ideas. Cibber foreshadows the nineteenth-century approach in signalising the 'extraordinary zeal and ability' with which Defoe undertook the defence of the Revolution (p. 313). For John Tutchin, see No. 2 above.

[Defoe wrote] many other poetical pieces, and political, and polemical tracts, the greatest part of which are written with great force of thought, though in an unpolished irregular stile. The natural abilities of the author (for he was no scholar) seem to have been very high. He had a great knowledge of men and things, particularly what related to the government, and trade of these kingdoms. He wrote many pamphlets on both, which were generally well received, though his name was never prefixed. His imagination was fertile, strong, and lively, as may be collected from his many works of fancy, particularly his *Robinson Crusoe*, which was written in so natural a manner, and with so many probable incidents, that, for some time after its publication, it was

49

judged by most people to be a true story. It was indeed written upon a model entirely new, and the success and esteem it met with, may be ascertained by the many editions it has sold, and the sums of money which have been gained by it. Nor was he less remarkable in his writings of a serious and religious turn, witness his *Religious Courtship*, and his *Family Instructor*; both of which strongly inculcate the worship of God, the relative duties of husbands, wives, parents, and children, not in a dry dogmatic manner, but in a kind of dramatic way, which excites curiosity, keeps the attention awake, and is extremely interesting, and pathetic.

We have already seen, that in his political capacity he was a declared enemy to popery, and a bold defender of revolution principles. He was held in much esteem by many great men, and though he never enjoyed any regular post under the government, yet he was frequently employed in matters of trust and confidence, particularly in Scotland, where he several times was sent on affairs of great importance, especially those relative to the union of the kingdoms, of which he was one of the negotiators.

It is impossible to arrive at the knowledge of half the tracts and pamphlets which were written by this laborious man, as his name is not prefixed, and many of them being temporary, have perished like all other productions of that kind, when the subjects upon which they were written are forgot. His principal performances, perhaps, are these,

A Plan of Commerce, an esteemed Work, in one large vol. 8vo. of which a new edition was lately published.

Memoirs of the Plague, published in 1665.

Religious Courtship.

Family Instructor. Two Volumes.

History of Apparitions (under the name of Moreton.)

Robinson Crusoe. Two Volumes.

Political History of the Devil.

History of Magic.

Caledonia, a Poem in praise of Scotland.

De Jure Divino, a Poem.

English Tradesman, &c.

History of Colonel Jack.

Cleveland's Memoirs, &c. are also said to be his.

Considered as a poet, Daniel De Foe is not so eminent, as in a political light: he has taken no pains in versification; his ideas are masculine, his expressions coarse, and his numbers generally rough.

He seems rather to have studied to speak truth, by probing wounds to the bottom, than, by embellishing his versification, to give it a more elegant keenness. This, however, seems to have proceeded more from carelessness in that particular, than want of ability: for the following lines in his *True Born Englishman*, in which he makes Britannia rehearse the praises of her hero, King William, are harmoniously beautiful, and elegantly polished.

[quotes *The True-Born Englishman*, lines 893–912.]

What provocation De Foe had given to Pope we cannot determine, but he has not escaped the lash of that gentleman's pen. Mr. Pope in his second book of his *Dunciad* thus speaks of him;[1]

> Earless on high stood unabash'd De Foe,
> And Tutchin flagrant from the scourge below.

It may be remarked that he has joined him with Tutchin, a man whom judge Jeffries had ordered to be so inhumanly whipt through the market-towns, that, as we have already observed, he petitioned the King to be hanged. This severity soured his temper, and after the deposition and death of King James, he indulged his resentment in insulting his memory. This may be the reason why Pope has stigmatized him, and perhaps no better one can be given for his attacking De Foe, whom the author of the Notes to the *Dunciad* owns to have been a man of parts. De Foe can never, with any propriety, be ranked amongst the dunces; for whoever reads his works with candour and impartiality, must be convinced that he was a man of the strongest natural powers, a lively imagination, and solid judgment, which, joined with an unshaken probity in his moral conduct, and an invincible integrity in his political sphere, ought not only to screen him from the petulant attacks of satire, but transmit his name with some degree of applause to posterity.

De Foe, who enjoyed always a competence, and was seldom subject to the necessities of the poets, died at his house at Islington, in the year 1731.[2]

[1] *The Dunciad*, II. 139–40.

[2] An error: see No. 2h above.

6. Rousseau on *Robinson Crusoe*

1762

From the third book of *Émile, ou de l'éducation* (1762), the celebrated account of 'natural' upbringing by Jean-Jacques Rousseau (1712–78), novelist and social thinker. Translation by the editor.

I loathe books: they only teach you to speak about things of which you know nothing. It is said that Hermes engraved the elements of knowledge on columns, in order to protect his discoveries from a flood. If they had been thoroughly imprinted in men's heads, they would have been preserved there by tradition. A well-prepared mind is the monument on which human knowledge may be most permanently engraved. Might there not be a means of bringing together all those lessons scattered through so many books, of uniting them under a common object, so that they will be easy to take in, interesting to follow, and stimulating even at an early age? If one could devise a situation in which all the innate needs of mankind are vividly displayed to the child's mind, and in which the means to supply these needs are presented in turn, just as simply, then it must be through a lively and direct description of this state that one first exercises his imagination.

Yours, since you are an ardent philosopher, is already caught by this prospect. No need to lay out any great efforts, however: this situation has already been invented and described – and, without detriment to yourself, much better than you could have done it, at least more simply and truly. Since books are absolutely necessary, there is one which to my taste supplies the happiest introduction to natural education. This will be the first book my Émile will read. For a long time it will constitute his entire library by itself, and it will always retain a distinguished place there. It will be the text on which all our discussions of the natural sciences will be merely a gloss. It will serve as a check on the state of our judgment as we proceed, and in so far as our taste remains unspoilt, we shall always take pleasure in reading it. What is this wonderful book then? Is it Aristotle, or Pliny, or Buffon? No – it is *Robinson Crusoe.*

Robinson Crusoe on his island, alone, deprived of the help of his fellows and of all artificial aids, yet providing for his own support, for his own safety and even achieving a sort of well-being – this is a matter of interest for any age, which can be made enjoyable to children in a thousand ways. This is how we shall get an idea of the desert island I first used as a comparison. This state, I admit, is not that of man in society, and most probably it will not be Émile's: but it is through this state that he will come to value all others. The surest way of rising above prejudice and ordering one's opinions according to the real relations of things is to put oneself in the place of a solitary man, and to judge everything as he would, having regard to its particular utility.

Stripped of all its nonsense, beginning with Robinson's wreck off his island and ending with the arrival of the ship which is to take him away, this novel will be both instruction and delight to Émile during this period. I would like him to be quite infatuated with it; to busy himself constantly with his stockade, his goats and his crops. I want him to learn in detail everything one would have to know in such a case, not through books but through things. I want him to identify himself with Robinson, to see himself dressed in skins, with a big hat and a broadsword – the whole grotesque paraphernalia of his appearance, except the parasol which he will not need. I want him to take careful thought as to the appropriate steps if his stock of this or that should happen to run out: to examine the behaviour of his hero, to see if he has not forgotten something, or if he could have done better: to make a careful note of his mistakes, and profit from these by not falling into them in similar circumstances – for do not doubt that he has every intention of setting up an establishment of this kind. This is the genuine castle in Spain of this fortunate age, when the only blessings one recognises are freedom and the necessary.

What a gift this foolish game is for a clever man, who has only encouraged it in order to turn it to advantage! The child, when urged to equip himself for the island, will be keener to learn than the master to teach him. He will want to know everything useful, and nothing else; you will no longer have to guide him, only to restrain him. Moreover, we must hurry to set him up on the island, whilst it is enough in itself to satisfy him. For the day is coming when, if he wishes to live there still, it will not be alone; and when Friday, who scarcely concerns him now, will no longer suffice for any time.

7. The close of the century

1775-90

In the last quarter of the eighteenth century, Defoe's works received a number of notices in two leading journals, the *Monthly Review* and the *Gentleman's Magazine*. Since ignorance concerning Defoe was still widespread, these materials often carry with them an air of 'curious learning', rather than scholarship or critical rigour. But they are all the more typical of the period on that account. Contributors are identified, where possible, by reference to Nangle (see Bibliography).

Later items not reprinted here include a notice by John Noorthouck in M[onthly] R[eview], vi (December 1791), 466; and a review of Chalmers's *Life* in G[entleman's] M[agazine], lxi (April 1791), 346-8.

(a) *MR*, lii (March 1775), 274, on *Roxana*:

The History of Mademoiselle de Beleau; or, the New Roxana, the Fortunate Mistress, afterwards Countess of Wintselheim, published by *Daniel De Foe*. And from Papers found since his Decease, it appears was greatly altered by himself; and from the said Papers the present Work is produced.

Few novels are better known than the story of the Lewd Roxana; which, we see, is ascribed to the famous *De Foe*. It is not improbable that this is really one of Daniel's productions; for he wrote books of all kinds, *romantic* as well as *religious*; moral as well as immoral. History, politics, poetry; in short, all subjects were alike to Daniel. – The versatility of this man's genius procured him the admiration of the age in which he lived; but the breed of De Foes has so much increased, of late years, that hundreds of them are to be found in the garrets of Grubstreet, where they *draw nutrition, propagate* [novels and pamphlets] *and rot*: and nobody minds them.

(b) *GM*, liii (May 1783), on the eighth edition of the *Tour thro' Great Britain*:

The *Tour through Great Britain*, as originally written by, I think, Daniel de Foe, is an entertaining and useful book, describing faithfully the face of the country as it appeared about the year 1725; but the last edition is the strangest jumble and unconnected hodge-podge that ever was put together. The compiler has cut out paragraphs from books that have been since published, and tacked them to the original work, without any local knowledge, and with so little skill, as to make what was separately respectable become truly ridiculous by the strange admixture of it with the new materials. [Signed 'S'.]

(c) *MR*, lxx (May 1784), 382, on a new edition of *Memoirs of a Cavalier*; the notice is by the prolific reviewer Samuel Badcock (1747–88):

This is a republication of a very interesting work. The Author places you on the spot where he chuses you should stand, or leads you away ('nothing loth') where he chuses you should go. You are only afraid of coming to your journey's end too soon.

(d) *GM*, lv (November 1785), 882; lv (December 1785), 953:

'Philobiblios' inquires: 'Who was the author of that singular book, *Memoirs of a Cavalier*, I almost despair of learning. Some, I think, have ascribed it to Defoe. . . . I think *Robinson Crusoe* is allowed to have been the work of Defoe, but I know no particulars of Defoe's life, nor what other books he wrote. [The writer goes on to compare *Gulliver's Travels* with *Robinson Crusoe*, to the advantage of the latter.] The Dr. was an able satirist, Defoe might have founded a colony. [*Crusoe* is said to be] a book scarcely less known than *Don Quixote*.'

A reply mentions the *Journal of the Plague Year* and *Colonel Jack*, this last 'a work excellent in its kind, though little known; it contains much manner of low life, and much nature: this author appears never to have attempted any scene in high life, with which he was doubtless unacquainted, but his rank is very exalted as a writer of original genius.'

(e) *GM*, lix (November 1789), 992; a note by 'Borealis', suggesting that the editor of the *History of the Union* (George Chalmers) was unaware that Defoe also wrote *A New Voyage Round the World, Roxana, Memoirs of a Cavalier, Moll Flanders, Religious Courtship*, etc.:

All his productions in the romantic species, but especially the last-mentioned, are much in vogue among country readers; and, on account of their moral and religious tendency, they very probably in some measure counteract the pernicious effects produced by the too general circulation of modern novels, those occasional vehicles of impiety and infidelity.

(f) *MR*, lxxvii (December 1787), 459–61, on Chalmers's edition of the *History of the Union*; the notice is by the dissenting minister Jabez Hirons (1728–1812):

He [Defoe] passed through a great variety of fortune, and met with difficulties and ill-treatment not only from the party which he opposed, but also from that which he espoused. This, indeed, was really honourable to him: a sincere friend as he appears to have been to the cause of liberty, civil and religious, he could not always concur in the measures and principles of those who professed at least to prosecuting the same design. By this means, like many other worthy persons, he often fell under the censures of those with whom he appeared to be united. . . . He is chiefly known as an author: his *Robinson Crusoe*, which has passed through seventeen editions, and been translated into other languages, will still preserve his memory: but his distinguished sphere, or that to which he principally applied himself, appears to have been policy [i.e. politics] and trade. . . . The work [*History of the Union*] appears, to us, to be not only of the instructive, but even of the entertaining kind: the style is different from that of the present time, but by no means unpleasant. To those readers who wish for information concerning memorable events relative to their own country, this volume will doubtless be acceptable, as contributing both to their amusement and improvement.

(g) *MR*, iii (December 1790), 471; a review of Chalmers's *Life* by John Noorthouck (c. 1736–1816), a widely active miscellaneous writer:

It would be a curious subject of investigation for any acute observer . . . to inquire why it should be the cruel fate of most of those whose pens have been employed in the service of the public, to have justice studiously withheld from their characters, till they are beyond receiving any benefit from it; and when the men have sunk under anxieties, neglect, and injurious treatment, perhaps their memory, some time or other, receives the full payment of applause, with all the interest due on it! Three-score years after the death of the ingenious and well-informed Daniel De Foe, a gentleman 'during a period of convalescence', amuses himself in writing his life; and has taken laudable, and we think successful pains, to rescue his memory from undeserved obloquoy. All this is so far well; and Mr. Chalmers, we doubt not, enjoys the conscious pleasure peculiar to good minds, in performing a generous act: but living merit can derive very little comfort from the instance.

De Foe, with great abilities, extensive knowledge, and a ready pen, living in troublesome times, became a busy controversial writer: he steadily supported the Whig interest, but could not (and what considerate honest man can?) go all lengths with his party: therefore, while he provoked the hatred of the Tories, he could not gain the entire love of the Whigs; and between both, his character has been transmitted to us under various misrepresentations. Mr. Chalmers has, with industrious and commendable zeal, traced every circumstance, as well as the distance of time would permit, to set his character and conduct in a true light; which . . . he has happily effected; and, in particular, has satisfactorily vindicated his *Robinson Crusoe* from being a piracy of Alexander Selkirk's papers.

8. Dr Johnson on Defoe

1778–84

The few references to Defoe by the lexicographer and moralist Samuel Johnson (1709–84) indicate a comparatively restricted acquaintance, but by no means a lack of sympathy. Johnson told Boswell in 1772 that the narrative of Mrs Veal was now recognised to be a fabrication; but he seems to have been quite deceived by the *Memoirs of an English Officer*. The text of the first two extracts is taken from Boswell's *Life of Johnson*, ed. G. B. Hill and L. F. Powell (Oxford, 1934–50), whilst the third is taken from Mrs Piozzi's recollections in *Johnsonian Miscellanies*, ed. G. B. Hill (Oxford, 1897), vol. i, p. 332. It must date from Johnson's later years.

(a) Boswell's *Life*:

He [Johnson] told us, that he had given Mrs. Montague[1] a catalogue of all Daniel Defoe's works of imagination; most, if not all of which, as well as of his other works, he now enumerated, allowing a considerable share of merit to a man, who, bred a tradesman, had written so variously and so well. Indeed, his *Robinson Crusoe* is enough of itself to establish his reputation. (vol. iii, pp. 267–8.)

(b) Boswell's *Life*:

'But, (said his Lordship,) the best account of Lord Peterborough[2] that I have happened to meet with, is in *Captain Carleton's Memoirs*. Carleton was descended of an ancestor who had distinguished himself at the siege of Derry. He was an officer; and, what was rare at that time, had some knowledge of engineering.' Johnson said, he had never heard of the book. Lord Eliot[3] . . . procured a copy in London, and sent it to Johnson, who told Sir Joshua Reynolds that he was going to

---

[1] Elizabeth Montagu (1720–1800), famous as 'Queen of the Blues'.
[2] Charles Mordaunt, third Earl of Peterborough (1658–1735), soldier, magnifico and friend of the wits.
[3] Edward Eliot, first Baron Eliot (1727–1804).

bed when it came, but was so much pleased with it, that he sat up till
he had read it through, and found in it such an air of truth, that he
could not doubt of its authenticity; adding, with a smile . . . 'I did not
think *a young Lord* could have mentioned to me a book in the English
history that was not known to me.' (vol. iv, pp. 333–4.)

(c) *Johnsonian Miscellanies:*

Was there ever yet anything written by mere man that was wished
longer by its readers, excepting *Don Quixote, Robinson Crusoe,* and the
Pilgrim's Progress?

9. James Beattie on the 'new romance'

1783

James Beattie (1735–1803), Professor of Moral Philosophy at
Marischal College, was most famous in his lifetime for his poem
The Minstrel (1771–4). His essay 'On Fable and Romance' was a
pioneering attempt to grapple with the critical issues raised by the
new popularity of the novel. Beattie constructed a scheme which
covered religious and moral allegory (including *Gulliver* and the
Pilgrim's Progress); historical allegory (Arbuthnot's *John Bull*);
comic romance; and serious romance. It is under this last heading
that Beattie comes to discuss *Crusoe.*

Text from the original publication in Beattie's *Dissertations Moral
and Critical* (1783), pp. 566–7.

Some have thought, that a lovetale is necessary to make a romance
interesting. But *Robinson Crusoe,* though there is nothing of love in it,
is one of the most interesting narratives that ever was written; at least
in all that part which relates to the desert island: being founded on a
passion still more prevalent than that of love, the desire of self-

preservation; and therefore likely to engage the curiosity of every class of readers, both old and young, both learned and unlearned. . . .

Robinson Crusoe must be allowed by the most rigid moralist, to be one of those novels, which one may read, not only with pleasure, but also with profit. It breathes throughout a spirit of piety and benevolence: it sets in a very striking light . . . the importance of the mechanick arts, which they, who do not know what it is to be without them, are apt to undervalue: it fixes in the mind a lively idea of the horrors of solitude, and, consequently, of the sweets of social life, and of the blessings we derive from conversation, and mutual aid: and it shows, how, by labouring with one's own hands, one may secure independence, and open for oneself many sources of health and amusement. I agree, therefore, with Rousseau, that this is one of the best books that can be put into the hands of children. – The style is plain, but not elegant, nor perfectly grammatical: and the second part of the story is tiresome.

10. Hugh Blair on Defoe

1783

Hugh Blair (1718–1800), Scottish divine and critic, was Regius Professor of Rhetoric and Belles Lettres at Edinburgh from 1762. The extract is from Lecture XXXVII in Blair's *Lectures on Rhetoric and Belles Lettres* (1783), vol. ii, p. 309. In the preceding passage Blair had discussed French fiction, in particular Rousseau and Marivaux.

In this kind of Writing we are, it must be confessed, in Great Britain, inferior to the French. We neither relate so agreeably, nor draw characters with so much delicacy; yet we are not without some performances which discover the strength of the British genius. No fiction, in any language, was ever better supported than the *Adventures of Robinson*

Crusoe. While it is carried on with that appearance of truth and simplicity, which takes a strong hold of the imagination of all Readers, it suggests, at the same time, very useful instruction; by showing how much the native powers of man may be exerted for surmounting the difficulties of any external situation.

11. The beginnings of serious study

1785

The antiquarian and biographer George Chalmers (1742–1825) made a number of important contributions to Defoe studies. His pioneering *Life* was written in 1785, and later appended to editions of the *History of the Union* (1786) and of *Robinson Crusoe* (1790). Chalmers was the first to grapple seriously with the intractable problems in biography and bibliography which Defoe's career still sets, and his checklist of about eighty 'canonical' works and twenty supposititious items was an essential base for nineteenth-century reappraisals of Defoe. Chalmers's own criticism is not of outstanding interest but it is ahead of its time in its awareness of Defoe's whole achievement. Chalmers, unlike his predecessors, had a good idea of the scope and nature of Defoe's literary undertakings. The text follows that of the *Life* as appended to *Robinson Crusoe* (1790).

(a) On the *History of the Union:*

The subject of this work is the completion of a measure, which was carried into effect, notwithstanding obstructions apparently insurmountable, and tumults approaching to rebellion, and which has produced the ends designed, beyond expectation, whether we consider its influence on the Government, or its operation on the governed. The minuteness with which [Defoe] describes what he saw and heard on the turbulent stage, where he acted a conspicuous part, is extremely interesting to us, who wish to know what actually passed, however this circumstantiality may have disgusted contemporaneous readers. History is chiefly valuable as it transmits a faithful copy of the *manners* and *sentiments* of every age. This narrative of De Foe is a drama, in which he introduces the highest peers and the lowest peasants, speaking and acting, according as they were each actuated by their characteristic passions; and while the man of taste is amused by his *manner*, the man of business may draw instruction from the *documents*, which are appended to the end, and interspersed in every page. This publication had alone preserved his name, had his *Crusoe* pleased us less. (vol. ii, p. 401.)

(b) On the 'secondary' novels:

Of fictitious biography it is equally true, that by matchless art it may be made more instructive than a real life. Few of our writers have excelled De Foe in this kind of biographical narration, the great qualities of which are, to attract by the diversity of circumstances, and to instruct by the usefulness of examples. . . . The fortunes and misfortunes of *Moll Flanders* were made to gratify the world in 1721. De Foe was aware, that in relating a vicious life, it was necessary to make the best use of a bad story; and he artfully endeavours, that the reader shall be more pleased with the moral than the fable; with the application than the relation; with the end of the writer than the adventures of the person. There was published in 1721, a work of a similar tendency, the *Life of Colonel Jack*, who was born a gentleman but was bred a pickpocket. – Our Author is studious to convert his various adventures into a delightful field, where the reader might gather herbs, wholesome and medicinal, without the incommodation of plants, poisonous, or noxious. In 1724, appeared the *Life of Roxana*. Scenes of crimes can scarcely be represented in such a manner, says De Foe, but some make a criminal use of them; but when vice is painted in its low-prized colours, it is not to make people love what from the frightfulness of the figures they ought necessarily to hate. Yet, I am not convinced, that the world has been made much wiser, or better, by the perusal of these lives: they may have diverted the lower orders, but I doubt if they have much improved them; if however they have not made them better, they have not left them worse. But they do not exhibit many scenes which are welcome to cultivated minds. Of a very different quality are the *Memoirs of a Cavalier*, during the Civil

Wars in England, which seem to have been published without a date. This is a romance the likest to truth that ever was written. It is a narrative of great events, which is drawn with such simplicity, and enlivened with such reflections, as to inform the ignorant and entertain the wise. (vol. ii, pp. 428–9.)

(c) Concluding summary:

De Foe has not yet outlived his century, though he have outlived most of his contemporaries. Yet the time is come, when he must be acknowledged as one of the ablest, as he is one of the most captivating, writers, of which this island can boast. Before he can be admitted to this pre-eminence, he must be considered distinctly, as a poet, as a novelist, as a polemick, as a commercial writer, and as a grave historian.

As a poet, we must look to the end of his effusions rather than to his execution, ere we can allow him considerable praise. To mollify national animosities or to vindicate national rights, is certainly noble objects, which merit the vigour and imagination of Milton, or the flow and precision of Pope; but our Author's energy runs into harshness, and his sweetness is to be tasted in his prose more than in his poesy. If we regard the adventures of Crusoe, like the adventures of Telemachus, as a poem, his moral, his incidents, and his language, must lift him high on the poet's scale. His professed poems, whether we contemplate the propriety of sentiment, or the suavity of numbers, may indeed, without much loss of pleasure or instruction, be resigned to those, who, in imitation of Pope, poach in the fields of obsolete poetry for brilliant thoughts, felicities of phrase, or for happy rhymes.

As a novelist, every one will place him in the foremost rank, who considers his originality, his performance, and his purpose. *The Ship of Fools* had indeed been launched in early times; but, who like De Foe, had ever carried his reader to sea, in order to mend the heart, and regulate the practice of life, by shewing his readers the effects of adversity, or how they might equally be called to sustain his hero's trials, as they sailed round the world. But, without attractions, neither the originality, nor the end, can have any salutary consequence. This he had foreseen; and for this he has provided, by giving his adventures in a style so pleasing, because it is simple, and so interesting, because it is particular, that every one fancies he could write a similar language. It was, then, idle in Boyer[1] formerly, or in Smollet lately, to speak of

---

[1] Abel Boyer (1667–1729), a frequent critic of Defoe in his *Political State*, a monthly journal.

De Foe as *a party writer, in little estimation.* The writings of no Author since have run through more numerous editions. And he whose works have pleased generally and pleased long, must be deemed a writer of no small estimation; the people's verdict being the proper test of what they are the proper judges.

As a polemick, I fear we must regard our Author with less kindness, though it must be recollected, that he lived during a contentious period, when two parties distracted the nation, and writers indulged in great asperities. But, in opposition to reproach, let it ever be remembered, that he defended freedom, without anarchy; that he supported toleration, without libertinism; that he pleaded for moderation even amidst violence. With acuteness of intellect, with keenness of wit, with archness of diction, and pertinacity of design; it must be allowed that nature had qualified, in a high degree, De Foe for a disputant. His polemical treatises, whatever might have been their attractions once, may now be delivered without reserve to those who delight in polemical reading. De Foe, it must be allowed, was a party-writer: But, were not Swift and Prior, Steel and Addison, Halifax[1] and Bolingbroke, party-writers? De Foe, being a party-writer upon settled principles, did not change with the change of parties: Addison and Steel, Prior and Swift, connected as they were with persons, changed their note as persons were elevated or depressed.

As a commercial writer, De Foe is fairly entitled to stand in the foremost rank among his contemporaries, whatever may be their performances or their fame. Little would be his praise, to say of him, that he wrote on commercial legislation like Addison, who when he touches on Trade, sinks into imbecility, without knowledge of fact, or power of argument. The distinguishing characteristics of De Foe, as a commercial disquisitor, are originality and depth. He has many sentiments with regard to traffic, which are scattered through his Reviews, and which I never read in any other book. His *Giving Alms no Charity* is a capital performance, with the exception of one or two thoughts about the abridgment of labour by machinery, which are either half formed or half expressed. Were we to compare De Foe with D'Avenant, it would be found, that D'Avenant has more detail from official documents; that De Foe has more fact from wider inquiry. D'Avenant is more apt to consider laws in their particular application; De Foe more frequently investigates commercial legislation in its general effects. From the

---

[1] Probably Chalmers means George Savile, first Marquis of Halifax (1633–1695), author of *The Character of a Trimmer* (1688).

publications of D'Avenant it is sufficiently clear, that he was not very regardful of means or very attentive to consequences; De Foe is more correct in his motives, and more salutary in his ends. But, as a commercial prophet, De Foe must yield the palm to Child;[1] who foreseeing from experience that men's conduct must finally be directed by their principles, foretold the colonial revolt: De Foe, allowing his prejudices to obscure his sagacity, reprobated that suggestion, because he deemed interest a more strenuous prompter than enthusiasm. Were we however to form an opinion, not from special passages, but from whole performances, we must incline to De Foe, when compared with the ablest contemporary: we must allow him the preference, on recollection, that when he writes on commerce he seldom fails to insinuate some axiom of morals, or to inculcate some precept of religion.

As an historian, it will be found, that our Author had few equals in the English language, when he wrote. His *Memoirs of a Cavalier* shew how well he could execute the lighter narratives. His *History of the Union* evinces that he was equal to the higher department of historic composition. This is an account of a single event, difficult indeed in its execution, but beneficial certainly in its consequences. With extraordinary skill and information, our Author relates, not only the event, but the transactions which preceded, and the effects which followed. He is at once learned and intelligent. Considering the factiousness of the age, his candour is admirable. His moderation is exemplary. And if he spoke of James I. as a tyrant, he only exercised the prerogative, which our historians formerly enjoyed, of casting obloquy on an unfortunate race, in order to supply deficience of knowledge, of elegance, and of stile. In this instance De Foe allowed his prejudice to overpower his philosophy. If the language of his narrative want the dignity of the great historians of the current times, it has greater facility; if it be not always grammatical, it is generally precise; and if it be thought defective in strength, it must be allowed to excel in sweetness. (vol. ii, pp. 435–9.)

[1] Dr Charles Davenant (1656–1714), and Sir Josiah Child (1630–99), writers on political economy.

12. Scott on Defoe's life and works

1810, 1817

Sir Walter Scott's familiarity with Augustan literature is signalised by his editions of Dryden (1808) and Swift (1814). The edition of Defoe's novels, later including the 'miscellaneous works', put out from 1810 onwards by John Ballantyne, included some contributions by Scott. However, only a few of the notes are now attributed to him, and these are reproduced in excerpts (a) and (b). The long introduction is, however, his: the greater portion is reproduced in (c) below. Text from *The Miscellaneous Works of Sir Walter Scott, Bart.* (Edinburgh, 1834), vol. iv, pp. 248–81.

Among other comments, we might note a remark in Scott's review of his own *Tales of my Landlord* in the *Quarterly Review* for January 1817 – where he speaks of Defoe's 'liveliness of imagination, who excelled all others in dramatising a story, and presenting it as if in actual speech and action before the reader'. (*Prose Works*, Edinburgh, 1834–7, vol. xix, p. 41.) There is also an interesting comparison of Swift and Defoe in Scott's edition of the former: this can be found reprinted in *Swift: The Critical Heritage*, ed. Kathleen Williams (1970), pp. 307–8.

(a) On the *Journal of the Plague Year:*

The *History of the Great Plague in London* is one of that particular character of compositions which hovers between romance and history. Had he not been the author of *Robinson Crusoe*, De Foe would have deserved immortality for the genius which he has displayed in this work.

(b) On *Memoirs of a Cavalier:*

[This work must be allowed] to reflect additional lustre, even on the author of *Robinson Crusoe*. There is so much simplicity and apparent fidelity of statement throughout the novel, that the feelings are little indebted to those who would remove the veil;[1] and the former editors, perhaps, have acted not unwisely in leaving the circumstances of its authenticity in their original obscurity.

(c) General assessment of Defoe's achievement:

The preceding memoir[2] does not notice one half of his compositions, all, even the meanest of which, have something in them to distinguish them as the works of an extraordinary man. It cannot, therefore, be doubted, that he possessed a powerful memory to furnish him with materials, and a no less copious vein of imagination to weave them up into a web of his own, and supply the rich embroidery which in reality constitutes their chief value. De Foe does not display much acquaintance with classic learning, neither does it appear that his attendance on the Newington seminary had led him deep into the study of ancient languages. His own language is genuine English, often simple even to vulgarity, but always so distinctly impressive, that its very vulgarity had, as we shall presently show, an efficacy in giving an air of truth or probability to the facts and sentiments it conveys. Exclusive of politics, De Foe's studies led chiefly to those popular narratives, which are the amusement of children and of the lower classes; those accounts of travellers who have visited remote countries; of voyagers who have made discoveries of new lands and strange nations; of pirates and bucaniers who have acquired wealth by their desperate adventures on the ocean. . . . We are afraid we must impute to his long and repeated imprisonments, the opportunity of becoming acquainted with the secrets of thieves and mendicants, their acts of plunder, concealment, and escape. But whatever way he acquired his knowledge of low life, De Foe certainly possessed it in the most extensive sense, and applied it in the composition of several works of fiction, in the style termed by the Spaniards *Gusto Picaresco*, of which no man was ever a greater master. This class of the fictitious narrative may be termed the Romance of Roguery, the subjects being the adventures of thieves, rogues, vagabonds, and swindlers, including viragoes and courtezans. The improved taste of the present age has justly rejected this coarse species of amusement, which is, besides, calculated to do an infinite deal of mischief among the lower classes, as it presents in a comic, or even heroic

[1] i.e. regarding the existence or otherwise of a 'real' cavalier officer, whose manuscript was supposedly used by Defoe.
[2] By the publisher Ballantyne.

shape, the very crimes and vices to which they are otherwise most likely to be tempted. Nevertheless, the strange and blackguard scenes which De Foe describes, are fit to be compared to the gipsy-boys of the Spanish painter Murillo, which are so justly admired, as being, in truth of conception, and spirit of execution, the very *chef d'œuvres* of art, however low and loathsome the originals from which they are taken. Of this character is the *History of Colonel Jack*, for example, which had an immense popularity among the lower classes; that of *Moll Flanders*, a shoplifter and prostitute; that of *Mrs Christian Davis*, called *Mother Ross*; and that of *Roxana*, as she is termed, a courtezan in higher life. All of these contain strong marks of genius; in the last they are particularly predominant. But from the coarseness of the narrative, and the vice and vulgarity of the actors, the reader feels as a well-principled young man may do, when seduced by some entertaining and dissolute libertine into scenes of debauchery, that, though he may be amused, he must be not a little ashamed of that which furnishes the entertainment. So that, though we could select from these *picaresque* romances a good deal that is not a little amusing, we let them pass by, as we would persons, howsoever otherwise interesting, who may not be in character and manners entirely fit for good society.

A third species of composition, to which the author's active and vigorous genius was peculiarly adapted, was the account of great national convulsions, whether by war, or by the pestilence, or the tempest. These were tales which are sure, when even moderately well told, to arrest the attention, and which, narrated with that impression of reality which De Foe knew so well how to convey, make the hair bristle and the skin creep. In this manner he has written the *Memoirs of a Cavalier*, which have been often read and quoted as a real production of a real personage. Born himself almost immediately after the Restoration, De Foe must have known many of those who had been engaged in the civil turmoils of 1642–6, to which the period of these memoirs refers. He must have lived among them at that age when boys, such as we conceive De Foe must necessarily have been, cling to the knees of those who can tell them of the darings and the dangers of their youth, at a period when their own passions, and views of pressing forward in life, have not begun to operate upon their minds, and while they are still pleased to listen to the adventures which others have encountered on that stage, which they themselves have not yet entered upon. The *Memoirs of a Cavalier* have certainly been enriched with some such anecdotes as were likely to fire De Foe's active and powerful imagination, and hint to him in what colours the subject ought to be treated.

The contrast betwixt the soldiers of the celebrated Tilly, and those of the illustrious Gustavus Adolphus,[1] almost seems too minutely drawn to have been executed from any thing short of ocular testimony. But De Foe's genius has shown, in this and other instances, how completely he could assume the character he describes. . . .

[On the *Journal of the Plague Year*:] Undoubtedly De Foe embodied a number of traditions upon this subject with what he might actually have read, or of which he might otherwise have received direct evidence. . . . This dreadful disease, which, in the language of Scripture, might be described as 'the pestilence which walketh in darkness, and the destruction that wasteth at noon-day,' was indeed a fit subject for a pencil so veracious as that of De Foe; and, accordingly, he drew pictures almost too horrible to look upon.

It is a wonder how so excellent a subject as the Great Fire of London, should have escaped the notice of De Foe, so eager for subjects of a popular character. Yet we can hardly regret this, since besides the verses of Dryden in the *Annus Mirabilis*, the accounts by two contemporaries, Evelyn and Pepys, have sketched it in all its terrible brilliancy.

The Great Storm, which, on 26 November, 1703, in Addison's phrase, 'o'er pale Britannia pass'd,' was seized upon by De Foe as a subject for the exercise of his powers of description. But as it consists in a great measure of letters from the country, wretched pastoral poetry, (for De Foe was only a poet in prose,) and similar buckram and binding used by bookmakers, it does not do the genius of the author the same credit as the works before named.

A third species of composition, for which this multifarious author showed a strong predilection, was that upon theurgy, magic, ghost-seeing, witchcraft, and the occult sciences. De Foe dwells on such subjects with so much unction, as to leave us little doubt that he was to a certain point a believer in something resembling an immediate communication between the inhabitants of this world, and of that which we shall in future inhabit. He is particularly strong on the subject of secret forebodings, mysterious impressions, bodements of good or evil, which arise in our own mind, but which yet seem

---

[1] Tilly, marshal of the Imperial Forces; Gustavus Adolphus, King of Sweden, invaded Germany in 1630. Both were killed in 1632, in separate encounters forming part of the Thirty Years War.

impressed there by some external agent, and not to arise from the course of our natural reflections. Perhaps he even acted upon these supposed inspirations; for the following passage plainly refers to his own history, though, whether he speaks for the nonce, or means to be seriously understood, we cannot pretend to judge, though we incline to the latter opinion.

Whatever were De Foe's real sentiments on those mystic subjects, there is no doubt that he was fond of allowing his mind to dwell on them; and, either from his own taste, or because he reckoned them peculiarly calculated to attract the notice of a numerous class of readers, many of his popular publications turn upon supernatural visitation. Thus he wrote *An Essay on the history and reality of Apparitions; being an account of what they are, and what they are not; whence they come, and whence they come not; as also how we may distinguish between the apparitions of good and evil spirits, and how we ought to behave to them.* This *Essay on Apparitions* was afterwards published under the name of Morton. . . . De Foe's reasoning, if it can be called such, belongs to the Platonic System of Dr Henry More, but is not very consistent either with that or with itself. On the other hand, the examples, or, in other words, the stories of ghosts and magic, with which we are favoured, are remarkably well told, or, rather, we should say, composed, and that with an air of perfect veracity, which nobody so well knew how to preserve as our author. To this class of his writings must be added the *Life of Duncan Campbell, the Conjurer and Fortune-teller,* a fellow who pretended to be deaf and dumb, and to tell fortunes and whose reputation was such at the time, that De Foe thought his name would sell more than one book, and also wrote the *Spy on the Conjurer;* for, pressed by his circumstances to seek out such subjects as were popular for the moment, our author was apt to adhere to those which he had already treated with approbation. Thus, he not only wrote a second part to *Robinson Crusoe,* which is greatly inferior to the first part of that inimitable romance, but he drew a third draft on the popularity which it had acquired him, by a work of the mystical kind to which we have just alluded. This last seems the perfection of book-making. It is termed, *Serious Reflections during the Life of Robinson Crusoe, with his Vision of the Angelic World.* The contents are, in general, trite enough reflections upon moral subjects; and though Robinson Crusoe's solitary state is sometimes referred to, and the book is ornamented with a bird's eye view of the memorable island, yet it contains few observations that might not have been made by any shopkeeper living at Charing Cross.

Thus may the richest source of genius be exhausted, and the most plentiful flow of invention drained off to the very dregs.

Besides those three several species of romantic fiction, in each of which Daniel De Foe was a copious author, his unwearied pen was also turned to moral and philosophical subjects, to those which relate to the economy of life, to history, and to statistics and descriptive subjects. He wrote *Travels in North and South Britain*; he wrote a *History of the Union*; he wrote an incorrect *History of the Church of Scotland, from the Restoration to the Revolution*. None of these historical works are of much value, except, perhaps, the *History of the Union*, which is little more than a dry journal of what passed in the Scottish Parliament upon that remarkable occasion; yet De Foe must have had an interesting tale to tell, if he had chosen it. But, writing under Harley's patronage, he cramped his genius, probably, to avoid the risk of giving offence to the irritable Scottish nation. Among his numerous political tracts, the most interesting perhaps is, *The History of Addresses*,[1] which, written with great power of sarcasm, places in a ludicrous and contemptible light, that mode of communication between the people and the throne. All must recollect the story of Richard Cromwell, who, in removing from Whitehall, no longer his own, begged that particular care might be taken of a large chest, which contained, he said, 'all the lives and fortunes of England,' pledged, of course, in support of the Second Protector, by those who now saw him, with the utmost indifference, dragged from the seat of government.

It is not, however, of such political subjects that we have undertaken to treat. The multifarious author whose head imagined, and whose pen executed, such variety of works upon them, that it is a labour even to collect their names, must be now treated of solely in his character of a writer of fictitious composition.

And here, before proceeding to attempt a few observations on *Robinson Crusoe* in particular, it may be necessary to consider what is the particular charm, which carries the reader through, not that *chef-d'œuvre* alone, but others of De Foe's compositions, and inspires a reluctance to lay down the volume till the tale is finished; and the desire, not generally felt in the perusal of works of fiction, to read every sentence and word upon every leaf, instead of catching up as much of the story as may enable us to understand the conclusion.

It cannot be the beauty of the style which thus commands the reader's

---

[1] Now known to be the work not of Defoe, but of John Oldmixon.

attention; for that of De Foe, though often forcible, is rather rendered so by the interest of a particular situation than by the art of the writer. In general the language is loose and inaccurate, often tame and creeping, and almost always that of the lower classes in society. Neither does the charm depend upon the character of the incidents; for although in *Robinson Crusoe*, the incidents are very fine, yet in the *History of the Plague* the events are disgusting, and scarce less in those works where the scene lies in low life. Yet, like Pistol eating his leek, we go on growling and reading to the end of the volume, while we nod over many a more elegant subject, treated by authors who exhibit a far greater command of language. Neither can it be the artful conducting of the story, by which we are so much interested. De Foe seems to have written too rapidly to pay the least attention to this circumstance; the incidents are huddled together like paving-stones discharged from a cart, and have as little connexion between the one and the other. The scenes merely follow, without at all depending on each other. They are not like those of the regular drama, connected together by a regular commencement, continuation, and conclusion, but rather resemble the pictures in a showman's box, which have no relation further than as being enclosed within the same box, and subjected to the action of the same string.

To what, then, are we to ascribe this general charm attached to the romances of De Foe? We presume to answer, that it is chiefly to be ascribed to the unequalled dexterity with which our author has given an appearance of REALITY to the incidents which he narrates. Even De Foe's deficiencies in style, his homeliness of language, his rusticity of thought, expressive of what is called the *Crassa Minerva*, seem to claim credit for him as one who speaks the truth, the rather that we suppose he wants the skill to conceal or disguise it. The principle is almost too simple to need illustration; and yet, as it seems to include something of a paradox, since in fact it teaches that with the more art a story is told, the less likely it is to attract earnest attention, it may be proved by reference to common life. If we meet with a friend in the street, who tells us a story containing something beyond usual interest, and not of everyday occurrence, our feeling with respect to the truth of the story will be much influenced by the character of the narrator. If he is a man of wit or humour, and places the ludicrous part of the tale in the most prominent point of view, the hearer will be apt to recollect that his friend is a wag, and make some grains of allowance accordingly. On the other hand, supposing the person who communicates the narrative to be of a sentimental or enthusiastic character, with romantic ideas and a store of words to express them, you listen to his tale with a sort of suspicion that it is *too well* told to be truly told, and that though it may be at bottom real, yet it has been embroidered over by the flourishes of the narrator. But if the same fact be told by a man of plain sense, and sufficient knowledge of the world, the minuteness with which he tells the story, mixing up with it a number of circumstances, which are not otherwise connected with it, than as existing at the same moment, seems to guarantee the truth of what he says; and the bursts, whether of mirth or of emotion, which accompany the narrative, appear additional warrants of his fidelity, because neither is the usual mood of his mind. You believe, as coming from such a person, that which upon other information you might have thought an imposition, as Benedick credits the report of Beatrice's affection towards him, because 'the fellow with the grey beard said it.'[1]

In the testimony of such a person upon a subject which is at all interesting, we generally detect some point which ascertains the eye-witness, and some expression which would seem to have only occurred to an individual who had heard and seen the facts to which he speaks. Those who are in the habit of attending courts of justice, during the leading of evidence, frequently hear, not only from men or women of observation, but from 'iron-witted fools and unrespective boys,' such striking circumstances as the following: A horrible murder had been committed by a man upon a person whom he had invited into his house in friendship; they were alone together when the deed was done, and the murderer, throwing on his coat, hastily left the house before the deed was discovered. A child of twelve or thirteen years old gave evidence that she was playing in the under part of the dwelling, and heard the accused person run hastily down stairs, and stumble at the threshold. She said she was very much frightened at the noise she heard; and being asked whether she had ever before thought of being frightened by a man running hurriedly down stairs, she replied no; but the noise then made was like no other she had ever heard before. The poet of the most active imagination would hardly have dared to ascribe such impressive effects to the wild and precipitate retreat of guilt in making its escape from justice. This peculiar effect upon the child's imagination we might have doubted if we had read it in fiction, and yet how striking it becomes, heard from the mouth of the child herself!

It is no doubt true, that, in assuming this peculiar style of narrative,

[1] *Much Ado About Nothing*, ii. iii. 123.

the author does so at a certain risk. He debars himself from the graces of language, and the artifice of narrative; he must sometimes seem prolix, sometimes indistinct and obscure, though possessing occasional points of brilliancy; in which respect his story may resemble some old Catholic towns on the Continent, where the streets are left in general darkness, save at those favoured spots where lamps are kept burning before the altars of particular saints; whereas, a regularly composed narrative represents an English country town, so well lighted throughout, that no particular spot, scarce even the dwelling of Mr Mayor, or the window of the apothecary, can exhibit any glow of peculiar lustre. And certainly it is the last style which should be attempted by a writer of inferior genius; for though it be possible to disguise mediocrity by fine writing, it appears in all its native inanity, when it assumes the garb of simplicity. Besides this peculiar style of writing requires that the author possess King Fadlallah's secret of transmigrating from one body to another, and possessing himself of all the qualities which he finds in the assumed character, retaining his own taste and judgment to direct them.

Sometimes this is done, by the author avowedly taking upon himself an imaginary personage, and writing according to his supposed feelings and prejudices. What would be the Vicar of Wakefield's history unless told by the kindest and worthiest pedant that ever wore a cassock, namely the Vicar himself? And what would be the most interesting and affecting, as well as the most comic, passages of *Castle Rackrent*, if narrated by one who had a less regard for 'the family' than the immortal Thady, who, while he sees that none of the dynasty which he celebrates were perfectly right, has never been able to puzzle out wherein they were certainly wrong. Mr Galt's country Provost, and still more his reverend Annalist of the Parish, should be also distinguished in this class.[1] Wordsworth, himself, has assumed, in one of his affecting poems, the character of a sea-faring person retired to settle in the country.

These are, however, all characters of masquerade: We believe that of De Foe was entirely natural to him. The high-born Cavalier, for instance, speaks nearly the same species of language, and shows scarce a greater knowledge of society than Robinson Crusoe; only he has a cast of the grenadier about him, as the other has the trim of a seaman.

---

[1] Apart from Goldsmith's *Vicar of Wakefield* (1766), Scott alludes to Maria Edgeworth's *Castle Rackrent* (1800), and two novels by John Galt, *Annals of the Parish* (1821) and *The Provost* (1822).

It is greatly to be doubted whether De Foe could have changed his colloquial, circuitous, and periphrastic style for any other, whether more coarse or more elegant. We have little doubt it was connected with his nature, and the particular turn of his thoughts and ordinary expressions, and that he did not succeed so much by writing in an assumed manner, as by giving full scope to his own.

The subject is so interesting, that it is worth while examining it a little more closely; with which view we have reprinted, as illustrating our commentary on what may be called the *plausible* style of composition, *The True History of the Apparition of one Mrs Veal the next day after her Death, to one Mrs Bargrave, at Canterbury, the eighth of September, 1705, which Apparition recommends the perusal of Drelincourt's Book of Consolation against the Fears of Death.* We are induced to this, because the account of the origin of the pamphlet is curious, the pamphlet itself short, and, though once highly popular, now little read or known, and particularly because De Foe has put in force, within these few pages, peculiar specimens of his art of recommending the most improbable narrative, by his specious and serious mode of telling it.

[Scott paraphrases *The Apparition of Mrs Veal* and explains Defoe's method in the pamphlet.]

... The air of writing with all the plausibility of truth must, in almost every case, have its own peculiar value; as we admire the paintings of some Flemish artists, where, though the subjects drawn are mean and disagreeable, and such as in nature we would not wish to study or look close upon, yet the skill with which they are represented by the painter gives an interest to the imitation upon canvass which the original entirely wants. But, on the other hand, when the power of exact and circumstantial delineation is applied to objects which we are anxiously desirous to see in their proper shape and colours, we have a double source of pleasure, both in the art of the painter, and in the interest which we take in the subject represented. Thus the style of probability with which De Foe invested his narratives, was perhaps ill bestowed, or rather wasted, upon some of the works which he thought proper to produce, and cannot recommend to us the subject of *Colonel Jack* and *Moll Flanders*; but, on the other hand, the same talent throws an air of truth about the delightful history of *Robinson Crusoe*, which we never could have believed it possible to have united with so extraordinary a situation as is assigned to the hero. All the usual scaffolding and machinery employed in composing fictitious history are carefully discarded. The early incidents of the tale, which in ordinary

works of invention are usually thrown out as pegs to hang the conclusion upon, are in this work only touched upon, and suffered to drop
out of sight. Robinson, for example, never hears any thing more of
his elder brother, who enters Lockhart's Dragoons in the beginning
of the work, and who, in any common romance, would certainly have
appeared before the conclusion. We lose sight at once and for ever of
the interesting Xury; and the whole earlier adventures of our voyager
vanish, not to be recalled to our recollection by the subsequent course
of the story. His father – the good old merchant of Hull – all the other
persons who have been originally active in the drama – vanish from
the scene, and appear not again. This is not the case in the ordinary
romance, where the author, however luxuriant his invention, does not
willingly quit possession of the creatures of his imagination, till they
have rendered him some services upon the scene; whereas in common
life, it rarely happens that our early acquaintances exercise much
influence upon the fortunes of our future life.

Our friend Robinson, thereafter, in the course of his roving and restless life, is at length thrown upon his Desert Island, a situation in which,
existing as a solitary being, he became an example of what the unassisted
energies of an individual of the human race can perform; and the author
has, with wonderful exactness, described him as acting and thinking
precisely as such a man must have thought and acted in such an extraordinary situation.

Pathos is not De Foe's general characteristic; he had too little delicacy
of mind; when it comes, it comes uncalled, and is created by the
circumstances, not sought for by the author. The excess, for instance,
of the natural longing for human society which Crusoe manifests while
on board of the stranded Spanish vessel, by falling into a sort of agony,
as he repeated the words, 'Oh, that but one man had been saved! – Oh,
that there had been but one!' is in the highest degree pathetic. The
agonizing reflections of the solitary, when he is in danger of being
driven to sea, in his rash attempt to circumnavigate his island, are also
affecting.

In like manner we may remark, that De Foe's genius did not approach
the grand or terrific. The battles, which he is fond of describing, are
told with the indifference of an old bucanier, and probably in the very
way in which he may have heard them recited by the actors. His
goblins, too, are generally a commonplace sort of spirits, that bring with
them very little of supernatural terror; and yet the fine incident of the
print of the naked foot on the sand, with Robinson Crusoe's terrors in

consequence, never fail to leave a powerful impression upon the reader. The supposed situation of his hero was peculiarly favourable to the circumstantial style of De Foe. Robinson Crusoe was placed in a condition where it was natural that the slightest event should make an impression on him; and De Foe was not an author who would leave the slightest event untold. When he mentions that two shoes were driven ashore, and adds that they were not neighbours, we feel it an incident of importance to the poor solitary.

The assistance which De Foe derived from Selkirk's history, seems of a very meagre kind. It is not certain that he was obliged to the real hermit of Juan Fernandez even for the original hint; for the putting mutineers or turbulent characters on shore upon solitary places, was a practice so general among the bucaniers, that there was a particular name for the punishment; it was called *marooning* a man. De Foe borrowed, perhaps, from the account in Woodes Rogers, the circumstance of the two huts, the abundance of goats, the clothing made out of their skins; and the turnips of Alexander Selkirk may have perhaps suggested the corn of Robinson Crusoe. Even these incidents, however, are so wrought up and heightened, and so much is added to make them interesting, that the bare circumstances occurring elsewhere, cannot be said to infringe upon the author's claim to originality. On the whole, indeed, Robinson Crusoe is put to so many more trials of ingenuity, his comforts are so much increased, his solitude is so much diversified, and his account of his thoughts and occupations so distinctly traced, that the course of the work embraces a far wider circle of investigation into human nature, than could be derived from that of Selkirk, who, for want of the tools and conveniences supplied to Crusoe by the wreck, relapses into a sort of savage state, which could have afforded little scope for delineation. It may, however, be observed, that De Foe may have known so much of Selkirk's history as to be aware how much his stormy passions were checked and tamed by his long course of solitude, and that, from being a kind of Will Atkins, a brawling dissolute seaman, he became (which was certainly the case) a grave, sober, reflective man. The manner in which Robinson Crusoe's moral sense and religious feeling are awakened and brought into action, are important passages in the work.

Amid these desultory remarks, it may be noticed, that, through all his romances, De Foe has made a great deal of the narrative depend upon lucky hits and accidents, which, as he is usually at some pains to explain, ought rather to be termed providential occurrences. This is coupled with a belief in spiritual communication in the way of strong internal suggestions, to which De Foe, as we have seen, was himself sufficiently willing to yield belief. Odd and surprising accidents do, indeed, frequently occur in human life; and when we hear them narrated, we are interested in them, not only from the natural tendency of the human mind towards the extraordinary and wonderful, but also because we have some disposition to receive as truths circumstances, which, from their improbability, do not seem likely to be invented. It is the kind of good fortune, too, which every one wishes to himself, which comes without exertion, and just at the moment it is wanted; so that it gives a sort of pleasure to be reminded of the possibility of its arrival even in fiction.

The continuation of Robinson Crusoe's history after he obtains the society of his man Friday, is less philosophical than that which turns our thoughts upon the efforts which a solitary individual may make for extending his own comforts in the melancholy situation in which he is placed, and upon the natural reflections suggested by the progress of his own mind. The character of Friday is nevertheless extremely pleasing; and the whole subsequent history of the shipwrecked Spaniards and the pirate vessel is highly interesting. Here certainly the *Memoirs of Robinson Crusoe* ought to have stopped. The Second Part, though containing many passages which display the author's genius, does not rise high in character above the *Memoirs of Captain Singleton,* or the other imaginary voyages of the author.

There scarce exists a work so popular as *Robinson Crusoe.* It is read eagerly by young people; and there is hardly an elf so devoid of imagination as not to have supposed for himself a solitary island in which he could act *Robinson Crusoe,* were it but in the corner of the nursery. To many it has given the decided turn of their lives, by sending them to sea. For the young mind is much less struck with the hardships of the anchorite's situation than with the animating exertions which he makes to overcome them; and *Robinson Crusoe* produces the same impression upon an adventurous spirit which the *Book of Martyrs* would do on a young devotee, or the *Newgate Calendar* upon an acolyte of Bridewell; both of which students are less terrified by the horrible manner in which the tale terminates, than animated by sympathy with the saints or depredators who are the heroes of their volume. Neither does a re-perusal of *Robinson Crusoe,* at a more advanced age, diminish our early impressions. The situation is such as every man may make his own, and, being possible in itself, is, by the exquisite art of the narrator, rendered as probable as it is interesting. It has the merit, too, of that species of accurate painting which can be looked at again and again with new pleasure.

Neither has the admiration of the work been confined to England, though Robinson Crusoe himself, with his rough good sense, his prejudices, and his obstinate determination not to sink under evils which can be surpassed by exertion, forms no bad specimen of the True-Born Englishman. The rage for imitating a work so popular seems to have risen to a degree of frenzy; and, by a mistake not peculiar to this particular class of the *servum pecus*, the imitators did not attempt to apply De Foe's manner of managing the narrative to some situation of a different kind, but seized upon and caricatured the principal incidents of the shipwrecked mariner and the solitary island. It is computed that within forty years from the appearance of the original work, no less than forty-one different *Robinsons* appeared, besides fifteen other imitations, in which other titles were used. Finally, though perhaps it is no great recommendation, the anti-social philosopher Rousseau will allow no other book than *Robinson Crusoe* in the hands of Emilius. Upon the whole, the work is as unlikely to lose its celebrity as it is to be equalled in its peculiar character by any other of similar excellence.

13. Coleridge on *Robinson Crusoe*

1818, c. 1830, 1832

Comments by Samuel Taylor Coleridge (1772–1834), poet and critic.

Extract (a) comes from the notes for Lecture XI, delivered on 3 March 1818, in Coleridge's famous series of lectures of that year. This lecture dealt with the *Arabian Nights* and other aspects of the supernatural, particularly in Oriental literature. Extract (b) comprises a selection from Coleridge's marginalia, found in a copy of the 1812 edition of *Robinson Crusoe*. They were made around 1830, and were reprinted by Hartley Coleridge in the *Literary Remains* (1836). Passage (c) comes from *Table Talk*, under 30 April 1832; and (d) from marginalia to Fuller's *Worthies of England*. The present text is based on *Coleridge's Miscellaneous Criticism*, ed. T. M. Raysor (1936).

(a) Lecture XI, 3 March 1818:

The charm of De Foe's works, especially of *Robinson Crusoe*, is founded on the same principle. It always interests, never agitates. Crusoe himself is merely a representative of humanity in general; neither his intellectual nor his moral qualities set him above the middle degree of mankind; his only prominent characteristic is the spirit of enterprise and wandering, which is, nevertheless, a very common disposition. You will observe that all that is wonderful in this tale is the result of external circumstances – of things which fortune brings to Crusoe's hand. (Raysor, p. 194.)

(b) *Robinson Crusoe* marginalia:

[He bid me observe it, and I should always find, that the calamities of life were shared among the upper and lower part of mankind; but that the middle station had the fewest disasters, and was not exposed to so many vicissitudes as the higher or lower part of mankind. Nay, they were not subjected to so many distempers and uneasinesses either of body or mind. . . .]

80

Rather malapropos from a gentleman laid up with the *gout*. Alas! the evil is that such is the pressure of the ranks on each other, and with exception of the ever-increasing class of paupers, so universal is the ambition of appearances, that morally and practically we scarcely have a middle class at present.

[I resolved not to think of going abroad any more, but to settle at home according to my father's desire. But alas! a few days wore it all off.]

A most impressive instance and illustration of my aphorism that the wise only possess ideas, but that the greater part of mankind are possessed by them. Robinson Crusoe was not conscious of the master impulse, because it *was* his master, and had taken full possession of him.

[But my ill fate pushed me on now with an obstinacy that nothing could resist; and though I had several times loud calls from my reason and my more composed judgment to go home, yet I had no power to do it. I know not what to call this, nor will I urge that it is a secret overruling decree that hurries us on to be the instruments of our own destruction, even though it be before us, and that we rush upon it with our eyes open.]

When once the mind, in despite of the remonstrating conscience, has abandoned its free power to a haunting impulse or idea, then whatever tends to give depth and vividness to this idea or indefinite imagination increases *its* despotism, and in the same proportion renders the reason and free will ineffectual. Now fearful calamities, sufferings, horrors, and hair-breadth escapes will have this effect far more than even sensual pleasure and prosperous incidents. Hence the evil consequences of sin in such cases, instead of retracting and deterring the sinner, goad him on to his destruction. This is the moral of Shakespeare's *Macbeth*, and this is the true solution of this paragraph, not any over-ruling decree of Divine wrath, but the tyranny of the sinner's own evil imagination which he has voluntarily chosen as his master. Compare the contemptuous Swift with the contemned De Foe, and how superior will the latter be found. But by what test? Even by this. The writer who makes me sympathise with his presentations with the *whole* of my being, is more estimable than the writer who calls forth and appeals to but a part of my being – my sense of the ludicrous for instance; and again, he who makes me forget my *specific* class, character, and circumstances, raises me into the universal man. Now this is De Foe's excellence. You become a man while you read.

[I smiled to myself at the sight of this money. 'O drug!' said I aloud, 'what art thou good for? . . . I have no manner of use for thee; even remain where

thou art, and go to the bottom as a creature whose life is not worth saving.'
However, upon second thoughts I took it away; and wrapping all this in a
piece of canvas, I began to think of making another raft.]

Worthy of Shakespeare; and yet the simple semi-colon after it, the
instant passing on without the least pause of reflex consciousness is
more exquisite and masterlike than the touch itself. A meaner writer,
a Marmontel,[1] would have put an '!' after 'away,' and have commenced
a new paragraph.

[... I must confess, my religious thankfulness to God's providence began to
abate too, upon the discovering that all this was nothing but what was common;
though I ought to have been as thankful for so strange the unforeseen a providence, as if it had been miraculous; for it was really the work of Providence....]

To make men feel the truth of this is one characteristic object of the
miracles worked by Moses – the providence miraculous, the miracles
providential.

[The growing up of the corn, as is hinted in my journal, had at first some
little influence upon me, and began to affect me with seriousness, as long as I
thought it had something miraculous in it....]

By far the ablest vindication of miracles that I have met with. It is
indeed the true ground, the proper purpose and intention of a miracle...

[I rather prayed to God as under great affliction and pressure of mind,
surrounded with danger, and in expectation every night of being murdered
and devoured before morning; and I must testify from my experience, that a
temper of peace, thankfulness, love, and affection, is much more the proper
frame for prayer than that of terror and discomposure; and that under the dread
of mischief impending, a man is no more fit for a comforting performance of
the duty of praying to God, than he is for repentance on a sick-bed. For these
discomposures affect the mind, as the others do the body; and the discomposure
of the mind must necessarily be as great a disability as that of the body, and
much greater, praying to God being properly an act of the mind, not of the
body.]

As justly conceived as it is beautifully expressed, and a mighty
motive for habitual prayer, for this cannot but facilitate the performance of rational prayer even in moments of urgent distress.

[... the very name of a Spaniard is reckoned to be frightful and terrible to all
people of humanity, or of Christian compassion; as if the Kingdom of Spain

[1] See note to p. 90.

were particularly eminent for the product of a race of men who were without principles of tenderness or the common bowels of pity to the miserable. . . .]

De Foe was a true philanthropist who had risen above the antipathies of nationality, but he was evidently partial to the Spanish character, which, however, it is not, I fear, possible to acquit of cruelty. – America, the Netherlands, the Inquisition, the late Guerilla warfare, etc., etc.

[The place I was in was a most delightful cavity or grotto of its kind, as could be expected, though perfectly dark. The floor was dry and level, and had a sort of a small loose gravel upon it. . . .]

How accurate an observer of nature De Foe was! The reader will at once recognise Prof. Buckland's caves and the diluvial gravel.*

[. . . I entered into a long discourse with him about the devil, the original of him, his rebellion against God, his enmity to man, the reason of it, his setting himself up in the dark parts of the world to be worshipped instead of God. . . .]

I presume that Milton's *Paradise Lost* must have been bound up with one of Crusoe's Bibles, or I should be puzzled to know where he found all this history of the Old Gentleman. Not a word of it in the Bible itself, I am quite sure. But to be serious, De Foe does not reflect that all these difficulties are attached to a mere fiction or at best an allegory, supported by a few popular phrases and figures of speech used incidentally or dramatically by the Evangelists, and that the existence of a personal intelligent evil being, the counterpart and antagonist of God, is in direct contradiction to the most express declarations of Holy Writ! 'Is there evil in the city and I have not done it? saith the Lord.' 'I do the evil and I do the good.'

[I have often heard persons of good judgment say, that all the stir people make in the world about ghosts and apparitions is owing to the strength of imagination, and the powerful operation of fancy in their minds; that there is no such thing as a spirit appearing, or a ghost walking, and the like.]

I cannot conceive a better definition of Body than Spirit appearing, or of a *flesh and blood man* than a rational spirit apparent. But a spirit *per se* appearing is tantamount to a spirit appearing without its appearances. As for ghosts it is enough for a man of common sense to observe

* The geologist Professor William Buckland (1784–1856) attracted attention by an article in the *Philosophical Transactions of the Royal Society* (1822) and later by his book *Reliquiae Diluvianae*, in which he was considered as a representative of science supporting the account of the Deluge in the Bible. Buckland treated the fine gravel which he found on the floor of various caves as evidence of a great deluge covering the entire earth [Raysor's note].

that a ghost and shadow are concluded in the same definition, viz., visibility without tangibility.

[But in the middle of all this felicity, one blow from unseen Providence unhinged me at once. . . . This blow was the loss of my wife. . . . She was . . . the stay of all my affairs, the centre of all my enterprises, the engine that, by her prudence, reduced me to that happy compass I was in, from the most extravagant and ruinous project that fluttered in my head, as above, and did more to guide my rambling genius than a mother's tears, a father's instruction, a friend's counsel, or my own reasoning powers could do.]

The stay of his affairs, the centre of his interests, the regulator of his schemes and movements, whom it soothed his pride to submit to and in complying with whose wishes the conscious sensation of his own *actions* will increase the impulse while it disguised the coercion of duty! The clinging dependent yet the strong supporter, the comforter, the comfort, and the soul's living home! This is De Foe's comprehensive character of the wife as she should be, and to the honour of womanhood be it spoken there are few neighbourhoods in which one name at least might not be found for the portrait.

These exquisite paragraphs in addition to others scattered, tho' with a sparing hand, thro' the novels, afford sufficient proof that De Foe was a first-rate master in periodic style, but with sound judgment and the fine tact of genius, had avoided it as adverse to, nay, incompatible with, the everyday matter-of-fact *realness* which forms the charm and character of all his romances. The *Robinson Crusoe* is like the vision of a happy nightmare such as a denizen of Elysium might be supposed to have from a little excess in his nectar and ambrosia supper. Our imagination is kept in full play, excited to the highest, yet all the while we are touching or touched by a common flesh and blood.

[. . . the ungrateful creatures began to be insolent and troublesome as before. . . .]

How should it be otherwise. They were idle, and when *we* will not sow *corn*, the *Devil* will be sure to sow *weeds* – nightshade, henbane, and Devil's-bit.

['How, Seignior A'tkins,' says he, 'would you murder us all?' . . . That hardened villain was so far from denying it, that he said it was true, and G—d d—m him if they would not do it still before they had done with them.]

Observe when a man has once abandoned himself to wickedness he cannot stop and does not join the devils till he has become a devil himself. Rebelling against his conscience he becomes a slave of his own furious will.

One excellence of De Foe among many is his sacrifice of lesser interest to the greater because more universal. Had he (as without any improbability he might have done) given his Robinson Crusoe any of the turn for natural history which forms so striking and delightful a feature in the equally uneducated Dampier – had he made him find out qualities and uses in the before (to him) unknown plants of the island, discover a substitute for hops, for instance, or describe birds, etc. – many delightful pages and incidents might have enriched the book; but then Crusoe would cease to be the universal representative, the person for whom every reader could substitute himself. But now nothing is done, thought, or suffered, or desired, but what every man can imagine himself doing, thinking, feeling, or wishing for.

Even so very easy a problem as that of finding a substitute for ink is with exquisite judgment made to baffle Crusoe's inventive faculties. Even in what he does he arrives at no excellence; he does not make basket work like Will Atkins. The carpentering, tailoring, pottery, are all just what will answer his purpose, and those are confined to needs that all men have, and comforts all men desire. Crusoe rises only where all men may be made to feel that they might and that they ought to rise – in religion, in resignation, in dependence on, and thankful acknowledgement of the divine mercy and goodness. (Raysor, pp. 292–300.)

(c) *Table Talk*, 30 April 1832:

I know no genuine Saxon English superior to Asgill's.[1] I think his and De Foe's irony often finer than Swift's. (Raysor, p. 409.)

(d) Fuller's *Worthies of England* marginalia:

[P. vii.] Shakespeare! Milton! Fuller! Defoe! Hogarth! As to the remaining mighty host of our great men, other countries have produced something like them. But these are uniques. England may challenge the world to shew a correspondent name to either of the five. I do not say that, with the exception of the first, names of equal glory may not be produced *in a different kind*. But these are genera, containing each only one individual. (Raysor, p. 273.)

[1] John Asgill (1659–1738), an eccentric and penurious man who wrote many pamphlets of Whiggish politics and deistic theology; receives a sneering mention in Swift's *Argument against the Abolition of Christianity*.

14. Charles Lamb on *The Complete English Tradesman* and the 'secondary' novels

1822, 1829

The essayist Charles Lamb (1775–1834) was consulted by Walter Wilson when the latter was preparing his biography of Defoe (see No. 16 below). In the life, Wilson made use of the letter quoted here, and also a separate discussion of the 'secondary' novels, which Lamb prepared in 1829. In a further letter, dated 24 February 1823, Lamb commented on *Roxana*. The text of these passages is taken from *The Works of Charles and Mary Lamb*, ed. E. V. Lucas (1903–5).

(a) Extract from Lamb's letter of 16 December 1822:

[Alluding to 'that curious book by Defoe, *The Complete English Tradesman*'.] The pompous detail, the studied analysis of every little mean art, every sneaking address, every trick and subterfuge (short of larceny) that is necessary to the tradesman's occupation, with the hundreds of anecdotes, dialogues (in Defoe's liveliest manner) interspersed . . . if you read it in an *ironical sense*, and as a piece of *covered satire*, make it one of the most amusing books which Defoe ever wrote, as much so as any of his best novels. It is difficult to say what his intention was in writing it. It is almost impossible to suppose him in earnest. Yet such is the bent of the book to narrow and degrade the heart, that . . . had I been living at that time, I certainly should have recommended to the Grand Jury of Middlesex, who presented the *Fable of the Bees*,[1] to have presented this book of Defoe's in preference, as of a far more vile and debasing tendency. (*Works*, vol. i, pp. 129–30.)

[1] The second edition of Bernard Mandeville's *Fable of the Bees*, a satiric allegory, was presented by the grand jury in July 1723. A *presentment* was an indictment by a grand jury of some offence which had come to their own notice.

(b) Lamb's remarks 'On the secondary novels of De Foe':

It happened not seldom that one work of some author has so trans-cendently surpassed in execution the rest of his compositions, that the world has agreed to pass a sentence of dismissal upon the latter, and to consign them to total neglect and oblivion. It has done wisely in this, not to suffer the contemplation of excellencies of a lower standard to abate, or stand in the way of the pleasure it has agreed to receive from the master-piece.

Again it has happened, that from no inferior merit of execution in the rest, but from superior good fortune in the choice of its subject, some single work shall have been suffered to eclipse, and cast into the shades the deserts of its less fortunate brethren. . . . But in no instance has this excluding partiality been exerted with more unfairness than against what may be termed the secondary novels or romances of De Foe.

While all ages and descriptions of people hang delighted over the *Adventures of Robinson Crusoe*, and shall continue to do so we trust while the world lasts, how few comparatively will bear to be told, that there exist other fictitious narratives by the same writer – four of them at least of no inferior interest, except what results from a less felicitous choice of situation. *Roxana – Singleton – Moll Flanders – Colonel Jack –* are all genuine offspring of the same father. They bear the veritable impress of De Foe. An unpractised midwife that would not swear to the nose, lip, forehead, and eye, of every one of them! They are in their way as full of incident, and some of them every bit as romantic; only they want the uninhabited Island, and the charm that has bewitched the world, of the striking solitary situation.

But are there no solitudes out of the cave and the desert? or cannot the heart in the midst of crowds feel frightfully alone? Singleton, on the world of waters, prowling about with pirates less merciful than the creatures of any howling wilderness; is he not alone, with the faces of men about him, but without a guide that can conduct him through the mists of educational and habitual ignorance; or a fellow-heart that can interpret to him the new-born yearnings and aspirations of an un-practised penitence? Or when the boy Colonel Jack, in the loneliness of the heart, (the worst solitude,) goes to hide his ill-purchased treasure in the hollow tree by night, and miraculously loses, and miraculously finds it again – whom hath he there to sympathise with him? or of what sort are his associates?

87

The narrative manner of De Foe has a naturalness about it beyond that of any other novel or romance writer. His fictions have all the air of true stories. It is impossible to believe, while you are reading them, that a real person is not narrating to you every where nothing but what really happened to himself. To this, the extreme *homeliness* of their style mainly contributes. We use the word in its best and heartiest sense – that which comes *home* to the reader. The narrators every where are chosen from low life, or have had their origin in it; therefore they tell their own tales, (Mr Coleridge has anticipated us in this remark,) as persons in their degree are observed to do, with infinite repetition, and an overacted exactness, lest the hearer should not have minded, or have forgotten, some things that had been told before. Hence the emphatic sentences marked in the good old (but deserted) Italic type; and hence, too, the frequent interposition of the reminding old colloquial parenthesis, 'I say' – 'mind' – and the like, when the story-teller repeats what, to a practised reader, might appear to have been sufficiently insisted upon before: which made an ingenious critic observe, that his works, in this kind, were excellent reading for the kitchen. And, in truth, the heroes and heroines of De Foe can never again hope to be popular with a much higher class of readers, than that of the servant-maid or the sailor; *Crusoe* keeps its rank only by tough prescription; Singleton, the Pirate – Colonel Jack, the thief – Moll Flanders, both thief and harlot – Roxana, harlot and something worse – would be startling ingredients in the bill of fare of modern literary delicacies. But, then, what pirates, what thieves, and what harlots, is *the thief, the harlot*, and *the pirate* of De Foe? We would not hesitate to say, that in no other book of fiction, where the lives of such characters are described, is guilt and delinquency made less seductive, or the suffering made more closely to follow the commission, or the penitence more earnest or more bleeding, or the intervening flashes of religious visitation, upon the rude and uninstructed soul, more meltingly and fearfully painted. They, in this, come near to the tenderness of Bunyan; while the livelier pictures and incidents in them, as in Hogarth or in Fielding, tend to diminish that 'fastidiousness to the concerns and pursuits of common life, which an unrestrained passion for the ideal and the sentimental is in danger of producing.' (*Works*, vol. i, pp. 325-7.)

15. Carlyle on Homer, Richardson and Defoe

1828

Thomas Carlyle (1795–1881) contributed a review of Lockhart's life of Burns to the *Edinburgh Review* 1828. In this he identified as a primary quality of great writing 'clearness of sight', that is, a certain graphic immediacy in vision and in presentation. Then follows the passage cited here. Text from *The Works of Thomas Carlyle*, ed. H. D. Traill (1896–1901), vol. xxvi, pp. 276–7.

Homer surpasses all men in this qualification: but strangely enough, at no great distance below him are Richardson and Defoe. It belongs, in truth, to what is called a lively mind; and gives no sure indication of the higher endowments that may exist along with it. In all the three cases we have mentioned, it is combined with great garrulity; their descriptions are detailed, ample and lovingly exact; Homer's fire burst through, from time to time, as if by accident; but Defoe and Richardson have no fire.

16. A major study

Walter Wilson (1781–1847), historian of the dissenting churches, brought out his three-volume *Memoirs of the Life and Times of Daniel De Foe* in 1830. Like Charles Lamb, whom he consulted in the preparation of this book (see No. 14), Wilson was a former clerk in the India Office. The biography remains an important source for students of Defoe, although it is exceedingly diffuse and frequently sidetracked by Wilson's ambition to portray Defoe as the staunchest of Nonconformists. Both faults were commonly remarked by reviewers. Yet Wilson's limitations in construction and in objectivity are largely offset by his knowledge, his sympathetic understanding and his thoroughgoing belief in Defoe as man and writer.

(a) On *Robinson Crusoe*:

Robinson Crusoe, in spite of all the efforts of envy and malevolence, has taken an honourable station in our literature. It has obtained a ready passport to the mansions of the rich, and the cottages of the poor, and communicated equal delight to all ranks and classes of the community. As a work of amusement, it is one of the first books put into the hands of youth; and there can be none more proper to insinuate instruction, whilst it administers delight. '*Robinson Crusoe*,' says Marmontel,[1] 'is the first book I ever read with exquisite pleasure, – and I believe every boy in Europe might say the same thing.' Whilst youth and ignorance have found ample scope for entertainment in the succession of incidents, told with all the simplicity and veri-similitude of real life, it has commended itself to the more enlightened, as one of those rare efforts of genius, that places its author in the first rank amongst the writers of invention. As a narrative replete with incidents, it stands unrivalled for its natural and easy transitions from one part of the story to another,

[1] Jean-François Marmontel (1723–99), author of sentimentalist fiction and drama.

unincumbered by irrelative matter, or display of useless ornament. The whole machinery is strictly subservient to the main object of the story, and its various parts are so nicely adjusted, that there is nothing wanting to complete the chain, nor to heighten the interest. Crusoe is strictly a child of Nature, assisted only by the circumstances that arose out of his peculiar situation and sphere of life. There is an air of plausibility, or rather reality, in all the particulars of the story, even to the minutest, that the reader reluctantly admits any part of it to be a fiction. When his mind is upon the stretch, it is absorbed in the fascinating description of scenes from real life; he is never astounded by improbabilities, nor disgusted by mawkish sensibility. His attention is fixed by one artless chain of natural incidents, such as may happen to any individual in a similar situation; but told in a concise manner, without decoration, and deriving their interest solely from the peculiar mode of telling the story.

The fine sentiments that abound in *Crusoe*, its delicate touches, and pure morality, are not the least parts of its beauties, and give it a decided superiority over every other work of the same description. Whilst it instructs us in the development of the human powers, under the guidance of natural reason, it points to the Almighty as the source from whence man derives his capacities, and to whom his homage should be directed. The reader of *Crusoe* is taught to be a religious, whilst he is an animal being. But his lessons of this kind are no where out of place; they are closely interwoven with the story, and are so just and pertinent in themselves, that they cannot be passed over, but the attention is irresistibly rivetted to them as an essential part of the narrative. So true are his pictures of human nature, so just his delineation of the passions, so skilful his transition from common matters to those of importance, and so artless his disposition of occurrences, that nothing can exceed its effect as a representation of life and manners, that comes home to the bosom of every reader. The intense interest excited by the work, may be owing partly to the minuteness with which the author details every incident that belongs to his narrative; to the charming simplicity in which he clothes his descriptions; and to the persuasion that hangs upon us whilst dwelling upon the story, that we are conversing with events and scenes which actually existed. Every reader of *Crusoe* is insensibly transported to his habitation; he is mixed up with all his affairs; enters into his labours and amusements; and participates in all the sympathies of his situation. Perhaps, few works have been more generally read, or more justly admired; few that have yielded such incessant amusement, and at the same time have developed so many lessons of practical instruction. It has been justly observed, that 'society is for ever indebted to the memory of De Foe, for his production of a work in which the ways of Providence are simply and pleasingly vindicated, and a lasting and useful moral is conveyed through the channel of an interesting and delightful story.'[1]

The marks of excellence that distinguished *Robinson Crusoe* beyond all other works in the same class, are so prominent, and present themselves in such a variety of shapes, that it has furnished ample scope for the diversified praise of ingenious men, according to the bent of their tastes and opinions. Some have eulogized it for its ingenuity; others, for its close adherence to nature, in the development of her resources amidst unexampled difficulties; and many for its moral and religious tendency. (*Memoirs*, vol. iii, pp. 441-4.)

(b) On *Moll Flanders:*

From the character of the incidents that compose the present narrative, De Foe was fully aware of the objections that would be urged against it by the scrupulous. To conceal a single fact, would have taken so much from the fidelity of the portrait; all that he could do, therefore, was to neutralize the poison, by furnishing the strongest antidotes. Accordingly, whilst he paints the courses of an every-day profligate in their natural colours, he shows us with the same faithfulness their natural tendency; and that, first or last, vice is sure to bring down its own punishment. His villains never prosper; but either come to an untimely end, or are brought to be penitents. In dressing up the present story, he tells us, he had taken care to exclude every thing that might be offensive; but conscious that he had a bad subject to work upon, he endeavours to interest the reader in the reflections arising out of it, that the moral might be more enticing than the fable. 'To give the history of a wicked life repented of, necessarily requires that the wicked part should be made as wicked as the real history of it will bear, to illustrate and give a beauty to the penitent part, which is certainly the best and brightest, if related with equal spirit and life.' Judging from the common experience of mankind, De Foe archly suspects that this part of his narrative will be less cordially received than the other. Should this be the case, he says, 'I must be allowed to say, 'tis because there is not the same taste and relish in the reading; and indeed it is too true, that the difference lies not in the real worth of the subject,

---

[1] From the Ballantyne edition of *Robinson Crusoe* – see headnote to No. 12.

so much as in the gust and palate of the reader.' But the work being intended for those who know how to make a good use of it, he adds, 'It is to be hoped, such readers will be much more pleased with the application than with the relation; with the end of the writer, than with the life of the person written of.'

Such is the object of the story of Moll Flanders, and it must be allowed to be executed in strict conformity with the writer's intentions. The events of her life are indeed coarse and disgusting; but they are exactly those of a person in her situation, led on from one degree of crime to another, and participating in all the miseries that may be expected to accompany such courses. In the midst of her career, this unhappy creature was not without those compunctions of conscience that often attend a life of guilt; and our author has pourtrayed the workings of her mind with great force and discrimination. But a perseverance in evil courses has a tendency to harden the heart, until it grows callous to conviction. So it was with our heroine; and the reflections suggested by it as soon as she found herself in Newgate, form a striking part of the narrative. The best part of her life is towards its close. 'Her application to a sober life and industrious management at last in Virginia, with her transported spouse, is a story fruitful of instruction to all the unfortunate creatures who are obliged to seek their re-establishment abroad, whether by the misery of transportation or other disaster; letting them know, that diligence and application have their due encouragement, even in the remotest part of the world, and that no case can be so low, so despicable, or so empty of prospect, but that an unwearied industry will go a great way to deliver us from it, and will in time raise the meanest creature to appear again in the world, and give him a new cast for his life.'

The story of Moll Flanders, although seriously told, and abounding in just reflections upon the danger of an habitual course of wickedness, is a book after all, that cannot be recommended for indiscriminate perusal. The scenes it unfolds are such as must be always unwelcome to a refined and well-cultivated mind; whilst with respect to others, it is to be feared that those who are pre-disposed to the oblique paths of vice and dishonesty, will be more alive to the facts of the story, than to the moral that is suspended to it. The life of a courtezan, however carefully told, if told faithfully, must contain much matter unfit to be presented to a virtuous mind. Moll Flanders is one of a low description; and gliding into the occupation of a shop-lifter, she became an adept in all the arts of her profession. The first part of her story renders her an object of pity, as the latter part of it does of respect; but the intermediate spaces are filled up by matters of a forbidding nature; and whatever lessons the whole may be calculated to afford to persons in a similar situation, it may be feared that they will weigh less with the obtuse and the profligate, than their dreams of present advantage. Those who take delight in exploring the annals of Newgate, without the moral, may here find the like scenes with the moral pointed. It is to the credit of De Foe, that he nowhere administers to the vicious taste of his reader, but takes every occasion of holding up vice to abhorrence. (*Memoirs*, vol. iii, pp. 490–2.)

(c) On *Colonel Jack*:

Many reflections of a moral and religious nature are interspersed through the volume, highly honourable to the piety and good understanding of the writer. Our Colonel, whose affairs prospered as they were directed by the hand of industry, found out at last, 'that it was honesty and virtue alone that made men rich and great, and gave them a fame as well as figure in the world; and that, therefore, he was to lay his foundation in these, expecting what might follow in time.' These thoughts led to many serious reflections upon the occurrences of his past life; his conscience becomes gradually awakened to the enormities he had committed; and he resolves henceforward to live like a reasonable being, and a good Christian. The circumstances which led to his convictions, the workings of his mind during their progress, and the happy means that were used for his illumination, are minutely described by our author, and are so many proofs of his great skill as a mental physiognomist. (*Memoirs*, vol. iii, pp. 498–9.)

(d) On *Memoirs of a Cavalier*:

From the foregoing particulars, the reader must allow that the Cavalier has composed his Memoirs with a spirit and vivacity that keep alive the attention, whilst he is charmed with the extreme simplicity of his narrative. His account of the civil wars, is distinguished by great candour and fairness; not concealing the errors of his own party, whilst he does justice to the bravery and the good conduct of his enemies. It is said to have been a favourite book with the great Lord Chatham, who long considered it an authentic history, and was in the habit of recommending it as the best account of the civil wars extant; nor was he a little mortified when told that it was a romance. It is indeed, as Mr Chalmers observes, 'a romance the likest to truth that ever was written'.

As a narrative of important events, containing a correct picture of the times, and enlivened by many just observations, it will be always read with a keen interest by those who may wish to occupy a spare hour in amusement or instruction. (*Memoirs*, vol. iii, p. 509.)

(e) On the *Journal of the Plague Year*:

It was one of the felicities of De Foe, to select such subjects for his pen, as would be of permanent interest; and such are all those pictures of life and manners that carry us back to former days, in the delineation of which he so greatly excelled. . . . In this affecting narrative, he has contrived to mix up so much that is authentic with the fabrications of his own brain, that it is impossible to distinguish the one from the other; and he has given to the whole such a likeness to the dreadful original, as to confound the sceptic, and encircle him in his enchantments. No one can take up the book without believing that it is the saddler of Whitechapel who is telling his own story; and that he was an eye-witness to all that he relates; that he actually saw the blazing stars which portended the calamity; that he witnessed the grass growing in the streets, reading the inscriptions upon the doors of the infected houses, heard the bell-men crying, 'Bring out your dead!' saw the dead-carts conveying the people to their graves, and was present at the digging of the pits in which they were deposited. In this, indeed, consists the charm of the narrative. It is not merely a record of the transactions that happened during the calamity, nor even of private circumstances that would escape the public eye; it is rather the familiar recital of a man's own observations upon all that passed before him, possessing all the minuteness of a log-book, without its dullness. The advantage derived from this mode of telling the story is, that it prepossesses the reader in a full belief of its reality. When a man sits down to record the events that happened in any given year, and crowds it with incidents, many of which are known to be true, we do not hesitate to give him credit for the remainder; and this more especially when he tells us, that he was upon the spot when such a thing happened, that he saw and spoke with the persons he describes, and relates the substance of the conversation. With the same unhesitating confidence we take up the book before us. It is not the journal of another person; there is not even the formality of a preface; but we open it, and come in contact at once with the author, who sees and hears all that he writes, and tells us so in the first person.

By adopting this familiar method of treating his subject, it cannot be doubted that De Foe secured to himself many advantages which he could not have hoped for in a formal history. Thus, whilst detailing incidents of importance, he will sometimes introduce a story, apparently trifling in itself, and by no means necessary to his main design; but merely to show, that he is willing to keep back nothing, or rather, must communicate every thing in the exact way that it happened. But, however trivial his incidents, or common-place his mode of relating them, they possess a secret charm that keeps the mind upon the full stretch, and gains it over to an unhesitating confidence in the relation. No one thinks of skipping over a single particle of his narrative, nor of exchanging for other words the homely language of the writer. In truth, the circumstantiality of De Foe never wearies; it rather adds to that intense consciousness of reality that hovers over every page of his writings. His *History of the Plague*, is one of those books in which he has carried his art to the greatest perfection. So faithful is the portrait of that distressing calamity, so entire its accordance with what has been delivered by other writers, so probable the circumstances of all the stories, and so artless the style in which they are delivered, that it would baffle the ingenuity of any one but De Foe, to frame a history with so many attributes of truth, upon the basis of fiction.

The propriety of such an alliance between history and fiction, more especially when so managed as to impose upon the most wary reader, has been called in question, and perhaps will scarcely admit of a satisfactory defence. Yet, who would sacrifice the *Memoirs of a Cavalier*, or the *Journal of the Plague Year*, to be disenchanted of so pleasing a delusion? De Foe well knew, that a dry detail of circumstances collected from the Bills of Mortality and the pamphlets of the day, would interest none but an antiquarian, the subject being of too repulsive a nature to invite general attention. By personating a citizen of London, who lived in the midst of the contagion, and was a spectator of the scenes he describes, he not only secured credit for his narrative, but was enabled to enliven it with numerous stories of probable occurrence, and with picturesque descriptions of the agitated feelings of the people. These, with the moral reflections which would naturally occur to persons in so distressing a situation, combine to render a story, in itself forbidding, not only readable, but highly attractive. The plain matter-of-fact style of the author, his undeviating simplicity, his well-timed lectures upon the uncertainty of life, and the air of serious piety that he communicates to his subject, concur not only to fix the attention of the reader, but to put into motion all the sympathies of his nature. As De

Foe was a mere child when the calamity happened, he could have no personal knowledge of the matters he has recorded. But the feelings arising from so awful a visitation would not subside suddenly. It would continue to be the talk of those who witnessed it for years afterwards, so that he must have been familiarized with the subject from his childhood; and as curiosity is most alive and the impressions strongest at that period, there can be no doubt that he treasured up many things in his memory, from the report of his parents and others, which he converted into useful materials as they passed through the operation of his own lively fancy. As it was a subject rendered peculiarly seasonable by the recent plague at Marseilles, so it was one that afforded him a fine opportunity for indulging in those religious feelings which it was so well calculated to awaken. De Foe is never so much at home as when he is inviting men to repentance and reformation; yet, he never goes out of his way for the purpose, but seizes upon incidents as they arise, and are calculated by their nature to give effect to his admonitions. ... It was his peculiar talent to seize upon any popular subject, and convert it, by his inimitable genius, into a fruitful source of amusement and instruction. From his history of the plague, notwithstanding its fictitious origin, we may derive more information, than from all the other publications upon the subject put together. He has collected all the facts attending the rise, progress, and termination of the malady, an accurate report of the number of deaths as published by authority, a faithful account of the regulations adopted to arrest and mitigate its fury, and numerous cases of infection, whether real or imaginary. But that which imparts life to the whole, and forms its distinguishing feature, is its descriptive imagery. The author's object is not so much to detail the deadly consequences of the disorder, as to delineate its effects upon the frighted minds of the inhabitants. These are depicted with all the genuine pathos of nature, without any aim at effect, but with the ease and simplicity of real life. The numerous incidents that follow in rapid succession, fraught as they are with human misery, present, at the same time, an accurate picture of life and manners in the metropolis, at the period referred to. The style and dress, the language and ideas, are exactly those of a citizen of London at the latter end of the 17th century. (*Memoirs*, vol. iii, pp. 511–16.)

(f) On *Religious Courtship*:

In discussing a subject of so much importance to young persons of both sexes, and one that required to be handled with great nicety, De Foe was well aware, that precept would be of less weight than example; that whilst the world refused to be instructed by a didactic treatise, it might be disposed to listen to a familiar story. He therefore chose to convey his ideas in this more inviting form, that by raising the curiosity of the reader he might the more effectually fix him with the moral. Historical dialogues, when written with spirit, are particularly acceptable to the inferior classes, and to young people in general, who make themselves parties to the conversation, and can fix the subject, with a slight effort, upon their memories. The familiar style of the present work, its deep acquaintance with human nature, and the exquisite moral feeling that pervades every page, render it peculiarly adapted to steal instruction upon the young and the uninformed, and to leave an abiding impression upon the heart. If this and the other moralities of De Foe were substituted for the modern novels that have so pernicious an influence in raising up false pictures to the mind, and unfitting it for sober contemplation, the experience of the present writer can vouch for their being equally attractive, whilst no one can doubt the incalculable superiority of their permanent effect.

Upon a story so well known as that which furnishes the materials for the present work, it would be needless to dwell. Those who are not acquainted with it may repair their neglect, as it is easily accessible; and they will find their reward. The author's deep knowledge of human nature, enabled him to decipher the motives that influence mankind, and to delineate the passions as they operate upon the mind, or influence the conduct. He had studied religion with all the attention due to its importance; and feeling its moral influence himself, he was qualified to trace its workings upon others. The reader that can peruse this narrative without instruction, has yet an important lesson to learn; and if he is disposed to give the subject his attention, he can scarcely hope for a more faithful or intelligent instructor. (*Memoirs*, vol. iii, pp. 521-2.)

(g) 'Remarks on De Foe as a Novelist':

The merits of De Foe, as a writer of fictitious narrative, are fully established by the works recorded in the foregoing chapters. These efforts of genius gave a new and decided turn to his reputation, and raised him to a proud superiority over other writers in the same class. Yet the year 1724 gave birth to a romance, which for originality of invention, for accuracy of painting, and for utility of purpose, was not exceeded by any of the former. In the story of *Roxana*, there are incidents, indeed, that cannot be welcome to a virtuous mind; but the fault is in the subject rather than in the author, whose aim is to describe human nature as it is, for the purpose of contrasting it with what it should be. This fidelity of design will not always admit of an agreeable outline; and it was the humour of De Foe to employ his pen upon those subjects that present the broad features of life in their full deformity. In ordinary cases, this would be considered a mark of bad taste; but De Foe had always some important end to legitimate his choice. He was the last man to administer fuel to a flame that he sought rather to extinguish. He never tells a story for mere amusement, nor does he go out of his way to obtrude reflections for the purpose of correcting it. His facts, however disreputable to virtue, are always subservient to it in the long run: he tells his story for the sake of the moral, which forms a con-stituent part, and yet so inartificially produced, as to be essential to the narrative. As a correct painter of life and manners, he was under the necessity of taking the world as he found it; as a moralist, he was desirous of leaving it better. He therefore selected those parts from the great drama that he thought most susceptible of improvement, and converted them into sources of instruction, in a form that would be most accessible to the generality of readers. His knowledge of the world had taught him, that those who would not listen to a grave discourse, might be allured by an eventful story; that whilst to the former they gave only the unwilling assent of the judgment, its exemplification would go far towards fixing it upon the heart. Such a result, however, is not to be produced by a forced delineation of the passions, nor by pictures of life that do violence to truth. These, indeed, have been the common resort of novelists, whose aim at effect has betrayed them into a departure from the ordinary operations of nature, and producing a degree of excitement that requires to be kept alive by fresh stimulants; but as the illusion vanishes, the mind falls a prey to grief and disappointment. De Foe never attempts the *beau ideal* of human life. His characters are those of ordinary occurrence, his portraits strictly natural, and his sketches of manners exactly such as existed at the period he describes. (*Memoirs*, vol. iii, pp. 524–6.)

(h) On *Roxana*:

The history of the beautiful Roxana, in the original dress that De Foe bestowed upon it, is one of those rare efforts of genius that occasionally blaze upon the world, to relieve it from the surrounding dullness. In rich natural painting, combining all the charms of simplicity with the most exquisite pathos, it is surpassed by none of his preceding works, and it is the subject only that renders it less acceptable than *Robinson Crusoe*. The genius that inspired the one, has put forth the same energies in the other, producing an equally striking effect, and illustrating alike the peculiar talents of the writer. From the nature of the facts developed in Roxana, her story will be less inviting to many readers than if she had been a virtuous character; and for this reason, its circulation will be restricted by prudence. Scenes of vice, however cautiously described, are never welcome to a virtuous mind, which feels an instinctive withdrawing from the degraded part of the species. But tales of real life, even when partially repulsive, if rendered subservient to the interests of virtue, may have their utility; although, to the young especially, there is always danger that the moral will be less attractive than the story. Of this De Foe was well aware, and therefore takes all imaginable pains to guard against any improprieties of expression that could prompt a vicious mind. 'Scenes of crime,' says he, 'can scarce be represented in such a manner, but some may make a criminal use of them; but when vice is painted in its low-prized colours, 'tis not to make people fall in love with it, but to expose it; and if the reader makes a wrong use of the figures, the wickedness is his own.' In the mean time, there are sufficient materials in the work, to extract improvement from a vicious story. De Foe instructs us, that a prosperous wickedness has a worm at its root, which blights the bud of enjoyment, and spreads a canker through the whole circulation. The terrors of a guilty conscience, lacerated by remorse, and haunted with the fears of future retribution, spring up in the paths of forbidden pleasure; and their workings in the mind of our heroine are delineated with a power that strikes the reader with awe, and constrains him to visit his own conscience with serious reflections. In such descriptions De Foe particularly excelled. He never labours at the pathetic, but produces all the effect without the assistance of art. The compunctions of Roxana are the spontaneous effusions of a mind oppressed with guilt, and feelingly alive to its alarming consequences. In the midst of her gaiety, she sees the *handwriting upon the wall*, which strikes a dart through her liver, and poisons the cup of enjoyment. But her miseries do not end here. She becomes the victim of her own vices, and reads her sin in her punishment. With De Foe the prosperity of the wicked always comes to an end, even in this life. The children of Roxana, whom she had deserted in their childhood, and who trace her out by a chain of events as singular as they are delightfully told, become eventually the cause of her ruin; her ill-gotten gains are swept from her at a blow;

and she descends from the pinnacle of greatness, to the depths of poverty and disgrace. Although the incidents that compose this instructive narrative, derive all their interest from the contrivances of the writer, yet we may believe him when he says, 'That the foundation is laid in truth of fact'. It is not improbable that the original of the picture may have had an existence in the gay court of Charles II; but be this as it may, it is certain that the effect is greatly heightened by her being made to tell her own story. In this, indeed, consists its magical influence, persuading the reader that he is conversing with the very person, and receiving from her own lips the recital of her misfortunes.

Although Roxana has passed under the same ban of proscription as Moll Flanders, yet there is an essential difference in the character of the two stories. The latter is an epitome of vice in low life, exhibiting the homely features of the class to which she belongs. Roxana, on the contrary, is a high-bred courtezan, and however revolting her story, she presents less grossness than is common to many of her order. She is just such a sort of person as may be supposed to have figured in the gay and licentious days of Charles II; when a thorough-bred loyalist, whether in court or city, would have thought it a breach of good manners to be considered better than his prince. It is true, that in the empire of vice, the moralist knows no distinction of ranks. In its personal consequences, the rich and the poor meet upon one common ground, and the more eminent the station, the more baneful is the influence; but it is equally true, that in proportion to the refinements or life, its exhibition will be usually more or less disgusting. In Roxana, we have a portraiture of manners in the upper classes of society; whilst her maid Amy, who performs a minor part in her adventures, belongs to the same class as Moll Flanders. (*Memoirs*, vol. iii, pp. 528–30.)

(i) On *The Complete English Tradesman:*

If his former writings had not given abundant evidence of the fact, these volumes are sufficient to shew the penetration of the writer, and that he was an accurate painter of life and manners in the middle classes of society. Although the lapse of a century has necessarily produced a considerable change both in habits and manners, yet the instruction conveyed in *The Compleat Tradesman* will be always seasonable; and this, not merely as it respects the class of persons to whom it is addressed. The caustic satire of the writer reaches to the buyer as well as the seller, and he may see how much the honesty of the one is affected by the dealings of the other. Few persons, perhaps, would expect to meet with amusement upon so dull a subject as trade; yet, inspired by the genius of De Foe, it has furnished materials for one of the most entertaining works in the English language. (*Memoirs*, vol. iii, pp. 586–7.)

(j) Summary:

We must now consider De Foe's pretensions as a writer, and the bare catalogue of his works will be sufficient to show, that, like the elder Scipio, 'he was never more employed than when at leisure, nor less solitary than when alone'. That he possessed talents of no ordinary cast, is a sentiment now so fully established, as to triumph over every contemporary effort to destroy his fame. 'Though his abilities, in certain respects, were generally acknowledged, full justice was far from being done to his reputation, either during his life, or for a considerable time after his decease. By some persons he has been spoken of with contempt, and others have regarded him as a ready miscellaneous writer; but the world is at last become sensible of his great and various talents.' De Foe affords one out of many examples, that literary merit, however oppressed for a time by the influence of party, is sure, at length, to find its proper place in the estimation of mankind. He has now outlived his century, when, as Mr Chalmers observes, 'he must be acknowledged as one of the ablest, as he was one of the most captivating, writers, of which this island can boast'.

For the qualities that constitute the basis of his fame, De Foe was more indebted to nature, than to any acquired endowments. Being shut out from the universities by barbarous statutes, his education was defective, and his learning rather various than profound. He appears, however, to have had a respectable acquaintance with the ancient and modern languages, was well read in history, and had improved himself by an extensive acquaintance with the world. Few men were better versed in the controversies of his time, whether political or ecclesiastical; or possessed more adroitness in the management of an argument. To extraordinary energy of mind, he united the most perfect self-possession; being as provoking by his coolness, as his pertinacity was galling. He possessed a large share of that dry, caustic wit, which gave a peculiar force to his language, and told more significantly than whole pages of sentiment. Perfect master of his own resources, he adapts himself to the humour of his opponents. When they argue fairly, he reasons with acuteness, vigour, and judgment; but when they lose their temper, he laughs at their weakness, and answers their railings by sarcasm. Unfettered by the opinions of other writers, and unawed by the authority of custom and precedent, he never fails to avow his convictions; justly considering that true wisdom consists in the right adaptation of means to existing circumstances, and that novelty should be no bar to improvement. In canvassing the most important subjects of human inquiry, he had to contend with strong prejudices, fortified by imposing sanctions, and defended with bitterness. To encounter them required skill, knowledge, and perseverance; and these De Foe possessed in an eminent degree. It will be found, upon a candid examination, that his sentiments upon most subjects are distinguished by good sense, and a profound acquaintance with human nature; and that his writings, generally, have for their object the diffusion of knowledge and happiness, and the advancement of the best interests of mankind.

De Foe paid but little attention to the graces of composition. He wrote too fast to study correctness, and seems to have read more for the purpose of storing his mind with ideas, than to express them tastefully. His style is often negligent, and sometimes coarse and verbose. Yet there are many fine passages in his writings, distinguished alike for vigour of thought, smoothness of language, and even elegance of expression; but his usual characteristics are plainness and simplicity. He writes with ease, and generally expresses himself with force and perspicuity; and whilst he pleases by his familiarity, he is often so impressive as to awaken the deepest attention, and to produce impressions that are never effaced. Many of his works appear to have been composed upon the spur of the moment, and the materials gathered from the inexhaustible stores of a retentive memory. Having read and thought much upon almost every subject, he was never at a loss for ideas; and so accurate was his recollection, that he often quotes at a distance from his books, with all the freshness of a recent impression. But De Foe was a perfectly original writer. He gathered his knowledge from men as well as from books; and the use that he made of it, discovers equal penetration and judgment. He was not only a keen observer of passing events, but dives into the recesses of the human heart. Whilst the surface of nature furnished him with pictures for delineation, its study enabled him to develope the secret springs that set it in motion. With a lively imagination, and powers of invention that have been rarely equalled, he brings up new worlds of ideas to the mind, that insensibly rivet the attention, and engage the best affections of the heart. Such was the acuteness of his perceptions, that he readily seizes upon every circumstance that constitutes an *item* in the great drama of life, and renders it available by his genius, either for amusement or instruction. Having studied nature in her own school, he acquired a knowledge of her capabilities; whilst he drew upon the resources of his own mind for those lessons of prudence which were suggested by her wants, or dictated by her teachings. In estimating the claims of De Foe to literary merit, it would be unjust to measure him by the standard of a more advanced period. Addison and Swift, to whom he was inferior in the graces of style, and even Johnson himself, with all his vigour and discernment, would be unable to bear such a test. 'To judge rightly of an author,' observes the last great writer, 'we must transport ourselves to his time, and examine what were the wants of his contemporaries, and what were his means of supplying them. That which is easy at one time, was difficult at another.' If De Foe was inferior to some of his contemporaries, it is sufficient that he did better than many with superior advantages; and this is his legitimate praise. . . .

Perhaps few writers obtained distinction in so many walks of literature, and still fewer who deserved it so well. In one department only can he be said to have failed. It will now be scarcely believed that De Foe took his station with the poets of his day; yet there were many who read and admired his verses. This might be partly owing to the excitement of the times, and the temporary nature of his subjects. The readers of poesy, however, will find little to gratify them in De Foe, beyond propriety of sentiment, keenness of satire, and benevolence of design; and these, probably, compensated with the vulgar for a want of harmony. . . . With the exception of the *True-Born Englishman*, in which are some tasteful and even elegant lines, his poetry would scarcely rescue his name from oblivion. The peculiar circumstances under which this poem was written, its political allusions, and its caustic satire, rendered it a favourite with the public long after the occasion that produced it, and raised a durable memorial to the author. From his perseverance in composing verses, it may be inferred that he was enamoured with the occupation, and thought better of them than has fallen to the judgment of posterity.

Whoever will be at the pains to examine his writings, must be satisfied that De Foe is intitled to take a high place amongst our English moralists. Whether he discusses politics or trade, history or manners, he converts it to the noble purpose of informing the judgment, or of ameliorating the heart. Not only his *Family Instructor*, and his *Religious Courtship*, which have for their specific object the awakening mankind to serious reflection; but his writings, generally, abound in prudential maxims, enforcing some sentiment of practical importance.

Such was his anxiety for reformation, that he never slips an opportunity of introducing some hint or caution, or of suggesting some remark in the way of admonition or satire, with a view to the correction of vice, and the inculcation of moral principles. Yet, he never goes out of his way for the purpose, but ingeniously contrives the moral to form a requisite part of his discourse. All his satires are written for the express purpose of exposing the follies of the age, and of inviting mankind to the regulation of their habits in conformity to the dictates of reason and religion. His prose writings, amidst the frequent ruggedness of their style, are rich in sentiment, and abound in sententious passages, that convey the soundest ideas upon some of the most important subjects of human inquiry. Whilst we respect his talents and revere his genius, it is impossible not to admire that purpose of instruction which is the end of all his performances. Although politics first raised his fame, and fiction has embalmed it with posterity, yet it should not be forgotten, that he was one of the ablest moralists of his age. If Johnson surpassed him in purity of diction, he only equals him in energy of thought and propriety of sentiment.

As a writer of fiction, whether we consider the originality of his genius, the simplicity of his design, or the utility of his moral, De Foe is now universally acknowledged to stand in the foremost ground. That his inventive powers were of the first order, no one can doubt; nor that he possessed the art above most other men, of infusing into his performances all the genuine pathos of nature, without the least apparent effort or exaggeration. Although he is now most known by the first great effort of his genius, *Robinson Crusoe*, yet in many of his other works he carries his art to the highest perfection. In these we discover the same unpretending simplicity, a like utility of purpose, and an undeviating likeness to real life. However uninviting his subject, the attention is insensibly chained down by the intense interest it excites, and the reader is inspired with a reluctance to lay down the story until the whole is finished. Much criticism has been employed to decipher the charm that rivets the faculties, and creates so much interest and delight. There have been writers who bring to their aid greater purity of language, and more attractive subjects for their discourse; but how few of them can be read with the same absorbing attention, and from which of them can be extracted so much nutriment for reflection? Whilst in ordinary cases, a single perusal is amply sufficient, and often more than can be conquered without weariness, we return to the pages of De Foe with renewed delight, and read him to the close with an appetite that refuses to be satiated. Whether the charm consist in the artificial structure of his story, in the minuteness and quick transition of incidents, or in that intense persuasion of reality which every where exists, or in a combination of these together, the effect is no less certain than it is striking; and however it may be explained, presents a rare occurrence in the history of literature. As De Foe wrote for the common people, who form the most numerous class of readers, he selected his subjects in accommodation to their habits and ideas; and his language is the fittest in the world to recommend them to their attention. Let the same stories be told in the classical style of our purest writers, and they would at once lose their impressive attraction; the charm would be broken, and they would bear about the same comparison with the great original, as Patrick's *Parable of the Pilgrim*,[1] by the side of the *Pilgrim's Progress*. It is the homely matter-of-fact style of De Foe, wholly free from artificial ornament and unincumbered by any aim at effect, that obtains credit with the reader. He is conscious of no disguise, nor is there any in fact; for the matters detailed bear all the marks of authenticity, and are related exactly as they would have occurred, had they actually taken place. It has been justly observed, by a distinguished living writer, that 'It is the last style which should be attempted by a writer of inferior genius; for though it be possible to disguise mediocrity by fine writing, it appears in all its native inanity when it assumes the garb of simplicity'.[2] (*Memoirs*, vol. iii, pp. 624–36.)

[1] *The Parable of the Pilgrim* (1664), by Simon Patrick (1626–1707).
[2] Quoted from Scott, vol. iv, p. 265 (see No. 12).

17. Hazlitt on Defoe

1830

The critic William Hazlitt (1775–1829) mentioned Defoe on a number of occasions. In his published *Lectures on the English Comic Writers* (1818) he briefly instanced *Colonel Jack* as representative of the 'secondary' novels, and stated that it left 'an impression on the mind more like that of things than words'. In *Blackwood's Edinburgh Magazine* for February 1818, ii, 556–62, a lecture entitled 'Of Poetry in General' is reported by an unnamed correspondent. In this, *Robinson Crusoe* is aligned with *Pilgrim's Progress* and Boccaccio, the three writers producing work 'coming nearest to poetry without being so'. Hazlitt describes them as 'poetry in *kind*', worthy to be married to the highest poetic language.

The extract reproduced here is taken from a review of Wilson's life in the *Edinburgh Review*, 1 (January 1830), 397–425. It is reprinted in Hazlitt's collected works, e.g. the edition by A. R. Waller and A. Glover (1904), vol. x, pp. 355–85. The present text follows the *Edinburgh Review*, l, 420–3.

We pass on to his Novels, and are sorry that we must hasten over them. We owe them to the ill odour into which he had fallen as a politician. His fate with his party reminds one a little of the reception which the heroine of the *Heart of Mid-Lothian* met with from her sister, because she would not tell a lie for her; yet both were faithful and true to their cause.[1] Being laid aside by the Whigs, as a suspected person, and not choosing to go over to the other side, he retired to Stoke-Newington, where, as already mentioned, he had an attack of apoplexy, which had nearly proved fatal to him. Recovering, however, and his activity of mind not suffering him to be idle, he turned his thoughts into a new channel, and, as if to change the scene entirely, set about writing Romances. The first work that could come under this title was *The*

---

[1] Alluding to Jeanie Deans and her sister Effie in Scott's *Heart of Midlothian* (1818).

Family Instructor; – a sort of controversial narrative, in which an argument is held through three volumes, and a feverish interest is worked up to the most tragic height, on 'the abomination' (as it was at that time thought by many people, and among others by Defoe) of letting young people go to the play. The implied horror of dramatic exhibitions, in connexion with the dramatic effect of the work itself, leaves a curious impression. Defoe's polemical talents are brought to bear to very good purpose in this performance, which was in the form of Letters; and it is curious to mark the eagerness with which his pen, after having been taken up for so many years with dry debates and doctrinal points, flies for relief to the details and incidents of private life. His mind was equally tenacious of facts and arguments, and fastened on each, in its turn, with the same strong and unremitting grasp. *Robinson Crusoe*, published in 1719, was the first of his performances in the acknowledged shape of a romance; and from this time he brought out one or two every year to the end of his life. As it was the first, it was decidedly the best; it gave full scope to his genius; and the subject mastered his prevailing bias to religious controversy, and the depravity of social life, by confining him to the unsophisticated views of nature and the human heart. His other works of fiction have not been read, (in comparison) – and one reason is, that many of them, at least, are hardly fit to be read, whatever may be said to the contrary. We shall go a little into the theory of this.

We do not think a person brought up and trammelled all his life in the strictest notions of religion and morality, and looking at the world, and all that was ordinarily passing in it, as little better than a contamination, is, *a priori*, the properest person to write novels: it is going out of his way – it is 'meddling with the unclean thing'. Extremes meet, and all extremes are bad. According to our author's overstrained Puritanical notions, there were but two choices, God or the Devil – Sinners and Saints – the Methodist meeting or the Brothel – the school of the press-yard of Newgate, or attendance on the refreshing ministry of some learned and pious dissenting Divine. As the smallest falling off from faith, or grace, or the most trifling peccadillo, was to be reprobated and punished with the utmost severity, no wonder that the worst turn was given to every thing; and that the imagination having once overstepped the formidable line, gave a loose to its habitual nervous dread, by indulging in the blackest and most frightful pictures of the corruptions incident to human nature. It was as well (in the cant phrase) 'to be in for a sheep as a lamb,' as it cost nothing more – the sin might at least be startling and uncommon; and hence we find, in this style of writing, nothing but an alternation of religious horrors and raptures, (though these are generally rare, as being a less tempting bait,) and the grossest scenes of vice and debauchery: we have either saintly, spotless purity, or all is rotten to the core. How else can we account for it, that all Defoe's characters (with one or two exceptions for form's sake) are of the worst and lowest description – the refuse of the prisons and the stews – thieves, prostitutes, vagabonds, and pirates – as if he wanted to make himself amends for the restraint under which he had laboured 'all the fore-end of his time' as a moral and religious character, by acting over every excess of grossness and profligacy by proxy! How else can we comprehend that he should really think there was a salutary moral lesson couched under the history of *Moll Flanders*; or that his romance of *Roxana, or the Fortunate Mistress*, who rolls in wealth and pleasure from one end of the book to the other, and is quit for a little death-bed repentance and a few lip-deep professions of the vanity of wordly joys, showed, in a striking point of view, the advantages of virtue, and the disadvantages of vice? It cannot be said, however, that these works have an *immoral* tendency. The author has contrived to neutralise the question; and (as far as in him lay) made vice and virtue equally contemptible or revolting. In going through his pages, we are inclined to vary Mr Burke's well-known paradox, that 'vice, by losing all its grossness, loses half its evil,'[1] and say that vice, by losing all its refinement, loses all its attraction. We have in them only the pleasure of sinning, and the dread of punishment here or hereafter; – gross sensuality, and whining repentance. The morality is that of the inmates of a house of correction; the piety, that of malefactors in the condemned hole. There is no sentiment, no atmosphere of imagination, no 'purple light' thrown round virtue or vice; – all is either the physical gratification on the one hand, or a selfish calculation of consequences on the other. This is the necessary effect of allowing nothing to the frailty of human nature; – of never strewing the flowers of fancy in the path of pleasure, but always looking that way with a sort of terror as to forbidden ground: nothing is left of the common and mixed enjoyments and pursuits of human life but the coarsest and criminal part; and we have either a sour, cynical, sordid self-denial, or (in the despair of attaining this) a reckless and unqualified abandonment of all decency and character alike: – it is hard to say which is the most repulsive. Defoe runs equally into extremes in his male characters as

[1] From Edmund Burke's *Reflections on the Revolution in France* (1790), p. 113.

in his heroines. *Captain Singleton* is a hardened, brutal desperado, without one redeeming trait, or almost human feeling; and, in spite of what Mr Lamb says of his lonely musings and agonies of a conscience-stricken repentance, we find nothing of this in the text: the captain is always merry and well if there is any mischief going on; and his only qualm is, after he has retired from his trade of plunder and murder on the high seas, and is afraid of being assassinated for his ill-gotten wealth, and does not know how to dispose of it. Defoe (whatever his intentions may be) is led, by the force of truth and circumstances, to give the Devil his due – he puts no gratuitous remorse into his adventurer's mouth, nor spoils the *keeping* by expressing one relenting pang, any more than his hero would have done in reality. This is, indeed, the excellence of Defoe's representations, that they are perfect *fac-similes* of the characters he chooses to pourtray; but then they are too often the worst specimens he can collect out of the dregs and sink of human nature. *Colonel Jack* is another instance, with more pleasantry, and a common vein of humanity; but still the author is flung into the same walk of flagrant vice and immorality; – as if his mind was haunted by the entire opposition between grace and nature – and as if, out of the sphere of spiritual exercise and devout contemplation, the whole actual world was a necessary tissue of what was worthless and detestable.

We have, we hope, furnished a clue to his seeming contradiction between the character of the author and his works; and must proceed to a conclusion. Of these novels we may, nevertheless, add, for the satisfaction of the inquisitive reader, that *Moll Flanders* is utterly vile and detestable: Mrs Flanders was evidently born in sin. The best parts are the account of her childhood, which is pretty and affecting; the fluctuation of her feelings between remorse and hardened impenitence in Newgate; and the incident of her leading off the horse from the inn-door, though she had no place to put it in after she had stolen it. This was carrying the love of thieving to an *ideal* pitch, and making it perfectly disinterested and mechanical. *Roxana* is better – soaring a higher flight, instead of grovelling always in the mire of poverty and distress; but she has neither refinement nor a heart; we are only dazzled with the outward ostentation of jewels, finery and wealth. The scene where she dances in her Turkish dress before the king, and obtains the name of Roxana, is of the true romantic cast. The best parts of *Colonel Jack* are the early scenes, where there is a spirit of mirth and good fellowship thrown over the homely features of low and vicious life; – as where the hero and his companion are sitting at the three-halfpenny ordinary, and are delighted, even more than with their savoury fare, to hear the waiter cry, 'Coming, gentlemen, coming,' when they call for a cup of small-beer; and we rejoice when we are told as a notable event, that 'about this time the Colonel took upon him to wear a shirt'. The *Memoirs of a Cavalier* are an agreeable mixture of the style of history and fiction. These Memoirs, as is well known, imposed upon Lord Chatham as a true history. In his *History of Apparitions*, Defoe discovers a strong bias to a belief in the marvellous and preternatural: nor is this extraordinary, for, to say nothing of the general superstition of the times, his own impressions of whatever he chose to conceive are so vivid and literal, as almost to confound the distinction between reality and imagination. He could 'call spirits from the vasty deep,' and they 'would come when he did call for them'.[1] We have not room for an enumeration of even half his works of fiction. . . . After *Robinson Crusoe*, his *History of the Plague* is the finest of all his works. It has an epic grandeur, as well as heart-breaking familiarity, in its style and matter.

[1] See *1 Henry IV*, III. i. 52–4.

18. Two reviews of Wilson's *Memoirs*

1830

Passage (a) comes from a rather wandering, if graceful, essay in the *Westminster Review*, xiii (April 1830), 69–85. On the question of authorship, cf. Introduction, p. 19. The remaining extracts are taken from the *British Critic and Quarterly Theological Review*, viii (January 1830), 74, 91–2, 95, 100. For the High Church prejudices of this article, see Introduction, p. 19.

(a) *Westminster Review:*

It would be ridiculous to undervalue the poetical genius of a Pope, or the powerful irony of a Swift, but it may be doubted if the courageous exercise of their reasonable powers by men of the persevering and untameable spirit of De Foe has not done more to distinguish and exalt Great Britain than all the Horatian felicity or Cervantic humour these satirists have ever displayed. . . . *Robinson Crusoe* [shows that Defoe was possessed of] the very first order of imaginative power if not always felicitous in its application. (xiii, 79–81.)

(b) *British Critic:*

If the doctrine of metempsychosis were true . . . we could almost persuade ourselves that the spirit which now dwells in Cobbett, once animated De Foe. That is, as far as a large portion of its intellectual, not of its moral, qualities is concerned. The ancient Pamphleteer *commanded* the Pillory; the modern has done no more than repeatedly *deserved* it. The elder, when he was bankrupt, discharged the claims even of rapacious creditors to the uttermost farthing; the young laughed in the face of those easy friends from whom he had borrowed money, and justified his swindling appropriation of it by a luminous apology. The one believed in a God, and wrote in defence of Religion; the other – but it is more to our purpose to point their resemblance than their discrepances. Each strikes us as possessing that singular restlessness of disposition which is never so much in its element as when the waters around it are troubled; which prefers foul weather to sunshine; takes its rides of pleasure in a whirlwind; and even if it cannot 'direct the storm' never loses an opportunity of calling it up. Each has the peculiar talent of levelling argument, or what seems to be such, down to the apprehension of the unlettered, so that every ball shall tell by being aimed sufficiently low. In each may be found much cleverness, many shrewd anticipations, and some occasional plain truths, though 'dash'd and brew'd with lies'. Coarse and clamorous abuse, arrogant claims to integrity and independence for themselves, intolerant denial of it to all others, bold and unabashed assertions, and disregard of ultimate consequences, so as the immediate object may be obtained, are other divisions of their common stock – a capital upon which each might draw without fear of exhaustion. If these had been the whole of De Foe's possessions he would have been as utterly forgotten now as we may venture to predict his successor in the same walk [Cobbett] . . . most assuredly will be, within six months after his decease. But to these, De Foe added, in the heel of life, an exhibition of inventive power in which he has never yet been rivalled; and while the political incendiary has scarcely left a trace behind, the author of *Robinson Crusoe* belongs to the imperishable portion of our National Literature. . . .

He wrote a Pamphlet [*The Shortest Way*] in which the Irony was so carefully sustained, that those whom he intended to serve, tore him to pieces at first, for attacking them; and those whom he intended to attack, when the secret was revealed, finished by consigning him to Newgate. *The Shortest Way with the Dissenters* is said to have passed current with both parties for a serious production; and it is not the only piece of Irony which has met a similar fate. To joke with a serious face and yet to be understood, is the triumph of joking; and in this De Foe failed; much more, it must be confessed, from the dullness of his readers, than from any fault on his own side. . . . This, which in our days would be considered, at worst, an amusing banter, was magnified by party fury into a State offence. . . .

Perhaps one of the most singular parts of De Foe's character, is to be found in his pertinacious attachment to verse, a species of composition for which it may not be going too far to say that from the badness of his ear he was organically incompetent. Quarles is harmony itself when compared with his rhythm – Blackmore greatly exceeds him in fire of expression – Tusser in delicacy of sentiment. His choice of subject is not less remarkable than of the vehicle in which it was to be conveyed. What should we say if Algernon Sydney had written on Government in Trochaics? or if Locke, on a similar theme, had adopted the Spenserian stanza? Yet the *Jure Divino*, framed with much the same object as the sober Treatises of those great men, and intended to exhibit De Foe's notions as to the origin of our State Polity, to combat the doctrine of non-resistance and passive obedience, is clattered to the rough music of marrow-bone-and-cleaver rhyme, the only accompaniment which he had at command. 'The whole,' says his advertisement, 'will be near 100 sheets in folio, with large annotations, printed on the finest paper. No more to be printed than are subscribed for. The price to be ten shillings; half-a-crown only to be paid down, the remainder on delivery.' We may be spared from attempting any citation from this huge mass of dulness; the single work wherein the writer has wholly failed. . . .[1]

Of the Works, however, upon which his fame is mainly rested, it is little necessary here to speak; they are too well known and have been too often criticised to need fresh Review – and as our estimate of them, perhaps, in some degree, falls short of that which is almost universal and established by prescription, we are not sorry to escape an ungrateful task. He must be bold, indeed, who would venture to contend with rooted opinion and early association against the merits of *Robinson Crusoe*; not to extol which, would almost as much stamp an Englishman with the guilt of *lèse-literature*, as any impugnment of the sovereignty of Shakespeare himself. On the *Journal of the Plague Year*, we feel no such hesitation. It is the most lively Picture of Truth which ever proceeded from imagination: and in spite of every anachronism which forbids the belief, we cannot take it up, after a hundredth perusal, without yielding, before we have traversed twenty pages, to a full conviction that we are conversing with one who passed through and survived the horrors which he describes.

[1] Those mentioned in this paragraph are: Francis Quarles (1592–1644), emblematic poet; Richard Blackmore (see p. 39); Thomas Tusser (1524?–80), doggerel poet; Algernon Sidney (1622–83), republican writer; and the philosopher John Locke (1632–1704).

19. Wordsworth on *Robinson Crusoe*

c. 1840

William Wordsworth made few references to Defoe. In 1808 he argued that works such as *Crusoe* and *Pilgrim's Progress* might prove quite as serviceable in the cause of religious improvement as orthodox manuals such as *A Serious Call*. The more substantial passage which follows was reported by Robert Perceval Graves, a young Irish clergyman who became curate of Bowness and a close friend of Wordsworth in the poet's latter days. Text from *The Prose Works of William Wordsworth*, ed. A. B. Grosart (1876), vol. iii, p. 468.

He thought the charm of *Robinson Crusoe* [was not simply a matter of its 'naturalness'.] . . . the chief interest of the story arose from the extraordinary energy and resource of the hero under his difficult circumstances from their being so far beyond what it was natural to expect or what would have been exhibited by the average man, and that similarly the high pleasure derived from his successes and good fortunes arose from the peculiar source of these uncommon merits of his character.

20. Two verse tributes by W. S. Landor

c. 1840

First published in 1897, these poems probably date from the 1830s or 1840s, with the latter more likely than the former. The text here follows *The Complete Works of Walter Savage Landor*, ed. Stephen Wheeler (1935), vol. iii, p. 216.

Characteristic of Landor (1775–1864) in their vigorous independence, as well as their lapidary compression, these verses none the less foreshadow the increasing Victorian tendency to make of Defoe a figure of sentimental patriotism. Crusoe is seen as a representative man, embodying active, outgoing qualities and a kind of magnanimous self-help.

DANIEL DEFOE

Few will acknowledge all they owe
To persecuted, brave Defoe.
Achilles, in Homeric song,
May, or he may not, live so long
As Crusoe; few their strength had tried
Without so staunch and safe a guide.
What boy is there who never laid
Under his pillow, half afraid,
That precious volume, lest the morrow
For unlearnt lesson might bring sorrow?
But nobler lessons he has taught
Wide-awake scholars who fear'd naught:
A Rodney and a Nelson may
Without him not have won the day.

[THE SAME]

Strangers in vain enquire, for none can show
Where rests thy mutilated frame, Defoe!

Small men find room enough within St. Paul's,
The larger limb'd must rest outside the walls.
Be thou content, no name hath spred so wide
As thine, undamaged stil by time and tide.
Never hath early valour been imprest
On gallant Briton's highly-heaving breast
So deeply as by Crusoe; therefor Fame
O'er every sea shall waft your social name.

21. De Quincey on verisimilitude

1841

From an essay on 'Homer and the Homeridae', first published in
Blackwood's Magazine, October to December 1841. The text here
follows *The Collected Writings of Thomas De Quincey*, ed. David
Masson (Edinburgh, 1890), vol. vi, pp. 84–5. De Quincey (1785–
1859), critic and friend of the Lake Poets, wrote well on Dr
Johnson and other eighteenth-century topics.

De Foe is the only author known who has so plausibly circumstantiated
his false historical records as to make them pass for genuine, even with
literary men and critics. In his *Memoirs of a Cavalier,* one of his poorest
forgeries, he assumes the character of a soldier who had fought under
Gustavus Adolphus (1628–31), and afterwards (1642–45) in our own
Parliamentary War; in fact, he corresponds chronologically to Captain
Dalgetty. In other works he personates a sea-captain, a hosier, a
runaway apprentice, an officer under Lord Peterborough in his
Catalonian expedition. In this last character he imposed upon Dr
Johnson; and, by men better read in History than Dr Johnson, he has
actually been quoted as a regular historical authority. How did he
accomplish so difficult an end? Simply by inventing such little circum-

stantiations of any character or incident as seem, by their apparent inertness of effect, to verify themselves; for, where the reader is told that such a person was the posthumous son of a tanner, that his mother married afterwards a Presbyterian schoolmaster, who gave him a smattering of Latin, but, the schoolmaster dying of the plague, that he was compelled at sixteen to enlist for bread – in all this, as there is nothing at all amusing, we conclude that the author could have no reason to detain us with such particulars but simply because they were true. To invent, when nothing at all is gained by inventing, there seems no imaginable temptation. It never occurs to us that this very construction of the case, this very inference from such neutral details, was precisely the object which De Foe had in view – was the very thing which he counted on, and by which he meant to profit. He thus gains the opportunity of impressing upon his tales a double character: he makes them so amusing that girls read them for novels; and he gives them such an air of verisimilitude that men read them for histories.

22. John Forster on the *Review* and other matters

1845

From a long review of two editions of Defoe, in the *Edinburgh Review*, lxxxii (October 1845), 480–532: reprinted with additions in *Daniel De Foe and Charles Churchill* (1855), from which the present text is taken, and subsequently in *Historical and Biographical Essays*, vol. ii (1858).

Forster (1812–76), friend and biographer of Dickens, also wrote lives of Swift and Goldsmith.

(a) Extract from *Daniel De Foe and Charles Churchill*, introductory section:

It is with De Foe dead, as it was with De Foe living. He stands apart from the circle of the reigning wits of his time, and his name is not called over with theirs. What in this respect was formerly the fashion is the fashion still; and whether sought for in the Histories of Doctor Smollett or of Lord Mahon, his niche is vacant. His life, to be fairly presented, should be written as the 'Life and Strange Surprising Adventures of Daniel De Foe, who lived above Seventy Years all Alone, in the Island of Great Britain'. It might then be expected to compare, in vicissitude and interest, with his immortal romance; as written hitherto, it has only shared the fate of his manly but perishable polemics. (p. 2.)

(b) Extract from chapter IV, on the *Review*:

So, through all the vicissitudes of men and ministries, from 1704 to 1713, amid all the contentions and the shouts of party, he kept with this homely weapon his single-handed way, a solitary watchman at the portals of the commonwealth. Remarkable for its rich and various knowledge, its humour, its satire, its downright hearty earnestness, it is a yet more surprising monument of inexhaustible activity and energy. It seems to have been suggested to him, in the first instance, as a resource against the uncertainties of his imprisonment, and their disastrous effect on his trade speculations (he had lost by his late prosecution more than £4,000); and there is no doubt it assisted him in the support of his family for several of these years. But he had no efficient protection against its continued piracy. The thieves counted it by thousands, when worthy Mr Matthews the publisher could only account by hundreds; and hence the main and most substantial profit its writer derived from all the anxiety and toil it cost him, was expressed in the proud declaration of one of its latest Numbers. 'I have here espoused an honest interest, and have steadily adhered to it all my days. I never forsook it when it was oppressed; never made a gain by it when it was advanced; and, I thank God, it is not in the power of all the Courts and Parties in Christendom to bid a price high enough to buy me off from it, or make me desert it.'

The arrangement of its plan was not less original than that of its form. The path it struck out in periodical literature was, in this respect, entirely novel. It classed the minor and the larger morals; it mingled personal and public themes; it put the gravities of life in an entertaining form; and at once it discussed the politics, and corrected the vices, of the age. We may best indicate the manner in which this was done, by naming rapidly the subjects treated in the first volume, in addition to those of political concern. It condemned the fashionable practice of immoderate drinking; in various ways ridiculed the not less fashionable habit of swearing; inveighed against the laxity of marital ties; exposed the licentiousness of the stage; discussed, with great clearness and sound knowledge, questions affecting trade and the poor; laughed at the rage for gambling speculations: and waged inveterate war with that barbarous practice of the duel, in which De Foe had to confess, with shame, that he had once during his life been engaged. Its machinery for matters non-political was a so-called *Scandalous Club*, organized to hear complaints, and entrusted with the power of deciding them. Let us show how it acted. A gentleman appears before the Club, and complains of his wife. She is a bad wife; he cannot exactly tell why. There is a long examination, proving nothing; when suddenly a member of the Club begs pardon for the question, and asks if his worship was a good husband. His worship, greatly surprised at such a question, is again at a loss to answer. Whereupon, the Club pass three resolutions. 1. That most women that are bad wives are made so by bad husbands.

2. That this society will hear no complaints against a virtuous bad wife from a vicious good husband. 3. That he that has a bad wife, and can't find the reason of it in her, 'tis ten to one that he finds it in himself. And the decision finally is, that the gentleman is to go home, and be a good husband for at least three months; after which, if his wife is still uncured, they will proceed against her as they shall find cause. In this way, pleas and defences are heard on the various points that present themselves in the subjects named; and not seldom with a lively dramatic interest. The graver arguments and essays, too, have an easy, homely vigour, a lightness and pleasantry of tone, very different from the ponderous handling peculiar to the Ridpaths and the Dyers, the Tutchins and the Leslies. We open at an essay on Trade, which would delight Mr Cobden himself.[1] De Foe is arguing against impolitic restrictions. We think to plague the foreigner, he says; in reality, we but deprive ourselves. 'If you vex me, I'll eat no dinner, said I, when I was a little boy: till my mother taught me to be wiser by letting me stay till I was hungry.'

The reader will remember the time when this *Review* was planned. Ensign Steele was yet but a lounger in the lobbies of the theatres, and Addison had not emerged from his garret in the Haymarket. The details of common life had not yet been invested with the graces of literature, the social and polite moralities were still disregarded in the press, the world knew not the influence of my Lady Betty Modish, and Colonel Ranter still swore at the waiters. Where, then, shall we look for 'the first sprightly runnings' of *Tatlers* and *Spectators* if we have not found them in De Foe's *Review*? The earlier was indeed the ruder workman; but wit, originality, and knowledge were not less the tools he worked with; and the later 'twopenny authors,' as Mr Dennis is pleased to call them, found the way well struck out for their finer and more delicate art. What had been done for the citizen classes, they were to do for the beauties and the wits. They had watched the experiment, and seen its success. The *Review* was enormously popular. It was stolen, pirated, hawked about every where; and the writer, with few of the advantages, paid all the penalties of success. He complains that his name was made 'the hackney title of the times'. Hardly a penny or twopenny pamphlet was afterwards cried in the streets, or a broadside put forth appealing to the people, to which the scurrilous libeller, or witless dunce, had not forged that popular name. Nor was it without its influence on the course of events which now gradually changed the

[1] Richard Cobden (1804–65), apostle of free trade.

aspect and the policy of Godolphin's government. De Foe has claimed for himself large share in preparing a way for what were called the 'modern Whigs'; and the claim was undoubtedly well founded. (pp. 84–8.)

(c) Extract from concluding section:

After all the objections that may be justly made to his opinions, on the grounds of shortcoming or excess, we believe that in the main features of the career we have set before the reader, will be recognised a noble English example of the qualities most prized by Englishmen. De Foe is our only famous politician and man of letters, who represented, in its inflexible constancy, sturdy dogged resolution, unwearied perseverance, and obstinate contempt of danger and of tyranny, the great Middle-class English Character. We believe it to be no mere national pride to say, that, whether in its defects or its surpassing merits, the world has had none other to compare with it. He lived in the thickest stir of the conflict of the four most violent party reigns of English history; and if we have at last entered into peaceful possession of most part of the rights at issue in those party struggles, it the more becomes us to remember such a man with gratitude, and with wise consideration for what errors we may find in him. He was too much in the constant heat of the battle, to see all that we see now. He was not a philosopher himself; but he helped philosophy to some wise conclusion. He did not stand at the highest point of toleration, or of moral wisdom; but, with his masculine active arm, he helped to lift his successors over obstructions which had stayed his own advance. He stood, in his opinions and his actions, alone and apart from his fellow men; but it was to show his fellow men of later times the value of a juster and larger fellowship, and of more generous modes of action. And when he now retreated from the world Without to the world Within, in the solitariness of his unrewarded service and integrity, he had assuredly earned the right to challenge the higher recognition of Posterity. He was walking towards History with steady feet; and might look up into her awful face with a brow unabashed and undismayed. (pp. 132–3.)

23. George Borrow discovers *Crusoe*

1851

Extract from chapter III of the autobiographic *Lavengro* (1851), by George Borrow (1803–81). Borrow is describing the occasion when, at the age of six, he came on a packet of books left in the house by a neighbour.

I now took up the third book: it did not resemble the others, being longer and considerably thicker; the binding was of dingy calf-skin. I opened it, and as I did so another strange thrill of pleasure shot through my frame. The first object on which my eyes rested was a picture; it was exceedingly well executed, at least the scene which it represented made a vivid impression upon me, which would hardly have been the case had the artist not been faithful to nature. A wild scene it was – a heavy sea and rocky shore, with mountains in the background, above which the moon was peering. Not far from the shore, upon the water, was a boat with two figures in it, one of which stood at the bow, pointing with what I knew to be a gun at a dreadful shape in the water; fire was flashing from the muzzle of the gun, and the monster appeared to be transfixed. I almost thought I heard its cry. I remained motionless, gazing upon the picture, scarcely daring to draw my breath, lest the new and wondrous world should vanish of which I had now obtained a glimpse: 'Who are those people, and what could have brought them into that strange situation?' I asked of myself; and now the seed of curiosity, which had so long lain dormant, began to expand, and I vowed to myself to become speedily acquainted with the whole history of the people in the boat. After looking on the picture till every mark and line in it were familiar to me, I turned over various leaves till I came to another engraving; a new source of wonder – a low sandy beach on which the furious sea was breaking in mountain-like billows; cloud and rack deformed the firmament, which wore a dull and leaden-like hue; gulls and other aquatic fowls were toppling upon the blast, or skimming over the tops of the maddening waves – 'Mercy upon him! he must be drowned!' I exclaimed, as my eyes fell upon a poor wretch who appeared to be striving to reach the shore; he was upon his legs, but was evidently half smothered with the brine; high above his head curled a horrible billow, as if to engulf him for ever. 'He must be drowned! he must be drowned!' I almost shrieked, and dropped the book. I soon snatched it up again, and now my eye lighted on a third picture; again a shore, but what a sweet and lovely one, and how I wished to be treading it; there were beautiful shells lying on the smooth white sand, some were empty like those I had occasionally seen on marble mantelpieces, but out of others peered the heads and bodies of wondrous crayfish; a wood of thick green trees skirted the beach and partly shaded it from the rays of the sun, which shone hot above, while blue waves slightly crested with foam were gently curling against it; there was a human figure upon the beach, wild and uncouth, clad in the skins of animals, with a huge cap on his head, a hatchet at his girdle, and in his hand a gun; his feet and legs were bare; he stood in an attitude of horror and surprise; his body was bent far back, and his eyes, which seemed starting out of his head, were fixed upon a mark on the sand – a large distinct mark – a human footprint!

Reader, is it necessary to name the book which now stood open in my hand, and whose very prints, feeble expounders of its wondrous lines, had produced within me emotions strange and novel? Scarcely, for it was a book which has exerted over the minds of Englishmen an influence certainly greater than any other of modern times, which has been in most people's hands, and with the contents of which even those who cannot read are to a certain extent acquainted; a book from which the most luxuriant and fertile of our modern prose writers have drunk inspiration; a book, moreover, to which, from the hardy deeds which it narrates, and the spirit of strange and romantic enterprise which it tends to awaken, England owes many of her astonishing discoveries both by sea and land, and no inconsiderable part of her naval glory.

Hail to thee, spirit of De Foe! What does not my own poor self owe to thee? England has better bards than either Greece or Rome, yet I could spare them easier far than De Foe, 'unabashed De Foe,' as the hunchbacked rhymer styled him.

The true chord had now been touched; a raging curiosity with respect to the contents of the volume, whose engravings had fascinated my eye, burned within me, and I never rested until I had fully satisfied it; weeks succeeded weeks, months followed months, and the wondrous volume was my only study and principal source of amusement. For hours together I would sit poring over a page till I had become acquainted with the import of every line. My progress, slow enough at first, became by degrees more rapid, till at last, under 'a shoulder of mutton sail,' I found myself cantering before a steady breeze over an ocean of enchantment, so well pleased with my voyage that I cared not how long it might be ere it reached its termination.

And it was in this manner that I first took to the paths of knowledge.

24. The novelist assessed

1856

From a review of Bohn's edition of Defoe, in the *National Review*, iii (October 1856), 380–410. In his opening paragraphs the anony- mous reviewer discusses works such as *Memoirs of a Cavalier*, *Captain Singleton* and the *Journal of the Plague Year*, which he finds satisfactory only as history, not as personal narrative. In the remainder of the article, reproduced here, he turns to the novels 'proper'. See also Introduction, p. 21.

The proper novels of De Foe – *Roxana*, *Moll Flanders*, *Colonel Jack*, and above all, the first part of *Robinson Crusoe* – are of a much higher class. They are pure fictions; any elements of fact which may be included in them being, as it were, entirely dissolved and incorporated in a homogeneous work of imagination. The most marked feature in them, the one which first strikes every reader that looks at them, is their reality, their life-likeness. Perhaps this quality would have been less remarked had it been more balanced by other qualities more or less common in works of fiction. As it is, it stands sharply out as the characteristic of De Foe, and is the index to a genius not more remark- able for its wonderful power in this direction than it is for its absolute deficiencies in another. No where else does our literature show the trace of an imagination at once so vivid and so curiously limited. It is as if he had just one-half of that faculty we commonly call by this name. The imagination of Shakespeare is a universal solvent; at its touch the combined elements in man and circumstance fly apart, and reveal their secret and innermost constituent nature. This analytical power of genius, – a power, however, not of reasoning, but of insight, – furnishes the reservoir from which spring the fountains of creative genius; the more piercing that power, the clearer, the deeper, the more shining will be the knowledge it amasses, and thence the more fresh, the more vivid, the more true the creations that are informed by it. With this searching insight, dividing like a sword the spirit and body of things, a great poet unites a passionate interest in concrete wholes, the realities of the created world, the very things which actually do exist; and, out of the resources of his penetrative genius, to create new things like the old is the highest ambition of his nature. Every artistic mind grasps at individual wholes; but not to every one is given this power to reproduce them in the complex reality in which they exist in the living world. The most common poetic power is that which, by intermittent exertions of the faculty of insight or the sense of loveliness, grasps some fragment of the beauty of the universe and shakes out its hidden gold, or gathers some flying whisper of the world's harmonies and echoes it back in human language which illustrates some working passion; gives a picture to some fleeting landscape, a voice to a senti-ment, a mood, or an aspiration; or freezes into language subtler than marble some passing incident as it sweeps swiftly down the never-returning current of time. These are simply expressive, and scarcely in any true sense creative poets. Others have a passion for creation, without a strong sense of the beauty of concrete wholes. These personify abstract emotions, dwell among ideas as contrasted with things; if they create a man, they make him only the incarnation of a single passion, or of a set of opinions and feelings; they don't feel that this is defective, that they are vivifying phantoms which want flesh and blood; their imagination does not grasp at a passionate man, but at passions which it endows with the attributes of man. Such a genius delights in allegory more or less transparent. It rushes into personification – often of the thinnest description. Collins attempted a drama – he might as well have tried to square the circle; the idea of a man never once probably presented itself to his mind; yet he could not help wrapping up in a hasty sketchy personification every idea that presented itself to him.

When the traveller in the desert is likely to want water, he says[1]

> Bethink thee, Hassan, where shall thirst assuage,
> When fails this cruise, his unrelenting rage.

Spenser was a genius of this order; he is most at home and at his best when he is expending the glorious richness of his fancy in giving external form and appropriate environment to a passion or a vice, or some yet more abstract idea – as in his fine procession of Love, or that description of Mammon[2]–

> An uncouth savage and uncivil wight,
> Of griesly hew and fowle ill-favour'd sight;
> His face with smoke was tand and eies were bleard,
> His head and beard with sout were ill bedight,
> His cole-blacke hands did seeme to have ben seard
> In smythe's fire-spitting forge, and nayles like clawes appeard.

> His yron cote, all overgrowne with rust,
> Was underneath enveloped with gold;
> Whose glistring glosse, darkned with filthy dust,
> Well yet appeared to have beene of old
> A work of rich entayle and curious mould,
> Woven with antickes and wyld ymagery;
> And in his lap a masse of coyne he told,
> And turned upside downe, to feede his eye
> And covetous desire with his huge threasury.

By the wayside leading to which

> There sat infernale Paine
> And fast beside him sat tumultuous Strife;
> The one in hand an yron whip did strayne,
> The other brandished a bloody knife;
> And both did gnash their teeth, and both did threaten life.

> On th' other side in one consort there sate
> Cruell Revenge, and rancorous Despight,
> Disloyall Treason, and hart-burning Hate;
> But gnawing Gealosy, out of their sight
> Sitting alone, his bitter lips did bight;

---

[1] William Collins, 'Hassan: or the Camel Driver', ll. 17-18, in his *Persian Eclogues* (1742).
[2] *Faerie Queene*, II. vii. 3-4, 21-2.

And trembling Feare still to and fro did fly,
And found no place where safe he shroud him might:
Lamenting Sorrow did in darknes lye;
And Shame his ugly face did hide from living eye.

But Spenser's Red-Cross Knights, his Artigalls, his Guyons, are only coats of armour inspired with special ideas; even the girl-huntress Belphœbe, his loveliest portraiture, is but the fair embodiment of fresh woodland virginity and pure animal spirits. Shelley, more intellectual, more subtle, yet less broad, was a poet of the same order, exercising his imagination on the qualities of things and facts, never on things and facts themselves.

Now De Foe is the very reverse of this turn of mind, and stands in striking contrast to it. His genius is still more one-sided, and occupies us t the ground which is left bare by such poets as Spenser and Shelley. He has nothing whatever of the solvent power. The strange underlying forces and essences which these minds love to contemplate as the component elements of the world have no interest for him. He abides in the concrete; he has no analytical perception whatever. Never was there a man to whom a yellow primrose was less of any thing more than a yellow primrose. He is always occupied with the absolute existent realities of the world; with men as he saw them move in actual life; with facts as they actually happened. He never conceives abstract passions: his only idea of anger is a particular man in a passion. He has an enormous reconstructive and a very narrow creative imagination. He takes up things just as he finds them; and when he wants to create, he re-sorts them, or at most makes others exactly like them. He loses much by these limits to his nature. What he gains on the other side is that life-likeness we spoke of in his art: the narrow range of his vision is compensated by its vividness. It is a mistake to say that the wonderful power he has of convincing you that his characters really lived in the flesh, and that all he tells you did really happen just as he says it did, arises from the minuteness of his detail. It is not the detail that causes the distinctness of the reflection in the reader's mind; it is the sharpness of the original image. A mind like De Foe's works by details; it is one of its defects that it does so. A greater genius can flash out as sharp and full an image of a concrete man as any of De Foe's, and unencumbered with useless minutiæ. It can at once seize the very essence of some special attribute of human nature, and embody it in a complete and individual man. It can give you Claudio, Angelo, Lucio, Isabella, within the limits of five acts; and in doing so it furnishes, under stringent restrictions of form and in limited space, a greater variety of character than can be found within the whole range of De Foe's novels, and leaves as distinct an image of each man as we can form of the heroes of his most laboured autobiographical narratives. We don't say as familiar; but as distinct and as complete. De Foe thus arrives by means of details at a result which may be reached independently of them; and his power lies not in his love of minute circumstance, but in the close and tenacious grasp of his imagination – in the constant and distinct presence before his own mind of the conception that controls and guides his minutiæ. Richardson is far more detailed in his narration than De Foe, far more universally circumstantial, more diffuse, if possible, more tiresome; every matter that he has occasion to handle, whether important or unimportant, is elaborated with the same patient microscopic attention; he is thrice as tedious as De Foe; and yet his characters are infinitely inferior in life-likeness. Lovelace is a character more striking and more complex than Roxana or Robinson Crusoe; but you do not believe in his existence in the same way: he is more of a man in a book. De Foe's detail is a more partial and discriminating one than that of Richardson. True he loves it for its own sake, and it is sometimes superfluous; but it is always under control, and duly subordinated to the effect he wishes to produce. If we read him attentively, we shall be as much struck with what he omits as with what he inserts.

Totally destitute of the power to fathom any intricacies of human nature, Defoe is familiar with its external manifestations. He may have no conscious picture of *character*; but he has a keen eye for traits of character, and a very vivid idea of *persons*. He takes a man and his life in the gross, as it were, and sets them down in writing; but as it is his characteristic to be mainly occupied with the life, not the man, so this too becomes the main source of the reader's interest. It is not Robinson Crusoe we care about, but the account of his adventures, the solution of the problem of how to live under the circumstances. His name calls up the idea not of a man, but of a story. Say 'Lear,' and you think of a man; you have the image of the white-haired king – the central point, about which the division of his kingdom, the disaffection of his daughters, the terrors of the tempest, the soft pity and sad death of Cordelia, group themselves in subordinate place: say 'Robinson Crusoe,' and you see a desert island, with a man upon it ingeniously adapting his mode of life to his resources; the imagination of a solitary existence, reproduced in a special form with wonderful vividness, consistency, and particularity, – this is the source of our interest. It would be to impugn the verdict of all mankind to say *Robinson Crusoe* was not a great work of genius. It is a work of genius – a most remarkable one – but of a low order of genius. The universal admiration it has obtained may be the admiration of men: but it is founded on the liking of boys. Few educated men or women would care to read it for the first time after the age of five-and-twenty. Even Lamb could say it only 'holds its place by tough prescription'.[1] The boy revels in it. It furnishes him with food for his imagination in the very direction in which, of all others, it loves to occupy itself. It is not that he cares for Robinson Crusoe, – that dull, ingenious, seafaring creature, with his strange mixture of cowardice and boldness, his unleavened, coarsely sagacious, mechanic nature, his keen trade-instincts, and his rude religious experiences; the boy becomes his own Robinson Crusoe – it is little Tom Smith himself, curled up in a remote corner of the playground, who makes those troublesome voyages on the raft, and rejoices over the goods he saves from the wreck; who contrives his palisade and twisted cables to protect his cave; clothes himself so quaintly in goat-skins; is terrified at the savages; and rejoices in his jurisdiction over the docile Friday, whom he thinks would be better than a dog, and almost as good as a pony. He does not care a farthing about Crusoe as a separate person for himself. This is one reason why he rejects the religious reflections, as a strange and undesirable element in a work otherwise so fascinating. He cannot enter into Crusoe's sense of wickedness, and does not feel the least concern for his soul. If a grown man reads the book in after years, it is to recall the sensations of youth, or curiously to examine the secret of the unbounded popularity it has enjoyed. How much this popularity is due to the happy choice of his subject, we may better estimate when we remember that the popular *Robinson Crusoe* is in reality only a part of the work, and the work itself only one of many others, not less well executed, from the same hand. No other man in the world could have drawn so absolutely living a picture of the desert-island life; but the same man has exercised the same power over more complex incidents, and the works are little read. *Moll Flanders* and *Roxana* and part of *Colonel Jack* are not inferior efforts of the same genius that wrote *Robinson Crusoe*; but the subject-matter is perhaps less well adapted for the sort of genius, and they are defaced by much both of narrated incident and expression which unfits them for the delicacy of modern readers. They are pictures of the career of vice. This is unfortunate; for had De Foe occupied himself with the

[1] See No. 14 above.

domestic life of his period, and drawn his persons and incidents thence, he would have presented us with a more vivid glimpse into the life of his times than any author has ever done. Miss Austen is not unlike De Foe in some of the main aspects of her genius, though as much his superior in handling character as she is inferior in knowledge and vigour. Had he done as she has done, – had he drawn the Sir Walter Elliots and General Tilneys, the Captain Wentworths and Henry Craufords, the Elizabeths, Anns, and Fannys of his time, – had he introduced us to the country-houses of Anne's or George I's time, as she has done to the Mansfield Parks and Longbourns of George III's, and brought to bear on them his superior sharpness of detail and wider scope of circumstantiality, – we should have gained a clearer idea of how people really lived in those days than can now be derived from all other sources of information put together. But De Foe as deliberately chooses his materials outside the field of ordinary social life as Miss Austen sedulously restricts herself within it. The latter deals with baronets, dyspeptics, young ladies, and amiable or self-sufficient clergymen. She represents the condition of man as regulated by marriage with settlements; her widest contrasts of life are between Bath and Wiltshire, Plymouth and the Hall; she walks gently through the well-trimmed 'shrubberies' of existence, and does not trust herself ever to peep over the park-palings. De Foe goes down the ragged lanes, tramps through gorse and heather, sits by the side of the duck-pond, and studies the aspect of the dunghill. Thieves and harlots, convicts, pirates, soldiers, and merchant-adventurers, are his *dramatis personae*. He has never attempted to draw a respectable man; or if the narrative of the *History of the Plague* be an exception, he is placed amid terrors that dislocate society and strip him of all the conventional properties which would naturally belong to him. He gives you no picture of the manners and the life of his times except incidentally, and by showing what strange things were compatible with them, and what sort of life those led who were outcasts from them. There are men who live in the framework of society. These are the respectable men of all classes; they accept the state of things into which they were born. To them the arrangements of society are not laws which may be broken, but conditions of the problem of life; they never feel the slightest temptation to infringe them. They are insensible to any hampering control from them: in fact, they are not controlled by them; conforming always to them, they have grown up into them as into a mould, which cannot press them because they fit it. These are the men who become lord mayors and presidents of council, who are respected by their neighbours and preside at quarter-sessions; men who, being bred tailors, aspire to be master-tailors; who, being lawyers, think of a puisne judgeship and never of jurisprudence; who are good church-goers in the country, or if born dissenters, adhere to their own communion; men who are capable of thinking and acting for themselves in all matters in which there is not an already fixed social canon of thought and social rule of action. Such minds give consistence, stability, and endurance to society: they inhabit, they constitute its substance, There are others whose character and destiny it is to dwell, as it were, in the interstices of that substance: they are impatient of the forms of social life; they shake off its artificial restrictions; they dare opinion; they love social adventure; they lead a freer life than the others, but a more dangerous one; escaping from constraint, they lose support; refusing the control of others, they lose a protection against themselves: they form a dangerous habit of disregarding authority and breaking through rules; not conforming to custom, they lose many of the advantages of experience; and, deprived of external guards, are apt to find themselves on some sudden occasion not sufficient to themselves.

De Foe always chooses his heroes and heroines from among this latter class – often from among the lowest specimens of it; and the social conditions of his time offered him greater temptations for so doing than can operate on any writer in our times. The rules of modern society are by far less stringent and oppressive than those of an earlier time; but they extend much wider, and exercise on the whole a much more binding force. It is not that they extend to more classes than they used to do. In the beginning of the eighteenth century the different classes, more widely separated than they now are, had each its peculiar traditions and ideas as to how life ought to be conducted; and the tradesman was bound by as formal and exacting a code of social propriety as the peer. But the very markedness of the distinction between classes left a wider field in the intervals between them for the occupation of those who were not definitely included within them. In the present day class-distinctions are much less abrupt, the borders between various ranks melt insensibly one into another; and social opinion, though not without its distinctions, is much more uniform both in its character and in its distribution. It is less of a chain binding the parts, and more of a net enveloping the whole; there is less formality, and more decorum; there is more freedom within the rules, but far more difficulty in escaping from them. It is scarcely possible now to exist as De Foe represents men doing – evading the social restraints, living in the world and yet out of society; dodging social laws, and shifting one's social relations, as may prove convenient for the time. It is the same with legal restraints. Formerly punishments were vastly more severe than they now are; but the chances of avoiding them altogether were far greater, the criminal had a much more varied and extensive field than he now enjoys. If you were taken stealing a watch out of a shop in good Queen Anne's reign, you were pretty sure to be hanged. But then, unless you were taken in the act, there was little or no danger of your being taken at all: whereas now you are sure not be hanged; but, on the other hand, you have not a moment's peace of mind – A1 may at any moment disturb the harmony of a cheerful supper-party by tapping you on the shoulder, and telling you you are wanted about that little job in Fleet Street. The thief's life was formerly one of more varied enterprise than it now is: it is a profession which has gone down in the world. It no longer offers any temptations to a man of spirit. The main difficulty now lies, not in committing the robbery – this the modern police don't so much care to prevent – but in escaping detection afterwards, which they have made very difficult. Hence a shifting skulking character attaches to the business. A man who makes robbery his occupation finds no opportunity of relaxing in the society of innocent men; he cannot shake off the shop; he is confined within the atmosphere of his crimes. He cannot put his predatory habits off and on, and persuade himself that he is playing with them. In former times there was a reality corresponding more or less accurately to the high-spirited, adventurous, generous thief of romance; but the gentleman-thief, such as he was, is no more. The difficulty of stopping travellers by the Great Western, and the organised detective industry of Mr Maine's forces, have narrowed the limits of the art; and its professors are inevitably mean, base, and miserable.

De Foe puts his characters in degraded enough positions, and plunges them deep enough in the meanest criminality; but he was able to show them not absolutely dislocated from the regular order of society; they wind in and out from it, and retain some points of contact. There was then much less of a separate criminal class than now exists. It is still possible to use even the worst members of this class as subjects of fiction, but not if you work in the same way as De Foe does. You can't show *all* the life as he does. Dickens paints the Jew, Sykes, Nancy, and the Artful Dodger, but not their actual lives and daily habits. He never shows them as they really are: he only selects the terrible, the ludicrous, or the pathetic incidents and points of character, and shrouds the stained every-day career of wickedness in silence. But De Foe gives all this; to him one event is as important as another, nothing is too common-place, nothing too revolting for his pen, he slurs over nothing, all is put down in its naked deformity, and, where it is dull and trivial, in its naked dullness and triviality. Sir Walter Scott was the first to introduce a school of narration in direct contrast to this, and was, perhaps, the greatest master of it we have yet seen. He plays like sunlight over the summits of his subject, develops his story by selected scenes, throws into bright relief the distinguishing characteristics of the numerous *dramatis personæ* with which he crowds his canvas, and from the aspect in which they appear in special circumstances he skilfully gives you an insight into their whole nature. Think of the characters in any one of his best novels. Take *Kenilworth*: Elizabeth, Leicester, Amy Robsart, Varney, Mike Lambourne, Tony Foster, Jean, Giles Gosling, Goldthred, Wayland, Dick Sludge, the Pedagogue Tressilian, Sussex, Raleigh, Blount, with half a score more, all of them perfectly distinct lifelike images, some more laboured, others just indicated by some light passing touch of the master's hand; but all alike clear and cognisable. Observe the language they use. It seems the most characteristic in the world, and it is so; but it is not what such people did really talk, any more than Hamlet really employed blank verse. It is an artificial language of Scott's own, always true in its essence to the requirements of character, and just sufficiently pointed with a flavour of the times in which the story is laid to give it piquancy and vrai-semblance. There is an exquisite dexterity displayed in the employment of traditional and antiquarian knowledge, always used so as to give as true an effect as the author himself could conceive without any of the obscurity and pedantry of raw details. Scott has not the profound insight which a great dramatist requires, but he is essentially a dramatic artist in his mode of working. De Foe is just the reverse; his strokes are all the same thickness, and he labours on with line after line and touch after touch, intent only on exact copy, and careless of the expense either of time or labour. He never drops his subject for an instant to take it up again at a more interesting point; he tracks it like a slot-hound, with his nose close to the ground, through every bend and winding. He makes people talk as they really do talk. Scott makes a conversation of a few sentences convey what in actual life would probably occupy as many pages. De Foe gives you every word of it, traces it backwards and forwards through its repetitions, its half-utterances, its corrections, its misconceptions, its chance wanderings, its broken and re-united threads, just as people do really talk who wilfully or unconsciously are not very ready to catch one another's drift. *The Religious Courtship* occupies a pretty large volume. Most men would have found it difficult to spread the arguments over half-a-dozen pages. When a man of De Foe's vivid powers of conception tracks out with this slow perseverance the history of a life, it is impossible that we should not gather a very distinct idea of the person who lived it; it grows up in a quiet and insensible manner out of the events. We are not expressly admitted by the author into the interior nature of such a person, but we know all of him which can be gathered from a complete acquaintance with the minutest circumstances of his actions, and often even of his thoughts. We must use our own insight and judgment if we wish to know what really was the interior character of Moll Flanders, just as we must have done had we met her in life, – not altogether a pleasant sort of person. None of his heroes or heroines are. Roxana is not pleasant; Colonel Jack is decidedly not pleasant; Robinson Crusoe is not the man to make a friend of; perhaps De Foe himself was not.

All these people are modelled on himself, and differ but slightly, except in their circumstances, from one another. Every man's imagination of other men gives you some clue to his own nature. You see the bent of it, at any rate. A man writing fiction is something like one in a dream, drifted hither and thither by the spontaneous working of his instincts and aspirations. He feeds his fancy by giving free play to the various elements in his disposition; and in so doing he reveals more or less, not himself – for he is what his own controlling will and the discipline of circumstance has made him – but his natural constitution, that which may rightly be called his genius, though the word is habitually used with a more contracted signification. This unconscious self-revelation is remarkably full and explicit in De Foe, because, not penetrating into the interior of other men, he was thrown very much on the resources within himself. All his characters are woven out of the same thread; they may differ in many ways, but in certain characteristics, and those the most deep-seated, they are like one another and like the author. It is the innermost part of his nature which a man can least shake off in his writings.

De Foe was a self-occupied man; more, however, by nature than in his life. He was never a self-seeking man; on the contrary, his whole life was a sacrifice of his own interests to those of truth and what he conceived the welfare of his country. Few men have left such a memorial

of disinterested labour as his *Review*, written exclusively by himself,
and published thrice a week, for many years, without profit or advantage; and by its uncompromising rejection of party-interests and
single-eyed adherence to his own convictions, bringing odium on his
head from Whigs and Tories alike, laying him bare to the attacks of his
enemies, exposing him to countless dangers, and actually subjecting
him to the grossest injuries, – slanders, law-suits, and imprisonment.
Yet this *Review* itself bears evidence to the nature of the man in his
anxious self-vindications, the constant reference to his own personal
position, and his often and openly expressed sense of the importance
of his labours.

The author earnestly desired, and to his utmost endeavoured, to be for ever
concealed: not that he was ashamed of the work, or sees any reason yet to be so;
professing to have a firm belief, that he was not without a more than ordinary
presence and assistance of the Divine Spirit in the performance. But being fully
satisfied with the prospect of doing good by it, he desired that his 'praise might
not be of men, but of God.'

To this end, he took such measures at first for effectually preserving the secret,
and for his entirely remaining in the obscurity he desired, that for some time
after the publication he continued unguessed at; and he flattered himself for a
while that he could be no further inquired after. 'But Satan hindered.'

The highest escape from the dominion of self may be said to have
been closed to De Foe. It is where the intellect and the will are in
constant activity under the control of the personal affections. Some
men, and more women, can lose themselves in others. It is a great
capacity to have; for in its highest direction and fullest development
it is what the truest exponents of the Christian faith have in all times
recognised as the fulfilment of the religious life. That is the service
which is perfect freedom; but as the slavery to self is the most binding
and oppressive of servitudes, so any degree of life in others insures,
paradoxical as it may seem, its corresponding measure of freedom.
This loss of self in others is not to be confounded with what in many
outward respects resembles it, though in reality its direct opposite – the
concentration of self in others; where one nature, often in the worst
indulgence of self-seeking, grafts itself on another, becomes dependent
without ceasing to be self-engrossed, and, sacrificing the natural conditions of growth, limits itself to the sustenance and health it can derive
from another stock, which often bears it as one of many branches whose
fall would not touch its life and scarce impair the fulness of its growth.
Both these forms of self-surrender require strong affections of some

sort. De Foe's affections were not strong; and he was neither in danger of the one, nor could avail himself of the other. It is true, as Mr Foster has forcibly stated, that De Foe lived alone in the world;[1] true, it is a noble thing to live alone in the isolation of great purposes, too great for the sympathy of a man's compeers; and that man's nature is the highest who feels most keenly the suffering of such an isolation – great as are its supports and consolations. But there is another loneliness, which comes from a want of warmth in the emotions, from an incapacity for strong individual attachments. Such a loneliness may be due to the deficiencies of a man's nature, not to the faults for which he is responsible; but it is an independence whose root is in wretchedness. Now De Foe lived partly, certainly, in the better isolation we speak of; but partly also in the latter. That he was not a man of strong or tender affections, his whole writings bear evidence. He never represents men as permanently bound together by affection. It costs him nothing uniformly to depict attachment as subordinate to interest. He shows husband and wife as united by common interests, common objects, or common duties; but rarely, if ever, by simple love. He has written one of the most moving passages that can be found in the range of English literature. It is the accidental meeting of a mother (a transported convict) with her son, born under tragic circumstances, and whom she had not seen since his earliest years. The father and the son pass by her accidentally in the plantation:

I had no mask; but I ruffled my hood so about my face that I depended upon it that after above twenty years' absence, and withal not expecting any thing of me in that part of the world, he would not be able to know me. – [This is the father.] – But I need not have used all that caution; for he was grown dim-sighted by some distemper which had fallen upon his eyes, and could but just see well enough to walk about, and not run against a tree or into a ditch. As they drew near to us, I said, 'Does he know you, Mrs. Owen?' – so they called the woman. 'Yes,' she said, 'if he hears me speak, he will know me; but he can't see well enough to know me or any body else.' And so she told me the story of his sight, as I have related. This made me secure; and so I threw open my hood again, and let them pass by me. It was a wretched thing for a mother thus to see her own son, a handsome comely young gentleman in flourishing circumstances, and durst not make herself known to him, and durst not take any notice of him. Let any mother of children that reads this consider it, and but think with what anguish of mind I restrained myself; what yearnings of soul I had in me to embrace him and weep over him; and how I thought all my entrails burned

---

[1] This and the following reference should read 'Forster'. See *Daniel Defoe and Charles Churchill*, pp. 139–40, as cited in No. 22.

within me; that my very bowels moved, and I knew not what to do; as I now know not how to express those agonies. When he went from me, I stood gazing and trembling, and looking after him as long as I could see him; then, sitting down on the grass, just at a place I had marked, I made as if I lay down to rest me; but turned from her, and lying on my face wept, and kissed the ground that he had set his foot on.

This is intense, if not refined, pathos; but it is the description, not of affection, but of the maternal instincts; and his power of entering, as he sometimes does, into this and similar instincts makes his silence on the subject of the more voluntary affections only the more remarkable. Another proof of the want of susceptibility in his own nature in this respect lies in the fact that he was not acutely sensible, as most men would have been, to the isolation of his position. It is true, as Mr Foster says, that *Robinson Crusoe* could only have been written by a man of solitude and self-sustainment; but the passage he quotes from the preface to *Crusoe's Serious Reflections* in which the author urges the analogy between the life of his hero and his own, marks decisively how little he felt that solitude. He indicates the analogy between the experiences of his own life and the adventures of Crusoe in every particular, excepting just his residence on the desert island:

The adventures of Robinson Crusoe, [he says,] are one whole scene of real life of eight-and-twenty years, spent in the most wandering, desolate, and afflicting circumstances that ever a man went through, and in which I have lived so long a life of wonders in continual storms; fought with the worst kind of savages and man-eaters by unaccountable surprising incidents; fed by miracles greater than that of the ravens; suffered all manner of violences and oppressions, injurious reproaches, contempt of men, attacks of devils, corrections from heaven, and oppositions on earth; have had innumerable ups and downs in matters of fortune; been in worse slavery than Turkish; escaped by as exquisite management as that in the story of Xury and the boat of Salee; been taken up ill at sea in distress; raised again, and depressed again, and that oftener, perhaps, in one man's life, than ever was known before; shipwrecked often, though more by land than by sea; – in a word, there is not a circumstance in the imaginary story but has its just allusion to a real story, and chimes part for part, and step for step, with the inimitable life of Robinson Crusoe.

In his novels we see what might have been the character of De Foe, had not the conscientiousness of his will raised it above the tendencies of his nature. Crusoe may be said to be only deeply self-engrossed; but Moll Flanders, Roxana, Colonel Jack, and Singleton, are selfish to the last extremes of baseness: their whole lives are only one struggle to secure their own interests, regardless not only of the welfare of others, but of gratitude, natural affection, and decency. It may be said that this is only what is to be expected if a man is writing with unsparing exactness and fidelity the lives of thieves and harlots; but this is a trait that pervades them all so universally, and shows itself so exactly in the same kind of way, that it evidently has a deeper root than mere appropriateness to the characters of those represented. Moreover De Foe is far from representing his characters as utterly depraved; and he is always anxious to point a moral. It seems strange to our juster notions of things, – and perhaps he wilfully deceived himself a little, – but he seems to have believed that he wrote these elaborate pictures of vice and wickedness with a direct moral purpose. 'Throughout the infinite variety of this book,' says he in the preface to *Moll Flanders*, 'this fundamental is most strictly adhered to: there is not a wicked action in any part of it, but is first or last rendered unhappy and unfortunate; there is not a superlative villain brought upon the stage, but either he is brought to an unhappy end, or brought to be a penitent; there is not an ill thing mentioned but it is condemned even in the relation, nor a virtuous just thing but it carries its praise along with it. Upon this foundation this book is recommended to the reader as a work from every part of which something may be learned; and some just and religious inference is drawn, by which the reader will have something of instruction, if he pleases to make use of it.' Thus (though these professions are not very adequately carried out) we see what the author's intentions were; but though vices and dishonesties meet with a thin share of reprobation, and are followed sooner or later by remorseful repentance, a depravity of selfishness, which to the reader seems far more abhorrent, is passed over in all the silence of complete unconsciousness. And with their selfishness and their insufficient affections, De Foe's characters have that solitary independent course through life which naturally results from these defects, and which reflects back in an exaggerated form the independent solitariness of De Foe's own life. Moll Flanders, Roxana, Singleton, Colonel Jack, all stand quite alone in the world. They are all single separate molecules, shifting to and fro in the wide sands of life – touching others, but never for a moment incorporated with them; they all live as using the world for themselves, and standing off from its binding influences; they grasp at others for a momentary assistance, but they never allow another's claim to interfere with their own liberty; they seize with the affections, but are never bound by them; they may cling to another life, but it is with a reserved power of disengagement, as a limpet clings to a rock; they never strike root in it, and grow from it, like a plant.

To turn to another point, in which the works give a glimpse into the interior of the writer. De Foe was very unfortunate as a trader; the same strong imagination acting on practical subjects as is displayed in his novels, made him a reformer in society and also a speculator in business. He would seem to have been the very man to succeed in the latter function; and his failure was probably due, as indeed he himself hints, to a distracting and overbalanced interest in the former direction, and to the literary habits it engendered. Whatever was the cause of his misfortunes, he showed himself in all his reverses a man of unblemished honesty and integrity. More, he showed himself often and under strong temptations a disinterested man. Yet in his heart he must have had an intense love of property; in his novels he lets his passion for it run free. He gloats over money or bales of silk, over spices and pearls; no sums are too large for him, no items too minute; he delights in putting the values down in separate lines, and totting up the columns. He revels in doubloons and pistoles and 'pieces of eight'. Little inventories have an especial charm for him; he always tells you exactly what his thieves' winnings amount to, and cannot for the life of him help looking at stealing as a sort of business, and secretly rejoicing when the profits come in. When he describes three young pickpockets going out, he has a certain reluctant sympathy with the 'dexterous young rogues;' and tells us: 'The list of their purchase the first night was as follows':

1. A white handkerchief from a country wench, as she was staring up at a jack-pudding; there was 3s. 6d. and a row of pins tied up in one end of it.

2. A coloured handkerchief, out of a young country fellow's pocket, as he was buying a china orange.

3. A riband purse with 11s. 3d. and a silver thimble in it, out of a young woman's pocket, just as a fellow offered to pick her up.

N.B. She missed her purse presently; but, not seeing the thief, charged the man with it that would have picked her up, and cried out, 'A pickpocket!' And he fell into the hands of the mob; but, being known in the street, he got off with great difficulty.

4. A knife and fork, that a couple of boys had just bought, and were going home with; the young rogue that took it got it within the minute after the boy had put it in his pocket.

5. A little silver box with 7s. in it, all in small silver, – 1d., 2d., 3d., 4d. pieces.

N.B. This it seems a maid pulled out of her pocket, to pay at her going into the booth to see a show; and the little rogue got his hand in and fetched it off, just as she put it up again.

6. Another silk handkerchief, out of a gentleman's pocket.

7. Another.

8. A jointed baby, and a little looking-glass, stolen off a toyseller's stall in the fair.

The account of how the little Colonel Jack and his friend the small Major dined on the proceeds of this enterprise is not to the purpose; but is so happy an illustration of De Foe's wonderful power of realising the minutest traits in a person he has once conceived, that we cannot forbear quoting it:

When we had thus fitted ourselves, I said, 'Hark ye, Major Jack, you and I never had any money in our lives before, and we never had a good dinner in all our lives: what if we should go somewhere and get some victuals? I am very hungry.'

'So we will, then,' says the Major, 'I am hungry too.' So we went to a boiling-cook's in Rosemary Lane, where we treated ourselves nobly; and, as I thought with myself, we began to live like gentlemen, for we had three-pennyworth of boiled beef, two-pennyworth of pudding, a penny brick (as they call it, or loaf), and a whole pint of strong beer; which was seven-pence in all.

N.B. We had each of us a good mess of charming beef-broth into the bargain; and, which cheered my heart wonderfully, all the while we were at dinner, the maid and the boy in the house, every time they passed by the open box where we sat at our dinner, would look in and cry, 'Gentlemen, do you call?' and, 'Do ye call, gentlemen?' I say this was as good to me as all my dinner.

In his more fortunate days, after he has reached man's estate, Colonel Jack makes his fortune in Virginia; and De Foe finds full indulgence for his fancy in making him trade with immense profits to Cuba and the coast of Mexico. There too, as in many other cases, he makes opportunities for the giving of presents, and rejoices in laying them out on the table and telling you how much every thing cost:

This bale was, in general, made up of several smaller bales, which I had directed, so that I might have room to make presents, equally sorted as the circumstance might direct me. However, they were all considerable, and I reckoned the whole bale cost me near 200*l*. sterling in England; and, though my present circumstances required some limits to my bounty in making presents, yet the obligation I was under being so much the greater, especially to this one friendly generous Spaniard, I thought I could not do better than, by opening two of the smaller bales, join them together, and make my gift something suitable to the benefactor, and to the respect he had shown me; accordingly I took two bales, and, laying the goods together, the contents were as follows:

Two pieces of fine English broadcloth, the finest that could be got in London, divided, as was that which I gave to the governor, at the Havannah, into fine crimson in grain, fine light mixtures, and fine black.

Four pieces of fine Holland, of 7s. to 8s. per ell in London.

Twelve pieces of fine silk drugget and duroys, for men's wear.

Six pieces of broad silks, two damasks, two brocaded silks, and two mantuas.

With a box of ribands, and a box of lace; the last cost about 40l. sterling in England.

This handsome parcel I laid open in my apartment; and brought him up-stairs one morning, on pretence to drink chocolate with me, which he ordinarily did; when, as we drank chocolate, and were merry, I said to him, – though I had sold him almost all my cargo, and taken his money, yet the truth was, that I ought not to have sold them to him, but to have laid them all at his feet, for that it was to his direction I owed the having any thing saved at all.

He smiled, and, with a great deal of friendship in his face, told me, that not to have paid me for them would have been to have plundered a shipwreck, which had been worse than to have robbed an hospital.

At last I told him I had two requests to make to him, which must not be denied. I told him I had a small present to make him, which I would give him a reason why he should not refuse to accept; and the second request I would make after the first was granted. He said he would have accepted my present from me, if I had not been under a disaster; but, as it was, it would be cruel and ungenerous. But, I told him, he was obliged to hear my reason for his accepting it. Then I told him that this parcel was made up for him by name, by my wife and I in Virginia, and his name set on the marks of the bale; and accordingly I showed him the marks, which was indeed on one of the bales, but I had doubled it now, as above, so that I told him these were his own proper goods; and, in short, I pressed him so to receive them, that he made a bow; and I said no more, but ordered my negro, – that is to say, his negro that waited on me, – to carry them all, except the two boxes, into his apartments, but would not let him see the particulars till they were all carried away.

After he was gone, about a quarter of an hour, he came in raving, and almost swearing, and in a great passion, but I could easily see he was exceedingly pleased; and told me, had he known the particulars, he would never have suffered them to have gone as he did; and at last used the very same compliment that the governor at the Havannah used, viz. that it was a present fit for a viceroy of Mexico rather than for him.

In the substance of their constitution, still more than in special traits, do De Foe's fictitious personages echo back their creator. They have all a certain squareness and solidity; they are all of hardy and stubborn materials. They put you in mind of timber; they have no sensibility, no pliancy. The events of life make just such an impression as blows on a heavy balk of wood; they bear the brunt and carry the dent it leaves, but the blow has no perceptible effect on them. The roughest treatment does but blunt their edges and tear off a few splinters. Theirs is never the elasticity which recovers from a blow, but the tough fibrous nature which a blow cannot permanently injure. Robinson Crusoe is the only one of De Foe's heroes who is at all sensible to the injuries of fortune; and even he is only a little stunned by the worst that befalls him, and less by actual evils than the imagination of them – as when he sees the footprint on the sand. De Foe himself passed through a life crowded with troubles, but a small part of which would have shattered, or even killed, many men; but they neither broke nor bowed him. Yet he had neither the levity which offers no resistance, nor the spring which casts off all the effect; he knew all he had gone through; he remembered the details of his sufferings; he felt, and even deeply, but dully. He was pachydermatous, tough, and tenacious of life. Sensitiveness is generally a part of imaginative genius; the same organisation which renders a man sensible to the finer and more elusive influences which surround him, exposes a trembling sensibility to the touch of pain or annoyance, so that sometimes he becomes like him who was

> As a nerve, o'er which do creep
> The else unfelt oppressions of the world.

But De Foe's genius had nothing of this character; and as his nature qualified him to deal only with the grosser and more obvious facts of existence, so, on the other hand, it required a hard blow to hurt him. 'Thirteen times,' says he, 'I have been rich and poor'; but he bore the vicissitudes of fortune with a cheerful sedateness which never failed him. He worked and lived, not like a winged Pegasus trampling the air, but like a serious laborious ox, dragging the slow plough through the long furrows, and rolling round a patient reproachful eye in answer to injury. There was nobleness too as well as constitutional phlegm in this patience of De Foe's; for it was certainly based, not only on his imperturbability of disposition, but in great measure on a trustful acceptance of God's will, and a just reliance on the goodness of the cause he advocated. His courage was of the same class. It was great, and did not fail him in arduous trials. Fear never could put him out of the course he felt called upon to follow. Still he recognised discretion as the better part of valour; he had no love of danger; and if it could be avoided without undue compromise, he was always willing to accept the terms. He had little or nothing of what we call spirit; no sensitiveness on the point of personal honour; injustice did not raise a fire in him, but a steady and resolute temper of resistance; injuries could never excite in him a desire for revenge; he replied to them by calm expostulation, or that sort of satire whose sting lies in its truthfulness, – a very thorough laying bare to day of his adversaries' weak points. Swift, with his fierce gladiatorial spirit, struck him insultingly a backhanded blow; to which De Foe replied in a tone that rises something above his usual heavy strain, and which shows the fair, temperate, political tradesman in a far better light than the arrogant, conscienceless, political churchman. Among his contemporaries, the constancy with which he endured persecution, and the steady disregard of threats and indignities with which he persisted in his purposes, won him the reputation of 'a man of true courage'. For himself he lays claim only to a good cause:

Fame, a lying jade, would talk me up for I know not what of courage; and they call me a fighting fellow. I despise the flattery; I profess to know nothing of it, further than truth makes any man bold; and I acknowledge, that give me but a bad cause, and I am the greatest coward in the world. Truth inspires nature; and as in defence of truth no honest man can be a coward, so no man of sense can be bold when he is in the wrong. He that is honest must be brave; and it is my opinion that a coward cannot be an honest man. In defence of truth, I think (pardon me that I dare go no further, for who knows himself?) – I say I think I could dare to die; but a child may beat me if I am in the wrong. Guilt gives trembling to the hands, blushing to the face, and fills the heart with amazement and terror. I question whether there is much, if any, difference between bravery and cowardice, but what is founded in the principle they are engaged for; and I no more believe any man is born a coward than that he is born a knave. Truth makes a man of courage, and guilt makes that man a coward.

This courage of the conscience, totally unaccompanied by any love of danger, or of combat for its own sake, might be illustrated from many pages of De Foe's novels. It is in his life, however, that we must look to see his sturdy and obstinate yet temperate nonconformist spirit, and that direct uncalculating energy, that unquestioning conviction, that intense reliance on the effect of one's own individual exertion, that power of standing alone and acting unsupported, which have given, not to the government or the higher gentry, but to the body of the English nation, its distinctive and peculiar type of character; and which De Foe possessed in a degree so remarkable, as to make him stand out perhaps of all Englishmen the most English our history can show.

In all his writings we trace an intellect corresponding to the nature we have endeavoured to describe. Like that, it was somewhat coarse in grain and confined in scope, but vigorous and powerful. A sort of Benjamin's portion of retail tradesman's mind, preserving the vulgar proportions and moving under the common conditions, but on a higher level of power, – a vessel of larger capacity and nobler uses, yet made of the same clay as the meanest. He has shrewd instincts, but cumbrous thoughts; he can express himself as fully, and even as fast, as you please; but not concisely. His ideas are heavy malleable metal, and he loves to hammer them out; his mind moves easily, but without spring, and he is a heavy hand at a joke. No one likes to call him dull, and there is a vigour in all he writes which redeems him from the charge; but tedious and intolerably self-repeating he undeniably is. This is a defect, however, which shows less in his novels than elsewhere. He is a master in the art of narration, and for the mere telling of a story, does it better and more simply than any writer we have. His style in his novels is well adapted to the level of his subject. In itself it scarcely deserves the commendation it has received. It is like the manners of a farmer at an Inn: a man of the best breeding could not be more at his ease; but it is because he submits to no artificial restraint whatever. In his works, written expressly for amusement or instruction, the plainness of his writing suits well with his plain rude way of treating his subject, and his complete insensibility to, and disregard of, any of its refinements or less obvious aspects. His shortcomings in this respect have been one great cause of the popularity these works have obtained, especially among the less-highly cultivated classes. Every reader feels competent to say as he reads, 'This is true and lifelike,' – to follow his arguments, and to comprehend his reflections. It is this which made Lamb say he was 'good kitchen reading'. Fielding is any thing but kitchen reading. A man must take pains with his education, and have a cultivated mind, if he intends to read *Tom Jones* so as to appreciate it. It has been called vulgar; it may contain vulgarities, but it is the least level to common capacities of any novel in the language; and De Foe's novels are perhaps the most so. The wonderful thing is, the wealth of the mine he lays bare at this low level, and on these universal conditions. There must be something very singular in a work which the chimney-sweep and the peer both understand and both find interesting, – which the latter at any rate admires, and the former fully enjoys. This would be an easy triumph if it were gained by an appeal to, or a description of, the common feelings; but the characteristic of De Foe is, that he has written books universally popular, whose interest is quite independent of this universal resource. His memory was a remarkable one, and he was widely and accurately informed in all those matters which a man learns by observation; and he had a signal power of gathering up that sort of information which is knowledge at first-hand, without requiring to be digested, and which is got through eye and ear rather than through books. His education had been good, but he appears simply to have mastered languages for practical use; to have accumulated the facts, not to have studied the ideas, conveyed in them. Though a wide reader, he was never interested in other men's thoughts, – if he cites them, it is simply as authorities. When he himself thinks, it is (with rare exceptions) to direct practical issues; then he is sagacious, acute – even wise in broad every-day matters. Only in one direction did he indulge in any speculative thought, and only in this one direction did his imagination break through its ordinary matter-of-fact boundaries. He had a singular interest in the world of spirits. He wrote a *History of the Devil*; and it is hard to say what object he proposed to himself in this amazingly tiresome, confused, lumbering work; a strange sort of half-serious, half-burlesque attempt to track the course of the great enemy's operations, criticising 'Mr Milton's' account of his fall, counting up how many names he has in Scripture, and apologising for still calling him 'plain devil'; pursuing him through Jewish history, and partly through profane; inquiring – 'What may probably be the great business this black emperor has at present upon his hands, either in this world or out of it, and by what agents he works'; and finally, discussing 'his last scene of liberty', and 'what may be supposed to be his end'. His *Life of Duncan Campbell* is another extraordinary production of the same class. It professes to be the history of a famous deaf and dumb wise man, who in those days had set up as a fortune-teller in London; and seriously accounts for his powers of penetrating futurity as derived from the second-sight and intercourse with the spiritual world. What grains of truth there may be in the book as a biography, and how far it is jest or grave hoaxing, and how far serious; how much of it the author himself believed, – it is impossible to tell. One can never say of De Foe, whether he was so fond of fiction he could never write unmixed truth, or so fond of exact truth as to spoil his hoaxes by making them too real. There is no joke in making people believe any thing short of what, at bottom, is a clear and palpable absurdity; and we are far from sharing in the modern astonishment, either that the public should at first have thought the famous tract on *The Shortest Way with the Dissenters* was written in earnest, or that both dissenters and Tories should have felt incensed against the author when it was found to be ironical. Much of it is common Tory argument and assertion, seriously and forcibly put; and the exaggeration of the conclusion scarcely, if at all, overstepped the limits of what might have proceeded from the pen of a high-flying Tory enthusiast. The whole thing had no point except as coming from a dissenter, and bore no evidence of doing so in the title-page or elsewhere. To have it written at all must have rubbed the sores of the dissenters; and to find it was written in travestie exasperated their oppressors. The *History of the Apparition of Mrs. Veal* is a very circumstantial ghost-story, and now we think it a very good joke; but it was not meant as a joke, any more than the cures of bad legs we see in the advertisements of quack ointments are meant as jokes. Very likely De Foe, in his own breast, enjoyed a grave sort of chuckle at the humour of making the apparition of 'a maiden gentlewoman of about thirty years of age, who for some years past had been troubled with fits,' appear to Mrs Bargrave, and recommend the perusal of Drelincourt's *Book of Consolations against the Fear of Death*; but he never meant the public to share his amusement. It is one of the most remarkable exhibitions ever seen of a power of giving an exact air of reality to imagined facts. Its old formal precise air, our knowledge that it was got up to sell the book to which it was prefixed, and of the extraordinary success it had, amuse us who are in the secret. But De Foe did not mean it to amuse; he meant it to convince; he deliberately intended it as an imposition, and a most successful one it proved. There are plenty more such ghost-stories scattered through De Foe's works. Take the following, with its terrific vocal conclusion, as a specimen:

In the year 1711, one Mrs. Stephens and her daughter were, together with Mr. Campbell, at the house of Mr. Ramells, a very great and noted weaver at Haggerstone; where the rainy weather detained them till late at night. Just after the clock struck twelve, they all of them went to the door to see if the rain had ceased, being extremely desirous to get home. As soon as ever they had opened the door and were all got together, there appeared before them a thing all in white; the face seemed of a dismal pallid hue, but the eyes thereof fiery and flaming, like beacons, and of a saucer size. It made its approaches to them, till it came up within the space of about three yards of them; there it fixed and stood like a figure agaze for some minutes; and they all stood likewise stiff, like the figure, frozen with fear, motionless, and speechless. When all of a sudden it vanished from their eyes; and that apparition to the sight was succeeded by a noise, or the appearance of a noise, like that which is occasioned by the fighting of twenty mastiff dogs.

All we can say as to De Foe's way of regarding these and similar supernatural, or quasi-supernatural occurrences, as we choose to think them, is, that it is clear he was not prepared entirely to disbelieve; but these sort of stories, accompanied by direct strenuous assertions as to their truth in fact, and grave argument as to their bearing on unbelief, are chiefly remarkable for our present purpose as a further indication of the strange sort of confusion there seems to have been in De Foe's mind between real fact and possible fact. His imagination is so strong, that its facts seem to him of equal weight with those of memory or knowledge; and he appears scarcely to recognise the boundary between truth and fiction. His characters, as usual, carry the tendency a step further. They lie, to suit their purposes, at every turn, and without scruple or remorse.

De Foe was a man of strong religious convictions, and there is scarcely one of his writings which does not bear the impress of his deep sense of the all-outweighing importance of a religious life; and he can even venture to affirm, in one of his vindicatory articles in his *Review*, that *Ad Te, quacunque vocas*, has been the rule of his own life. He had a strong sense of direct inspiration, even as guiding to or deterring from particular actions. Neither his genius nor his heart, however, were such as to give him any profound insight into a sense of spiritual relations. He had that sort of temperament which can feel and sympathise with sudden and violent accesses of somewhat coarse religious emotion, with too much sense and staidness on the one hand, and too much conscientiousness on the other, to make him guilty either of the unseemly excesses, or the discordant self-indulgence, which distinguish the debased forms of so-called Evangelicism. All his characters repent in the same way; they are suddenly stricken with an overwhelming sense, not so much of their guilt as of their crimes; they are appalled to think themselves outcasts from God; they lay down their evil habits generally when circumstances have removed the temptation to pursue them; repent in a summary manner, and become without difficulty sincere penitents and religious characters. He has no sense of the temptations, the trials, the difficulties with which the souls of most men find themselves surrounded after they have once left home with Bunyan's pilgrim. He knows that strait is the gate, and sharp the struggle necessary to pass it; but he always seems to forget that narrow is the way even after the gate is passed.

We have strict conventional rules in England as to what are to be considered readable books for society at large. It is scarcely necessary to say, that De Foe's novels are quite outside this pale. It is not that they were written with the least idea either of pandering to a vicious nature, or shocking an innocent one; but they deal frankly with matters about which our better modern taste is silent, and use language which shocks modern refinement.

It is only fair, however, to say, they are in their essence wholesome, decent, and, above all, cleanly. They have neither the varnished prurience of Richardson, the disgusting filth of Swift, nor the somewhat too indulgent and sympathising warmth of Fielding; they are plain-spoken and gross, but that is the worst of them; and though the obvious and hammered moralities of the author seem valueless enough, it is to be remembered that the class whose rudeness would make it impervious to injury from the absence of delicacy in these works, is just the one in a position to profit by their rough and primitive teaching. For those who seek it, they contain a deeper moral, not the less important because the writer was unconscious of its existence. They are warnings against the too common error of confounding crime and sin. They are the histories of criminals, who remind us at every page that they are human beings just like ourselves; that the forms of sin are often the result merely of circumstances; and that the aberration of the will, not the injury done to society, is the measure of a man's sinfulness. They show us among thieves and harlots the very same struggles against new temptations, the same slow declension and self-enfeebling wiles, which we have to experience and contend against in ourselves. We are too apt to think of the criminal outcasts of society as of persons removed from the ordinary conditions of humanity, and given up to a reprobate condition totally different from our own. One day we shall probably be surprised to find that, while right and wrong continue to differ infinitely, the various degrees of human sinfulness lie within much narrower limits than we, who measure by the external act, are at all accustomed to conceive. De Foe is a great teacher of charity; he always paints the remaining good with the growing evil, and never dares to show the most degraded and abandoned of his wretches as beyond the pale of repentance, or unattended by the merciful providences of God; nay, he can never bear to quit them at last, except in tears and penitence and in the entrance-gate at least of reconciliation.

25. The climate of the fifties

1856, 1858

The first three extracts are taken from an article 'Daniel De Foe', in the *Dublin University Magazine*, xlviii (July 1856), 57–71. The last item comes from the *British Quarterly Review*, xxvii (January 1858), 85–105, a review of Bohn's edition of the works.

(a) *Dublin University Magazine:*

His heroism was misunderstood. His moral constitution, like his wit, was beyond his era, and he was doomed to undergo the ill as well as the good of that fortune. Enemies hated him, and friends distrusted him. In his life he without doubt knew many who admired him, like honest Dunton, for his honesty, his subtlety, his daring, and his perseverance, but very few were the educated men who sincerely wished him well. He has been dead over a hundred and twenty years, and has now plenty of defenders, – Hazlitt, Lamb, Forster! What living (much more dead) man can want more applauders? (xlviii, 57.)

(b) *Dublin University Magazine:*

In what estimation are we to hold Defoe as a writer of fiction? And for what is the English novel indebted him? The latter question can be answered in a few words and with great precision. Defoe brought to the domain of imaginative prose-writing graphic descriptions of scenes, events and mental emotions, and quick, pointed conversations. (xlviii, 63.)

(c) *Dublin University Magazine:*
[Quotes *Colonel Jack*, Oxford English Novels, pp. 31–8.]

Who has read this extract without having the vision of Charles Dickens rise before his eyes?

Of *Robinson Crusoe* what necessity is there to speak? Who is not familiar with its pages? What schoolboy has not undergone a whipping for leaving his lessons unstudied while he has been sitting in the Solitary's hut, or spending an afternoon with 'man Friday'? How many in the decline of life have over the leaves of that wonder book grown young again! Charles Lamb says, 'next to the Holy Scriptures, it may be safely asserted that this delightful romance has, ever since it was written, excited the first and most powerful influence upon the juvenile mind of England, nor has its popularity been much less among any of the other nations of Christendom'. He might have added, 'and out of Christendom too'. It has been translated into Arabic; and Burckhart 'heard it read aloud among the wandering tribes in the cool hours of evening'. '*That* island,' a beautiful writer has observed, 'placed "far amidst the melancholy main," and remote from the track of human wanderings, remains to the last the greenest spot in memory. At whatever distance of time, the scene expands before us as clearly and distinctly as when we first beheld it; we still see the green savannahs and silent woods, which mortal footstep had never disturbed; its birds of strange wing, that had never heard the report of a gun; its goats browsing securely in the vale, or peeping over the heights, in alarm at the first sight of man. We can yet follow its forlorn inhabitant on tiptoe with suspended breath, prying curiously into every recess, glancing fearfully at every shade, starting at every sound, and then look forth with him upon the lone and boisterous ocean with the sickening feeling of an exile cut off for ever from all human intercourse. Our sympathy is more truly engaged by the poor shipwrecked mariner, than by the great, the lovely, and the illustrious of the earth. We find a more effectual wisdom in its homely reflections than is to be derived from the discourses of the learned and eloquent. The interest with which we converse with him in the retirement of his cave, or go abroad with him on the business of the day, is as various and powerful as the means by which it is kept up are simple and inartificial. So true is everything to nature, and such reality is there in every particular, that the slightest circumstance creates a sensation, and the print of a man's foot or shoe is the source of more genuine terror than all the strange sights and odd noises in the romances of Mrs Radcliffe.'

Children are charmed with the *story* of *Robinson Crusoe*; men of thought are not less delighted with the narrative, but they have recourse to it also as a book instructing them in some of the most valuable truths of philosophy. He must possess a far lower than a merely ordinary mind who leaves the perusal of this wonderful book without having acquired from it a new insight into his own nature, the means of avoiding the evil, and attaining to the good, – without having perceived how many infant faculties of his being might by training be made to assume grand proportions, and be endowed with vast strength. It is a great religious poem. It is 'the drama of solitude,' the object of which is to show that in the most wretched state of desertion there still remains within the human breast a power of life independent of external circumstances; and that where man is not, there God especially abides.

Why did not Defoe, with such an unexampled capability as a writer of fiction, occupy himself earnestly in his art? Why did he not expend thought, toil, and long years in elaborating two such works as *Robinson Crusoe*, or the commencement of *Colonel Jack*, instead of scribbling page after page, without consideration enough to avoid dulness, stories replete with obscenities he must have disapproved, and nonsense that he must have grinned at with contempt even while the pen was in his hand? Foster, in his graphic and fascinating sketch of Defoe and his times, bids us remember, when judging of *Moll Flanders* and *Roxana*, the tone of society at the time of their appearance. Without a doubt, measured by the standard of the vicious literature of the Restoration and the two succeeding ages, they do not especially sin against purity of morals. But in this we cannot find a valid apology for Defoe, who, in composing them, put his hand to works that all serious men of his own religious views must have regarded with warm disapproval. Defoe was not by profession amongst the frivolous or godless of his generation; he was loud in his condemnation of the stage, of gambling, and of debauchery; he not only knew that voluptuous excess was criminal, but he raised his voice to shame it out of society, – and yet he exercised his talents in depicting scenes of sensual enjoyment, which no virtuous nature can dwell on without pain, no vicious one without pleasure. What was his motive? Money.

Drelincourt's book of *Consolations against the fears of Death*, – one of the heaviest pieces of literature religion has given to the world, (and that is saying no little) – hung on hand, so that the publisher, much downcast, informed Defoe he should lose a considerable sum. 'Don't fear! – I'll make the edition go off,' said Defoe; and sitting down he wrote *A True Relation of the Apparition of one Mrs Veal, the next day after her death, to one Mrs Bargrave, at Canterbury, the 8th of September, 1705, which apparition recommends the perusal of Drelincourt's book of 'Consolations against the fears of Death'.* The ghost story startled and took captive the silly people the author intended, and knew so well how to hoax. A true, *bonâ fide* ghost of a respectable Mrs Veal had urged on mankind the study of Drelincourt. Forthwith the publisher's shop was crowded with purchasers, and the edition rapidly left his shelves. It is strange to me how Defoe's biographers and admirers delight in this story. It may show Defoe to advantage in an intellectual point of view, leading a crowd of John Bulls astray and all the while laughing at them; but as a proof of his mental power such testimony is valueless because unnecessary. That Mrs Veal's apparition was ingeniously told, no one will deny; but then it was a wilful falsehood, all the same for its cunning construction, and was framed to puff a bad book. Such a deed would aid the 'Woolly Horse' and 'Feejee Mermaid' in giving grace to a Barnum's life; but to think that Defoe could tell lies for a trade purpose, is more than a common pain.

And here we find the secret of this great man's shame. He was a man of somewhat expensive habits, continually entering into rash monetary speculations, and burdened with debts which *in honour* he felt himself bound to discharge. Of all men he was just the one to be called upon for large sums of wealth, and to have little in hand to meet such demands. His pen was a ready one at earning money; he could turn off any composition with facility: and as, just then, tales (highly seasoned) met with the best prices in the market, he wrote them as fast as his pen could run over the paper, and spiced them up to the palates of his employers. And what trash (dishonest quack gibberish to get pennies from the crowd) poured in unceasing flow from him, it grieves one to reflect. . . .

We have stated our thanks are due to Defoe for giving the English novel, graphic descriptions, and quick, pointed conversations. In one of the qualities of a novelist he was unaccountably deficient – not even coming up to his precursor Mrs Behn.[1] To the construction or the most vague conception of a plot he seems to have been quite inadequate. This may be accounted for partly by the fact that, from abstaining on religious grounds from the theatres, his mind had not been duly educated in this most difficult department of his art; and partly by the rapidity with which his 'histories' were evolved. Whatever may be the

[1] Aphra Behn (1640–89), dramatist and poet, also wrote fiction including *Oroonoko* (1688).

cause of the fault, that it exists few will be so rash as to question. All Defoe's novels, long as they are, are but a string of separate anecdotes related of one person, but having no other connection with each other. In no one of them are there forces at work that necessitate the conclusion of the story at a certain point. One meets with no mystery, no denouement in them. They go on and on, (usually at a brisk pace, with abundance of dramatic positions) till it apparently strikes the author he has written a good bookful, and then he winds up with a page and a half of 'so he lived happily all the rest of his days'; intermixed with some awkward moralizing by way of apology for the looseness of the bulk of the work. For example, *Roxana* might as well have been twice or half as long as it is.

One feature more of Defoe as a novelist. May he not be regarded as the first English writer of prose-fiction who pointed out the field of history to imaginative literature? His *Journal of the Plague Year*; his *Memoirs of a Cavalier*; and *The Memoirs of an English Officer who served in the Dutch War in 1672, to the peace of Utrecht in 1713, &c. &c. By Captain George Carlton*, were the pioneers of that army of which the Waverley Novels form the main body. The great Earl of Chatham used, before he discovered it to be a fiction, to speak of the *Memoirs of a Cavalier* as the best account of the civil wars extant. (xlviii, 68–70.)

(d) *British Quarterly Review:*

In criticising De Foe's life and works it is difficult to refrain from associating both with the principle of caste. There were, we take it, two men whom the great Puritan reaction brought forth, illustrating severally its two great phases – religious and political – Bunyan and De Foe. Bunyan's strong imagination, reacted on by the events of the hour, made him an earnest religionist. The associations of De Foe left him a political zealot. Their works are but types of their class. De Foe is Bunyan in the garb of a layman. Bunyan is De Foe in the pulpit. In the hands of a prophetic tinker human nature is represented in the form of a spiritual creation and in a spiritual capacity, full of energy, indeed, and inventive aspirations, but with aspirations set on things above, and with an energy that obeys an intuition less gross than that of sinew and nerve. With De Foe as exemplified in his *Crusoe* the powers of man are bent on the attainment of earthly objects – earthy. It is this practical spirit which distinguishes it from the more imaginative interest excited by the *Prisons of Pellico* and the *Picciola* of De Santaine. Not a little of its absorbing interest we are inclined to believe rests in reality on this unwitting admiration with which we watch the progressive triumph of man over matter, with which we see material nature, animals and savages, gradually succumbing to the coercive control of that peculiar contriving power, an excess of which has at different times produced a Franklyn and a Watt. The power of individualizing he shared in common with the author of the *Pilgrim's Progress*. Thus Bunyan's personifications are the most real, De Foe's characters the least fictitious. Bunyan was the last of that allegorical school which the piety or the superstition of the middle ages bequeathed to us. In this view the *Pilgrim's Progress* is not so much a novelty as a renaissance, and as he was the last, so he was the best. If we compare him to the author of *Visions of Piers Plowman*, *The Mirror for Magistrates*, or the *Faerie Queen*, we shall at once see the superiority of his skill in his emblematical characters. His allegorical personages, regarded as attributes, are as far superior to those of his predecessors as the Michael and Gabriel of Milton to the Bia and Kratos of Æschylus. For De Foe, there is no writer in the English language whose fictions wear the garb of fact so becomingly. The anecdotes connected with them are ample testimonies to his imposing powers of originality; for indeed no writer without originality could ever have beguiled the penetration of Chatham and Johnson. There is not a child who does not believe in the adventures of Crusoe as strongly as he believes in the history of Joseph.

In powers of realization we would compare him with Swift, not but that the Dean gains by the comparison. There is more skill, it is presumed, required to paint natural objects naturally, than to paint monstrous objects consistently. Swift undoubtedly has very vividly drawn the adventures of Lilliput, but he had the license which the unexplored province of the præternatural always gives. De Foe painted the familiar, and the execution is always within reach of criticism. Swift can only extract our wonder or excite our scepticism. De Foe has been tried by our experience, and has almost cheated us of our belief. If Swift had been an artist, and preserved the same characteristics, he would have illustrated the infernal terrors of Milton's Pandemonium to perfection; but it would have been reserved for the cunning art of a De Foe to engrave the natural delights of his Paradise.

As with all books that hold the popular affections, his *Crusoe* is remarkable for its simplicity, and indeed one might justly include in this remark all De Foe's works of fiction. The language employed and the style are Herodoteanly simple. It is to an eminent degree the language of the common people. One of his satirists in derision consigned the circulation of his pieces among all the old women in London from Tothill-street to Limehouse Hole,[1] and when it is remembered that this has been the fate of the *Pilgrim's Progress* it may be questioned whether the sarcasm is not a compliment. The *Crusoe* has been seriously attributed to the prison-hours of Harley; but it bears too much the impress of De Foe's character to admit of the least doubt of the authorship. The hero is strictly the model of an Independent. On every occasion the idiosyncracies of the Puritan peep out. The strictness with which in the midst of his solitude he kept the Sabbath, and the devotion with which he observed the anniversary of his shipwreck, might have been considered a protest against Laud's legislation for Sunday sports. The strong penitential agonies in which he reviewed his past career, his self-condemnation when suddenly enlightened, the vision of the avenger who descended from a great black cloud, in a bright flame of fire, making the earth to tremble at his step, and the air to flash lightning as he moved forward with his uplifted spear to kill him, remind us of the earnest confessions of the *Grace Abounding*. The curious arguments and hesitations which induced him several times to spare the wretches who only wanted to find him out to eat him, the comparison between himself and Saul in the midst of the Philistines, the thought that flashed across him on seeing the footprint in the sand that Satan had taken upon him human form in order to frighten him, the superstitious curiosity with which he observed that all the accidents of his life had been providentially arranged for a corresponding day in the year, clearly betray the pen of the author who sent such moral effusions as the *Family Instructor* and the *Religious Courtship* into the closets of kings. The conversation with Friday on the existence of evil in the world might have been held by De Foe any Sabbath from the pulpit in Surrey Chapel.

It seems rather paradoxical that he should be accused of want of imagination. It is certain he was no poet, though he himself was disposed to set a high poetical value on his metrical treatise, *De jure Divino*. Pope, in his *Treatise on Bathos*, assigned him his portion among the ostriches, which, though they could not fly, were yet able to outrun the fleetest horse; an idea more than once appropriated by a writer who, to use the words of Dryden, when he invades authors, invades them like a monarch, and whose skill converts theft into victory. Most of his imaginative productions are the result, not so much of a romantic fancy, as of a keen observation and a methodical reason. It will perhaps help

[1] See No. 3, p. 42 above.

to diminish our wonder at the lateness of their publication, if we can be convinced that his fictions draw as little upon the ideal, and as much upon experience, as fictions can possibly do. His education, doubtless, assisted him. As a volunteer in the service of constitutional government, his avocations must have carried him through scenes of stirring adventure. The Highlands were as familiar to him as his own Stoke Newington. And in England there was scarcely a province that he had not visited. From his trips across the Channel, and his occasional intercourse with such characters as Dampier, his genius might have derived the lawless encounters of the piracies of *Captain Singleton*. While his experience about the court of Charles II, or as a political refugee in the haunts of the metropolis, or in Newgate, must have brought before his observant eye many an original for the fortunate Roxana or the guilty Moll Flanders. To the wretchlessness of human nature his mind, like the mind of Crabbe and of Hogarth, must have been peculiarly sensitive. For, like Johnson's, it was a believing one. The Doctor, it is well known, believed in second sight, and almost believed in the Cock-lane Ghost. Nor is there want of evidence to show that De Foe himself shared in a rather characteristic conviction in the phenomena of dreams and in the spectral paraphernalia of the spiritual world.

It has been said that the discovery of the footprint on the sand was a poetical touch on the part of the author worthy of Shakspeare. But we may be quite sure that the author himself no more dreamt of setting himself up as a rival to him whose genius has given us the scene of Lady Macbeth's guilty start at the bloodstained hand, than the originator of the nursery rhymes on the Covetous King thought of making, according to Lord Macaulay, the best hexameter in the English language when he wrote –

The Queen was in her garden, making bread and honey.

Some have doubted whether from the presence of the practical element so strongly developed in his constitution he even possessed those lighter qualities, belonging more to the fancy than to the reason, which so admirably adapted Steele and Addison to be the arbiters of taste. Coleridge said he could select papers from his *Review* not inferior in wit and humour, and superior in style and thought, to the *Tatlers* and *Spectators*. But we are more disposed to allow him the attributes of solidity than of raciness. Under these heads he showed at once his superiority and his inferiority to Swift. Rhetorically speaking, the brilliant, easy, idiomatic style of the Dean place him, as a pamphleteer, beyond reach. But here his praise ends, and De Foe's begins. His writings are not those of a philosopher, but those of a partisan. We look in vain for evidence of a mind probing deep into the causes of things, uninfluenced by everything but an anxiety after truth. The reader of his works rises from their perusal with a perfect knowledge of the particular defects of particular men, but the motives of those men, the moral origin of those defects, are never touched upon. There is abundance of good satire, of hearty abuse, but no analysis of character, no appeal to the metaphysics of nature. This is doubtless partly to be attributed to the confined sphere of his composition. He wrote not for mankind, but for a class. His dealings were not with universal truths, but with local facts. Propositions were framed for him, and a distinct discourse of reasoning laid down. Hence in all his discussions, even in those which admit of more elaborate treatment, he clings to circumstances, discarding the cause for the simple effect. This is more evident in his larger treatises. In his furious invectives against the Whigs he abuses them, not because their legislation was based on false political conclusions, but because Somers and Godolphin were not Tories, and Lord Oxford and Dean Swift were. He promoted agitations among the Irish, not to redress the real grievances of Ireland, the animosities of class, the influences of a deteriorating religion, the absence of educational legislation, but simply because Irish coffers were being enriched by halfpence from a private mint. The contrast in De Foe would be best illustrated by a recurrence to his *Essay on Projects*. The author of the *Directions to Servants* could never have elevated his mind from the absorbing frivolities of politics to conceive it. It is with this *Essay* that De Foe's fame as a political economist is associated. It would not be fair to compare him to Bacon, or, what would be a more genial comparison, to Adam Smith. Yet it is certain that he comes nearer to the author of the *Wealth of Nations*, than do the economists of his own day, Child, Petty, or Davenant. It would hardly be believed that the man whose name has been overlooked by Smollett, by Lord Mahon, and as yet by Lord Macaulay, had anticipated Macadam and Howard, had laid the foundation of Bethlehem Asylum and Greenwich Academy, had published expositions of views on commerce not unworthy of the Free Trade Catechism, had suggested the reform of the national banking system, had proposed the establishment of provincial banks – and this, too, when not twenty years before the rise of shops in the country villages had been seriously deplored as the ruin of the great towns; and had projected a scheme for a commission of bankruptcy, for friendly societies, and for an institution for the education of females. It is not one of the least anomalies about his singular character and fate, that posterity should forget the merits of a writer who had, in his time, composed one of the most extraordinary books since the *Century of Inventions* or the *Principia*, and whose moth-eaten pages should one day help to mould the mind of such a philosopher as Franklin.

In closing a review of De Foe's career, one cannot help acknowledging that there is no writer in English literature whose characteristics bear more strongly the stamp of nationality. Everything about him is identified with that idiomatic creature we are accustomed to recognise as the portrait of an English citizen. Goldsmith is Irish all over. The artistic affability of Addison would rather suggest an association with the fellow-countrymen of Labruyère. The artificiality of Johnson's exterior compromises the earnestness of his spirit. The brusque and indomitable emphasis which Swift sometimes infused into his demeanour, comes nearest to him. But it is in De Foe alone we meet with the plain unembellished existence of the Anglo-Saxon element, exemplifying itself in its vigorous common sense, its epigrammatic expressiveness, its homely and prosaic reality. His individuality realises the philosophy of common life as thoroughly as that of Addison illustrates its amenities. His experience embodies, as it were, the chivalry of the middle class, the heroism of the bourgeoisie. Every page of his writings is impregnated with the spirit of rational industry, which he opposed to the sensualism around him, and of which he is the canonical exponent. Cobbett did not yield less to sentiment. Critics have decided that this unmusical deficiency in taste has ruined his reputation as a literary artist, that his versification is harsh, his characterization homely, his narration without variety. The remark might, indeed, be justly extended to his conduct in matters where other men, with more sensibility, would have escaped the imputation. The reason is plain. His speculations had not been elaborated in the studio. His academy had been the world. He had not been 'swaddled, rocked, and dandled,'[1] into a theorist. *Nitor in adversum*,[1] was his motto, as emphatically as it was Burke's. His sphere of contemplation was not in the realms of imagination, but of fact. His studies were identified, not with the ideal, but with the real. He had no sympathies with the prevailing tastes of the age. His powers were enlisted in another quarter; his subjects were of sterner stuff. The delicacies of criticism, the elegancies of the *belles lettres* he resigned to the wits who decided over their cups at Button's

[1] Ovid, *Metamorphoses*, ii, 72: 'I strive against opposition'.

on the merits of Pope's *Homer* and Tickell's; or to the fine gentlemen of White's who relieved the tedium of ombre with bets on the arrival of Sir Henry Newton's despatches from the Court of Tuscany with Filicaja's last Latin ode on Lord Somers. His standard was not *mode*, but utility. His character, accordingly shone, to use a Baconian expression, with a dry light. His mental and moral structure partook of the angular conformation peculiar to his sect. In his idiosyncracies the mechanical predominated. His ethics were those of a reformer, and were composed in the single word, progress. A century later in England he would have been called a Utilitarian, in Germany a Eudæmonist. (xxviii, 100–5.)

26. Taine on Defoe

1863

Hippolyte Taine (1828–93) produced his influential *Histoire de la Littérature Anglaise* in 1863. In this work he applied to Defoe his theory of the '*faculté maîtresse*' determining the nature of a given writer's output. Text from the translation by H. Van Laun (Edinburgh, 1873), vol. ii, pp. 153–7.

However we regard his life, we see only prolonged efforts and persecutions. Joy seems to be wanting; the idea of the beautiful never enters. When he comes to fiction, it is like a Presbyterian and a plebeian, with low subjects and moral aims, to treat of the adventures and reform the conduct of thieves and prostitutes, workmen and sailors. His whole delight was to think that he had a service to perform, and that he was performing it:

He that opposes his own judgment against the current of the times ought to be backed with unanswerable truth; and he that has truth on his side, is a fool as well as a coward, if he is afraid to own it, because of the multitude of other men's opinion. 'Tis hard for a man to say, all the world is mistaken, but himself. But if it be so, who can help it?

De Foe is like one of those brave, obscure, and useful soldiers who, with empty belly and burdened shoulders, go through their duties with their feet in the mud, pocket blows, receive day by day the fire of the enemy, and sometimes that of their friends into the bargain, and die sergeants, happy if it has been their lot to get hold of the legion of honour.

He had the kind of mind suitable to such a hard service, solid, exact, entirely destitute of refinement, enthusiasm, pleasantness.* His imagination was that of a man of business, not of an artist, crammed and, as it were, jammed down with facts. He tells them as they come to him, without arrangement or style, like a conversation, without dreaming of producing an effect or composing a phrase, employing technical terms and vulgar forms, repeating himself at need, using the same thing two or three times, not seeming to suspect that there are methods of amusing, touching, engrossing, or pleasing, with no desire but to pour out on paper the fulness of the information with which he is charged. Even in fiction his information is as precise as in history. He gives dates, year, month, and day; notes the wind, north-east, south-west, north-west; he writes a log-book, an invoice, attorneys' and shopkeepers' bills, the number of moidores, interest, specie payments, payments in kind, cost and sale prices, the share of the king, of religious houses, partners, brokers, net totals, statistics, the geography and hydrography of the island, so that the reader is tempted to take an atlas and draw for himself a little map of the place, to enter into all the details of the history as clearly and fully as the author. It seems as though he had performed all Crusoe's labours, so exactly does he describe them, with numbers, quantities, dimensions, like a carpenter, potter, or an old tar. Never was such a sense of the real before or since. Our realists of today, painters, anatomists, decidedly men of business, are very far from this naturalness; art and calculation crop out amidst their too minute descriptions. De Foe creates illusion; for it is not the eye which deceives us, but the mind, and that literally: his account of the great plague has more than once passed for true; and Lord Chatham took his *Memoirs of a Cavalier* for authentic. This was his aim. In the preface to the old edition of *Robinson Crusoe* it is said:

* See his dull poems, amongst others *Jure Divino*, a poem in twelve books, in defence of every man's birthright by nature. [Taine's note.]

The story is told . . . to the instruction of others by this example, and to justify and honour the wisdom of Providence. The editor believes the thing to be a just history of facts; neither is there any appearance of fiction in it.

All his talents lie in this, and thus even his imperfections aid him; his lack of art becomes a profound art; his negligence, repetitions, prolixity, contribute to the illusion: we cannot imagine that such and such a detail, so minute, so dull, is invented; an inventor would have suppressed it; it is too tedious to have been put in on purpose: art chooses, embellishes, interests; art, therefore, cannot have piled up this heap of dull and vulgar accidents; it is the truth.

Read, for instance, *A True Relation of the Apparition of one Mrs Veal, the next Day after her Death, to one Mrs Bargrave, at Canterbury, the 8th of September 1705; which Apparition recommends the perusal of Drelincourt's Book of Consolation against the Fear of Death.** The ancient threepenny little books, read by old needlewomen, are not more monotonous. There is such an array of circumstantial and guaranteed details, such a file of witnesses quoted, referred to, registered, compared, such a perfect appearance of tradesman-like honesty, coarse, vulgar common sense, that one would take the author for an honest retired hosier, with too little brains to invent a story; no writer careful of his reputation would have composed such nonsense. In fact, it was not his reputation that De Foe cared for; he had other motives in his head; we literary men of the present time cannot guess them, being literary men only. In short, he wanted to sell a pious book of Drelincourt, which would not sell of itself, and in addition, to confirm people in their belief by advocating the appearance of ghosts. It was the grand proof then brought to bear on sceptics. Grave Dr Johnson himself tried to see a ghost, and no event of that time was more appropriate to the belief of the middle class. Here, as elsewhere, De Foe, like Swift, is a man of action; effect, not noise touches him; he composed *Robinson Crusoe* to warn the impious, as Swift wrote the life of the last man hung to inspire thieves with terror. In this positive and religious age, amidst these political and puritan citizens, practice is of such importance as to reduce art to the condition of its tool.

Never was art the tool of a more moral or more English work. Crusoe is quite one of his race, and might instruct it in the present day. He has that force of will, inner enthusiasm, dull ferment of a violent examination which formerly produced the sea-kings, and now produces

* Compare Edgar Poe's *Case of M. Waldemar*. The American is a suffering artist; De Foe a sensible citizen. [Taine's note.]

emigrants and squatters. The misfortunes of his two brothers, the tears of his relatives, the advice of his friends, the remonstrances of his reason, the remorse of his conscience, are all unable to restrain him: there was 'a something fatal in his nature'; he had conceived the idea, he must go to sea. To no purpose is he seized with repentance during the first storm; he drowns in punch these 'fits' of conscience. To no purpose is he warned by shipwreck and a narrow escape from death; he is hardened, and grows obstinate. To no purpose captivity among the Moors and the possession of a fruitful plantation invite repose; the indomitable instinct returns; he was born to be his own destroyer, and embarks again. The ship goes down; he is cast alone on a desert island; then his native energy found its vent and its employment; like his descendants, the pioneers of Australia and America, he must re-create and re-master one by one the inventions and acquisitions of human industry; one by one he does so. Nothing represses his effort; neither possession nor weariness:

I had the biggest magazine of all kinds now that ever was laid up, I believe for one man; but I was not satisfied still; for, while the ship sat upright in that posture, I thought I ought to get everything out of her that I could. . . . I got most of the pieces of cable ashore, and some of the iron, though with infinite labour; for I was fain to dip for it into the water; a work which fatigued me very much. . . . I believe, verily, had the calm weather held, I should have brought away the whole ship, piece by piece.

In his eyes, work is natural. When, in order 'to barricade himself, he goes to cut the piles in the woods, and drives them into the earth, which cost a great deal of time and labour,' he says:

A very laborious and tedious work. But what need I have been concerned at the tediousness of any thing I had to do, seeing I had time enough to do it in? . . . My time or labour was little worth, and so it was as well employed one way as another.

Application and fatigue of head and arms give occupation to his superfluous activity and force; the mill must find grist to grind, without which, turning round empty, it would consume itself. He works, therefore, all day and night, at once carpenter, oarsman, porter, hunter, tiller of the ground, potter, tailor, milkman, basketmaker, grinder, baker, invincible in difficulties, disappointments, expenditure of time and toil. Having but a hatchet and an adze, it took him forty-two days to make a board. He occupied two months in making his first two jars; five months in making his first boat; then, 'by dint of hard labour', he levelled the ground from his timber-yard to the sea, tried to bring the sea up to his boat, and began to dig a canal; then, reckoning that he would require ten or twelve years to finish the task, he builds another boat at another place, with another canal half a mile long, four feet deep, six wide. He spends two years over it:

I bore with this. . . . I went through that by dint of hard labour. . . . Many weary stroke it had cost. . . . This will testify that I was not idle. . . . As I had learned not to despair of any thing. I never grudged my labour.

These strong expressions of indomitable patience are ever recurring. This hard race is framed for labour, as its sheep are for slaughter and its horses for the chase. Even now you may hear their mighty hatchet and pickaxe strokes in the claims of Melbourne and in the log-houses of the Salt Lake. The reason of their success is the same there as here; they do everything with calculation and method; they rationalise their energy, which is like a torrent they make a canal for. Crusoe sets to work only after deliberate calculation and reflection. When he seeks a spot for his tent, he enumerates the four conditions of the place he requires. When he wishes to escape despair, he draws up impartially, 'like debtor and creditor', the list of his advantages and disadvantages, putting them in two columns, active and passive, item for item, so that the balance is in his favour. His courage is only the servant of his common sense:

By stating and squaring everything by reason, and by making the most rational judgment of things, every man may be in time master of every mechanic art. I had never handled a tool in my life, and yet in time, by labour, application, and contrivance, I found at last that I wanted nothing but I could have made it, especially if I had had tools.

There is a grave and deep pleasure in this painful success, and in this personal acquisition. The squatter, like Crusoe, takes pleasure in things, not only because they are useful, but because they are his work. He feels himself a man, whilst finding all about him the sign of his labour and thought; he is pleased:

I had everything so ready at my hand, that it was a great pleasure to me to see all my goods in such order, and especially to find my stock of all necessaries so great.

He returns to his home willingly, because he is there a master and creator of all the comforts he has around him; he takes his meals there gravely and 'like a king'.

Such are the pleasures of home. A guest enters there to fortify these natural inclinations by the ascendency of duty. Religion appears, as it must, in emotions and visions: for this is not a calm soul; imagination breaks out into it at the least shock, and carries it to the threshold of madness. On the day when he saw the 'print of a naked man's foot on the shore', he stood 'like one thunderstruck', and fled 'like a hare to cover'; his ideas are in a whirl, he is no longer master of them; though he is hidden and barricaded, he thinks himself discovered; he intends 'to throw down the enclosures, turn all the tame cattle wild into the woods, dig up the corn-fields'. He has all kind of fancies; he asks himself if it is not the devil who has left this footmark; and reasons upon it:

I considered that the devil might have found out abundance of other ways to have terrified me; . . . that, as I lived quite on the other side of the island, he would never have been so simple to leave a mark in a place where it was ten thousand to one whether I should ever see it or not, and in the sand too, which the first surge of the sea upon a high wind would have defaced entirely. All this seemed inconsistent with the thing itself, and with all notions we usually entertain of the subtlety of the devil.

In this impassioned and uncultivated mind, which for eight years had continued without a thought, and as it were stupid, engrossed in manual labour and bodily wants, belief took root, fostered by anxiety and solitude. Amidst the risks of all-powerful nature, in this great uncertain upheaving, a Frenchman, a man bred like us, would cross his arms gloomily like a Stoic, or would wait like an epicure for the return of physical cheerfulness. As for Crusoe, at the sight of the ears of barley which have suddenly made their appearance, he weeps, and thinks at first 'that God had miraculously caused this grain to grow'. Another day he has a terrible vision: in a fever he repents of his sins; he opens the Bible, and finds these words, which 'were very apt to his case': 'Call upon me in the day of trouble; I will deliver thee, and thou shalt glorify me'. Prayer then rises to his lips, true prayer, the converse of the heart with a God who answers, and to whom we listen. He also read the words: 'I will never leave thee nor forsake thee'.

Immediately it occurred that these words were to me. Why else should they be directed in such a manner, just at the moment when I was mourning over my condition, as one forsaken of God and man?

Thenceforth spiritual life begins for him. To reach its very foundation, the squatter needs only his Bible; with it he carries out his faith, his theology, his worship; every evening he finds in it some application to his present condition: he is not alone; God speaks to him, and provides for his energy matter for a second labour to sustain and complete the first. For he now undertakes against his heart the combat which he has maintained against nature; he wants to conquer, transform, ameliorate, pacify the one as he has done with the other. Crusoe fasts, observes the Sabbath, three times a day he reads the Scripture, and says:

I gave humble and hearty thanks . . . that he (God) could fully make up to me the deficiencies of my solitary state, and the want of human society by his presence, and the communication of his grace to my soul, supporting, comforting, and encouraging me to depend upon his providence, and hope for his eternal presence hereafter.

In this disposition of mind there is nothing a man cannot endure or do; heart and hand come to the assistance of the arms; religion consecrates labour, piety feeds patience; and man, supported on one side by his instincts, on the other by his beliefs, finds himself able to clear the land, to people, to organise and civilise continents.

27. Karl Marx on *Robinson Crusoe*

1867

From part i, chapter I, 'Commodities', in the first volume of *Das Kapital*, published in 1867. The text is that of the standard translation by Samuel Moore and Edward Aveling, edited by Friedrich Engels (1915), vol. i, pp. 88–91.

Since Robinson Crusoe's experiences are a favourite theme with political economists, let us take a look at him on his island. Moderate though he be, yet some few wants he has to satisfy, and must therefore do a little useful work of various sorts, such as making tools and furniture, taming goats, fishing and hunting. Of his prayers and the like we take no account, since they are a source of pleasure to him, and he looks upon them as so much recreation. In spite of the variety of his work, he knows that his labour, whatever its form, is but the activity of one and the same Robinson, and consequently, that it consists of nothing but different modes of human labour. Necessity itself compels him to apportion his time accurately between his different kinds of work. Whether one kind occupies a greater space in his general activity than another, depends on the difficulties, greater or less as the case may be, to be overcome in attaining the useful effect aimed at. This our friend Robinson soon learns by experience, and having rescued a watch, ledger, and pen and ink from the wreck, commences, like a true-born Briton, to keep a set of books. His stock-book contains a list of the objects of utility that belong to him, of the operations necessary for their production; and lastly, of the labour time that definite quantities of those objects have, on an average, cost him. All the relations between Robinson and the objects that form this wealth of his own creation, are here so simple and clear as to be intelligible without exertion, even to Mr Sedley Taylor.[1] And yet those relations contain all that is essential to the determination of value.

Let us now transport ourselves from Robinson's island bathed in light to the European middle ages shrouded in darkness. Here, instead of the independent man, we find everyone dependent, serfs and lords, vassals and suzerains, laymen and clergy. Personal dependence here characterises the social relations of production just as much as it does the other spheres of life organized on the basis of that production. But for the very reason that personal dependence forms the groundwork of society, there is no necessity for labour and its products to assume a fantastic form different from their reality. They take the shape, in the transactions of society, of services in kind and payments in kind. Here the particular and natural form of labour, and not, as in a society based on production of commodities, its general abstract form is the immediate social form of labour. Compulsory labour is just as properly measured by time, as commodity-producing labour; but every serf knows that what he expends in the service of his lord, is a definite quantity of his own personal labour-power. The tithe to be rendered to the priest is more matter of fact than his blessing. No matter, then, what we may think of the parts played by the different classes of people themselves in this society, the social relations between individuals

---

Sedley Taylor (1834–1920), Fellow of Trinity College, Cambridge, writer on industrial ownership and on music; called by Engels 'this mannakin, a dabbler in the tamest of co-operative enterprises'.

in the performance of their labour, appear at all events as their own mutual personal relations, and are not disguised under the shape of social relations between the products of labour. . . .

Let us now picture to ourselves, by way of change, a community of free individuals, carrying on their work with the means of production in common, in which the labour-power of all the different individuals is consciously applied as the combined labour-power of the community. All the characteristics of Robinson's labour are here repeated, but with this difference, that they are social, instead of individual. Everything produced by him was exclusively the result of his own personal labour, and therefore simply an object of use for himself. The total product of our community is a social product. One portion serves as fresh means of production and remains social. But another portion is consumed by the members as means of subsistence. A distribution of this portion amongst them is consequently necessary. The mode of this distribution will vary with the productive organization of the community, and the degree of historical development attained by the producers. We will assume, but merely for the sake of a parallel with the production of commodities, that the share of each individual producer in the means of subsistence is determined by his labour-time. Labour-time would, in that case, play a double part. Its apportionment in accordance with a definite social plan maintains the proper proportion between the different kinds of work to be done and the various wants of the community. On the other hand, it also serves as a measure of the portion of the common labour borne by each individual and of his share in the part of the total product destined for individual consumption. The social relations of the individual producers, with regard both to their labour and to its products, are in this case perfectly simple and intelligible, and that with regard not only to production but also to distribution.

28. Leslie Stephen on Defoe

1868

From the essay, 'Defoe's Novels', first published in the *Cornhill Magazine*, xvii (1868). It was reprinted in Stephen's *Hours in a Library*, 1st series (1874). The text here is based on the revised edition of *Hours in a Library* (1892), vol. i, pp. 17–46.

Sir Leslie Stephen (1832–1904), editor of the *Dictionary of National Biography* and of the *Cornhill Magazine*, made a special study of the eighteenth century. His daughter, Virginia Woolf, was herself a distinguished critic of Defoe.

(a) *Hours in a Library:*

We may ask . . . what is the peculiar source of Defoe's power? He has little or no dramatic power, in the higher sense of the word, which implies sympathy with many characters and varying tones of mind. If he had written *Henry IV*, Falstaff, and Hotspur, and Prince Hal would all have been as like each other as are generally the first and second murderer. Nor is the mere fact that he tells a story with a strange appearance of veracity sufficient; for a story may be truth-like and yet deadly dull. Indeed, no candid critic can deny that this is the case with some of De Foe's narratives; as, for example, the latter part of *Colonel Jack*, where the details of management of a plantation in Virginia are sufficiently uninteresting in spite of the minute financial details. One device, which he occasionally employs with great force, suggests an occasional source of interest. It is generally reckoned as one of his most skilful tricks that in telling a story he cunningly leaves a few stray ends, which are never taken up. Such is the well-known incident of Xury, in *Robinson Crusoe*. This contrivance undoubtedly gives an appearance of authenticity, by increasing the resemblance to real narratives; it is like the trick of artificially roughening a stone after it has been fixed into a building, to give it the appearance of being fresh from the quarry. De Foe, however, frequently extracts a more valuable piece of service from these loose ends. The situation which has been most praised in

De Foe's novels is that which occurs at the end of *Roxana*. Roxana, after a life of wickedness, is at last married to a substantial merchant. She has saved, from the wages of sin, the convenient sum of 2,056*l.* a year, secured upon excellent mortgages. Her husband has 17,000*l.* in cash, after deducting a 'black article of 8,000 pistoles', due on account of a certain lawsuit in Paris, and 1,320*l.* a year in rent. There is a satisfaction about these definite sums which we seldom receive from the vague assertions of modern novelists. Unluckily, a girl turns up at this moment who shows great curiosity about Roxana's history. It soon becomes evident that she is, in fact, Roxana's daughter by a former and long since deserted husband; but she cannot be acknowledged without a revelation of her mother's subsequently most disreputable conduct. Now, Roxana has a devoted maid, who threatens to get rid, by fair means or foul, of this importunate daughter. Once she fails in her design, but confesses to her mistress that, if necessary, she will commit the murder. Roxana professes to be terribly shocked, but yet has a desire to be relieved at almost any price from her tormentor. The maid thereupon disappears again; soon afterwards the daughter disappears too; and Roxana is left in terrible doubt, tormented by the opposing anxieties that her maid may have murdered her daughter, or that her daughter may have escaped and revealed the mother's true character. Here is a telling situation for a sensation novelist; and the minuteness with which the story is worked out, whilst we are kept in suspense, supplies the place of the ordinary rant; to say nothing of the increased effect due to apparent veracity, in which certainly few sensation novelists can even venture a distant competition. The end of the story differs still more widely from modern art. Roxana has to go abroad with her husband, still in a state of doubt. Her maid after a time joins her, but gives no intimation as to the fate of the daughter; and the story concludes by a simple statement that Roxana afterwards fell into well-deserved misery. The mystery is certainly impressive; and Roxana is heartily afraid of the devil and the gallows, to say nothing of the chance of losing her fortune. Whether, as Lamb maintained, the conclusion in which the mystery is cleared up is a mere forgery, or was added by De Foe to satisfy the ill-judged curiosity of his readers, I do not profess to decide. Certainly it rather spoils the story; but in this, as in some other cases, one is often left in doubt as to the degree in which De Foe was conscious of his own merits. (vol. i, pp. 17–20.)

(b) Even De Foe's imagination recognised and delighted in a certain margin of mystery to this harsh world of facts and figures. He is generally too anxious to set everything before us in broad daylight; there is too little of the thoughts and emotions which inhabit the twilight of the mind; of those dim half-seen forms which exercise the strongest influence upon the imagination, and are the most tempting subjects for the poet's art. De Foe, in truth, was little enough of a poet. Sometimes by mere force of terse idiomatic language he rises into real poetry, as it was understood in the days when Pope and Dryden were our lawgivers. It is often really vigorous. The well-known verses –

> Wherever God erects a house of prayer,
> The devil always builds a chapel there –

which begin the *True-born Englishman*, or the really fine lines which occur in the *Hymn to the Pillory*, that 'hieroglyphic state machine, contrived to punish fancy in', and ending –

> Tell them that placed him here,
> They're scandals to the times,
> Are at a loss to find his guilt,
> *And can't commit his crimes* –

may stand for specimens of his best manner. More frequently he degenerates into the merest doggerel, *e.g.* –

> No man was ever yet so void of sense,
> As to debate the right of self-defence,
> A principle so grafted in the mind,
> With nature born, and does like nature bind;
> Twisted with reason, and with nature too,
> As neither one nor t'other can undo –

which is scarcely a happy specimen of the difficult art of reasoning in verse. His verse is at best vigorous epigrammatic writing, such as would now be converted into leading articles, twisted with more or less violence into rhyme. And yet there is a poetical side to his mind, or at least a susceptibility to poetical impressions of a certain order. And as a novelist is on the border-line between poetry and prose, and novels should be as it were prose saturated with poetry, we may expect to come in this direction upon the secret of Defoe's power. . . . The mysterious has a very strong though peculiar attraction for him. (vol. i, pp. 20–2.)

(c) When such a man spins us a yarn the conditions of its being interesting are tolerably simple. The first condition obviously is, that the plot must be a good one, and good in the sense that a representation in dumb-show must be sufficiently exciting, without the necessity of any explanation of motives. The novel of sentiment or passion or character would be altogether beyond his scope. He will accumulate any number of facts and details; but they must be such as will speak for themselves without the need of an interpreter. For this reason we do not imagine that *Roxana, Moll Flanders, Colonel Jack,* or *Captain Singleton* can fairly claim any higher interest than that which belongs to the ordinary police report, given with infinite fulness and vivacity of detail. In each of them there are one or two forcible situations. Roxana pursued by her daughter, Moll Flanders in prison, and Colonel Jack as a young boy of the streets, are powerful fragments, and well adapted for his peculiar method. He goes on heaping up little significant facts, till we are able to realise the situation powerfully, and we may then supply the sentiment for ourselves. But he never seems to know his own strength. He gives us at equal length, and with the utmost plain-speaking, the details of a number of other positions, which are neither interesting nor edifying. He is decent or coarse, just as he is dull or amusing, without knowing the difference. The details about the different connections formed by Roxana and Moll Flanders have no atom of sentiment, and are about as wearisome as the journal of a specially heartless lady of the same character would be at the present day. He has been praised for never gilding objectionable objects, or making vice attractive. To all appearance, he would have been totally unable to set about it. He has only one mode of telling a story, and he follows the thread of his narrative into the back-slums of London, or lodging-houses of doubtful character, or respectable places of trade, with the same equanimity, at a steady jog-trot of narrative. The absence of any passion or sentiment deprives such places of the one possible source of interest; and we must confess that two-thirds of each of these novels are deadly dull; the remainder, though exhibiting specimens of his genuine power, is not far enough from the commonplace to be specially attractive. In short, the merit of De Foe's narrative bears a direct proportion to the intrinsic merit of a plain statement of the facts; and, in the novels already mentioned, as there is nothing very surprising, certainly nothing unique, about the story, his treatment cannot raise it above a very moderate level. (vol. i, pp. 30–1.)

(d) Robinson Crusoe dwells but little upon the horrors of his position, and when he does is apt to get extremely prosy. We fancy that he could never have been in want of a solid sermon on Sunday, however much he may have missed the church-going bell. But in *Robinson Crusoe*, as in the *History of the Plague*, the story speaks for itself. To explain the horrors of living among thieves, we must have some picture of internal struggles, of a sense of honour opposed to temptation, and a pure mind in danger of contamination. De Foe's extremely straightforward and prosaic view of life prevents him from setting any such sentimental trials before us; the lad avoids the gallows, and in time becomes the honest master of a good plantation; and there's enough. But the horrors of abandonment on a desert island can be appreciated by the simplest sailor or schoolboy. The main thing is to bring out the situation plainly and forcibly, to tell us of the difficulties of making pots and pans, of catching goats and sowing corn, and of avoiding audacious cannibals. This task De Foe performs with unequalled spirit and vivacity. In his first discovery of a new art he shows the freshness so often conspicuous in first novels. The scenery was just that which had peculiar charms for his fancy; it was one of those half-true legends of which he had heard strange stories from seafaring men, and possibly from the acquaintances of his hero himself. He brings out the shrewd vigorous character of the Englishman thrown upon his own resources with evident enjoyment of his task. Indeed, De Foe tells us very emphatically that in Robinson Crusoe he saw a kind of allegory of his own fate. He had suffered from solitude of soul. Confinement in his prison is represented in the book by confinement in an island; and even a particular incident, here and there, such as the fright he receives one night from something in his bed, 'was word for word a history of what happened'. In other words, this novel too, like many of the best ever written, has in it the autobiographical element which makes a man speak from greater depths of feeling than in a purely imaginary story.

It would indeed be easy to show that the story, though in one sense marvellously like truth, is singularly wanting as a psychological study. Friday is no real savage, but a good English servant without plush. He says 'muchee' and 'speakee', but he becomes at once a civilized being. . . . This is comparatively a trifle; but Crusoe himself is all but impossible. Steele, indeed, gives an account of Selkirk, from which he infers that 'this plain man's story is a memorable example that he is happiest who confines his wants to natural necessities'; but the facts do not warrant this pet doctrine of an old-fashioned school. Selkirk's state of mind may be inferred from two or three facts. He had almost forgotten to talk; he had learnt to catch goats by hunting them on foot; and he had acquired the exceedingly difficult art of making fire by rubbing two sticks. In other words, his whole mind was absorbed in providing a few physical necessities, and he was rapidly becoming a savage – for a man who can't speak and can make fire is very near the Australian. We may infer, what is probable from other cases, that a man living fifteen years by himself, like Crusoe, would either go mad or sink into the semi-savage state. De Foe really describes a man in prison, not in solitary confinement. We should not be so pedantic as to call for accuracy in such matters; but the difference between the fiction and what we believe would have been the reality is significant. De Foe, even in *Robinson Crusoe*, gives a very inadequate picture of the mental torments to which his hero is exposed. He is frightened by a parrot calling him by name, and by the strangely picturesque incident of the footmark on the sand; but, on the whole, he takes his imprisonment with preternatural stolidity. His stay on the island produces the same state of mind as might be due to a dull Sunday in Scotland. For this reason, the want of power in describing emotion as compared with the amazing power of describing facts, *Robinson Crusoe* is a book for boys rather than men, and, as Lamb says, for the kitchen rather than for higher circles. It falls short of any high intellectual interest. When we leave the striking situation and get to the second part, with the Spaniards and Will Atkins talking natural theology to his wife, it sinks to the level of the secondary stories. But for people who are not too proud to take a rather low order of amusement *Robinson Crusoe* will always be one of the most charming of books. We have the romantic and adventurous incidents upon which the most unflinching realism can be set to work without danger of vulgarity. Here is precisely the story suited to De Foe's strength and weakness. He is forced to be artistic in spite of himself. He cannot lose the thread of the narrative and break it into disjointed fragments, for the limits of the island confine him as well as his hero. He cannot tire us with details, for all the details of such a story are interesting; it is made up of petty incidents, as much as the life of a prisoner reduced to taming flies, or making saws out of penknives. The island does as well as the Bastille for making trifles valuable to the sufferer and to us. The facts tell the story of themselves, without any demand for romantic power to press them home to us; and the efforts to give an air of authenticity to the story, which sometimes make us smile, and sometimes rather bore us, in other novels are all to the purpose; for there is a real point in putting such a story in the mouth of the sufferer, and in giving us for the time an illusory belief in his reality. It is one of the exceptional cases in which the poetical aspect of a position is brought out best by the most prosaic accuracy of detail; and we imagine that Robinson Crusoe's island, with all his small household torments, will always be more impressive than the more gorgeously coloured island of Enoch Arden. When we add that the whole book shows the freshness of a writer employed on his first novel – though at the mature age of fifty-eight; seeing in it an allegory of his own experience embodied in the scenes which most interested his imagination, we see some reasons why *Robinson Crusoe* should hold a distinct rank by itself amongst his works. As De Foe was a man of very powerful but very limited imagination – able to see certain aspects of things with extraordinary distinctness, but little able to rise above them – even his greatest book shows his weakness, and scarcely satisfies a grown-up man with a taste for high art . . . [but] to have pleased all the boys in England for near a hundred and fifty years is, after all, a remarkable feat. (vol. i, pp. 36–40.)

(e) But De Foe had never approached the conception of his art which afterwards became familiar. He had nothing to do with sentiment or psychology, those elements of interest came in with Richardson and Fielding; he was simply telling a true story and leaving his readers to feel what they pleased. It never even occurred to him, more than it occurs to the ordinary reporter, to analyse character or describe scenery or work up sentiment. He was simply a narrator of plain facts. He left poetry and reflection to Mr Pope or Mr Addison, as your straightforward annalist in a newspaper has no thoughts of rivalling Lord Tennyson or Mr Froude.[1] His narratives were fictitious only in the sense that the facts did not happen; but that trifling circumstance was to make no difference to the mode of writing them. The poetical element would have been as much out of place as it would have been in a merchant's ledger. He could not, indeed, help introducing a little moralising, for he was a typical English middle-class dissenter. Some of his simple-minded commentators have even given him credit, upon the strength of such passages, for lofty moral purpose. They fancy that his lives of criminals, real or imaginary, were intended to be tracts showing that vice leads to the gallows. No doubt, De Foe had the same kind of solid homespun morality as Hogarth, for example, which was not in its way a bad thing. But one need not be very cynical to believe

[1] James Anthony Froude (1818–84), historian and biographer of Carlyle.

that his real object in writing such books was to produce something that would sell, and that in the main he was neither more nor less moral than the last newspaper writer who has told us the story of a sensational murder.

De Foe, therefore, may be said to have stumbled almost unconsciously into novel-writing. He was merely aiming at true stories, which happened not to be true. But accidentally, or rather unconsciously, he could not help presenting us with a type of curious interest; for he necessarily described himself and the readers whose tastes he understood and shared so thoroughly. His statement that *Robinson Crusoe* was a kind of allegory was truer than he knew. In *Robinson Crusoe* is De Foe, and more than De Foe, for he is the typical Englishman of his time. He is the broad-shouldered, beef-eating John Bull, who has been shouldering his way through the world ever since. Drop him in a desert island, and he is just as sturdy and self-composed as if he were in Cheapside. Instead of shrieking or writing poetry, becoming a wild hunter or a religious hermit, he calmly sets about building a house and making pottery and laying out a farm. He does not accommodate himself to his surroundings; they have got to accommodate themselves to him. He meets a savage and at once annexes him, and preaches him such a sermon as he had heard from the exemplary Dr Doddridge.[1] Cannibals come to make a meal of him, and he calmly stamps them out with the means provided by civilisation. Long years of solitude produce no sort of effect upon him morally or mentally. He comes home as he went out, a solid keen tradesman, having, somehow or other, plenty of money in his pockets, and ready to undertake similar risks in the hope of making a little more. He has taken his own atmosphere with him to the remotest quarters. Wherever he has set down his solid foot, he has taken permanent possession of the country. The ancient religions of the primæval East or the quaint beliefs of savage tribes make no particular impression upon him, except a passing spasm of disgust at anybody having different superstitions from his own; and, being in the main a good-natured animal in a stolid way of his own, he is able to make use even of popish priests if they will help to found a new market for his commerce. The portrait is not the less effective because the artist was so far from intending it that he could not even conceive of anybody being differently constituted from himself. It shows us all the more vividly what was the manner of man represented by the stalwart Englishman of the day; what were the men who were building up vast systems of

---

[1] Philip Doddridge (1702–51), dissenting minister and teacher.

commerce and manufacture; shoving their intrusive persons into every quarter of the globe; evolving a great empire out of a few factories in the East; winning the American continent for the dominant English race; sweeping up Australia by the way as a convenient settlement for convicts; stamping firmly and decisively on all toes that got in their way; blundering enormously and preposterously, and yet always coming out steadily planted on their feet; eating roast beef and plum-pudding; drinking rum in the tropics; singing 'God Save the King' and intoning Watts's hymns under the nose of ancient dynasties and prehistoric priesthoods; managing always to get their own way, to force a reluctant world to take note of them as a great if rather disagreeable fact, and making it probable that, in long ages to come, the English of *Robinson Crusoe* will be the native language of inhabitants of every region under the sun. (vol. i, pp. 43–6.)

29. The biographer's view

1869

In 1869 William Lee, Superintending Inspector in the Board of Health, brought out *Daniel Defoe: His Life and Recently Discovered Writings*. The second and third volumes of this work contain extensive tracts of Defoe's journalism, hitherto unknown to his readers. The first volume is a life, the fullest and most accurate up to this date. Lee was not a literary critic of any great distinction, but he expresses articulately the contemporary view of Defoe, current among admirers less choosy and analytic than Leslie Stephen.

(a) On *The Family Instructor*:

I should waste the reader's time by commenting upon the contents of this admirable, unsectarian, though religious, Manual. Few, if any, seriously disposed persons are unacquainted with its value. It has found its way into the libraries of kings, and into the cottages of peasants: it has passed through innumerable editions, and is still popular; it has been made a blessing, under God, to thousands of souls, and will continue to be the same, wherever the English language is known, and so long as that which is pure and peaceable, shall continue to be lovely, and of good report. . . .

The [second] volume is in no sense inferior to its predecessor. It is equally unsectarian, catholic, and evangelical. It abounds in excellent maxims of piety and wisdom, calculated to arouse the attention, to enlighten the understanding, and kindle the best affections of the heart. The young have been attracted by the incidental narratives in this, and the companion volume; – to the old, they constitute a manual of social duty; – the sweet simplicity of the dialogue commends the work to the meanest capacity, – while the accurate delineation of human nature must extort praise, from the most refined and critical student. There are few books better adapted for the perusal of all to whom the education of the young is committed; the clergy of every denomination, – teachers of National and Sunday Schools, parents, children, and servants. And as Mr Wilson truly observes, 'if the author had written nothing else, these volumes alone possess a sufficient merit to give him a high place amongst English moralists'. (vol. i, pp. 248, 279.)

(b) On Defoe's creative fecundity:

Our Author was now in the fifty-eighth year of his age, and had already given to the world a greater number of distinct Works than any other living writer; yet his past labours, whether considered with respect to their number, – the marvellous capacity of his genius, – the astonishing rapidity of his composition, – or his title thereby to undying fame, – appear to sink into comparative insignificance, when we contemplate his productions during the twelve remaining years of his life. The inexhaustible fertility of his invention, – stimulating a hand and frame inured by long habit to the toil of composition, – has called forth the wonder and astonishment of many of the greatest writers and critics of modern times. But they were all unaware that in addition to the Herculean labours claiming their admiration, there were also, a monthly publication of nearly a hundred pages; a Paper published weekly; another appearing thrice a week; and, a great part of the time, a fourth, issued daily; besides about twenty biographical, historical, and political pamphlets, and several considerable volumes, then unknown to be his. So great an amount of intellectual toil would be incredible were not the facts before us, in the works themselves. Much of the time for recruiting exhausted Nature with necessary food and sleep, – all his goings and returnings – his seasons of social intercourse, if any, – in fact, during every waking moment, must that calm and clear head have been able to concentrate his faculties upon whatever subject engaged his pen at the time. Let the eye glance at the List of his works from the beginning of 1719 to 1724, – let the attention be directed to the short periods between the publication of successive volumes, – and adding thereto, his Journalistic labours, it may fairly be asked if the history of the world contains proof that an equally prolific literary genius has existed?

This is not the place in which to dilate upon the wide grasp of Defoe's mind, as exhibited in his later writings, – which included almost every branch of literature; nor to enlarge upon his peculiar and happy manner of treating every subject, so as to interest all ranks and classes of readers. (vol. i, pp. 290–1.)

(c) On *Captain Singleton*:

This work has been spoken of in comparatively disparaging terms by several of the biographers of Defoe. I take leave entirely to dissent from such judgment, and to say, that making allowance for the absence of that charm which, in some of his works, is due to the isolation of his hero, and the concentrated interest arising therefrom, Singleton comes in no sense behind the other literary creations of our author. It is true that the pirate is not an honest man, because that would be a contradiction of terms, but natural conscience is always at work, and the book itself abounds in moral reflections. Only the latter portion contains the piratical adventures of Singleton; and they are full of striking incidents, and of appropriate dialogue; each part, however, contributes to the unity of the whole, as a true representation of the times. The Quaker pirate is the moralist of the work, and was not introduced by Defoe, as an important character, without due consideration. Few men had better studied, or more highly respected, the body of Friends, called Quakers, whose religious and moral principles were closely allied to his own; but there were undoubtedly, in the reigns of Queen Anne and George I, professed Quakers, such as we know nothing of now. London had several who kept taverns, – one, who was an owner of race-horses, that ran for wagers on Banstead Downs; and several Quakers were transported, for burglaries and highway robberies. There is therefore no moral or literary improbability in Singleton's connection with one of that body, whose sister he afterward married. The titlepage of the book however, shows that Defoe considered the former part as the more important, containing the escape of the mutineers from Madagascar to Mozambique, and their subsequent marvellous journey by land across the most desolate and unknown part of the continent of Africa, to its western coast. I hold the conception and execution of this part of his work, considered in all the detail of its circumstances, to be one of the highest and most successful efforts of Defoe's genius. I have traced this route on the map of Africa, in Wyld's great Atlas of 1849; and where I find on the map *carte blanche* for more than a thousand miles, Defoe's Captain Singleton, of 1720, has guided me along the shores of the mighty Lakes, – which he declared to be the true sources of the Nile, – through dreary deserts, and across primeval mountains, – inhabited by many races of savage men, and more savage beasts; and the whole journey, to use his own words, – 'full of Adventures that were never heard or read of before'. This knowledge of the interior of Africa appears the more amazing since the recent researches of Livingstone, Baker, Grant, and other explorers, have confirmed what our author had so long before stated. (vol. i, pp. 335–6.)

(d) On the criminal lives; the sociological defence:

I have now to explain briefly . . . the motives and circumstances that induced [Defoe], at sixty years of age, to commence writing a series of volumes professedly recording the lives of notorious criminals, whose many offences and immoralities had subjected them to the penalties of the laws they had broken. His personal honesty and integrity, the purity of his life, nay even his high religious character, has never been called in question by any well-informed writer, and is attested by the excellence of his numerous moral works; – composed, not only previously, but interposed between, and continued after, the publication of those which are felt to be offensive to modern notions of delicacy. It has also excited inquiry how he became acquainted with the class of persons from whom alone he could have obtained such an intimate knowledge of their habits, manners, and associations; not only at home, – but in the Plantations to which they were transported, – as was requisite for the production of these works. As to the latter of these inquiries, the only answer has been based on the horrible manner in which prisoners were confined together in Newgate, almost without discrimination of offence, or of sex. It has been supposed that when Defoe was imprisoned for writing *The Shortest Way*, – in the beginning of the reign of Queen Anne, – he was compelled to associate ordinarily with the most abandoned of both sexes; and then acquired the knowledge that enabled him, nearly twenty years afterward, to write the books in question. I must state that there is not the slightest foundation for believing that he was ever subjected, against his will, to so barbarous an indignity. In the eyes even of those who condemned him, he had only written and published a libel; and the numerous works he composed while in prison, not only show upon what subjects his mind and attention were then engaged, but also that he was able to pursue his studies, without great disturbance. There is not a word to be found in any of his prison writings, or later productions, giving countenance to any assertion that he had been exposed, for more than a year, to degrading associations, which, with his sense of morality and religion, would have been worse than a thousand deaths.

Pecuniary motives, arising from straitened circumstances, have been assigned, as having induced him to write what his conscience might not approve. I must also strongly dissent from this, as a libel upon his moral character. Such humiliation of their hero, by his biographers, has arisen from their belief, that during the last fifteen years of his life, he was in poverty; and entirely dependent, for the support of himself and family, upon the sale of the books heretofore known as his writings. But when it is considered that all his children were now grown up, and some of them no longer a burden; that he appears to have been no longer harassed by his former pecuniary misfortunes; that he had an adequate income from the Government; that he was paid for his services in connection with three or four Journals, and periodical publications; and that, in addition, – his other works were a large and increasing source of revenue, – it will be readily believed that he had never been in such prosperity as now, since the death of King William III. It is undeniable that he composed these works and as he had not treasured up any degrading experiences of an imprisonment twenty years previously, nor was urged by necessity, we must conclude that he wrote them under circumstances not heretofore known, voluntarily, and from motives justified by his own enlightened conscience.

A glance at the moral, or immoral, condition of large classes of the people, during the latter part of the reign of Queen Anne, and the whole reign of George I, is requisite to a right judgment of this matter. To narrow the question as much as possible, we may leave out of consideration the leaven of depravity, which, commencing with the Court after the Restoration, had now leavened the mass of society. Nor need we do more than name, that somewhat similar influences in

France culminated, at the period with which we have now to do, in the Cartouchian organization of robbers and murderers. It will be sufficient to say of England, that her pirates, the offspring of the buccaneers, infested every sea in the known world; that the *Owlers* were leagued with justices and landed gentry in defrauding the Customs of the country, to an extent that would now be thought incredible; that the *Blacks*, who were organized in many of the western counties for burglaries, comprised substantial yeomen and well-to-do farmers in their numbers; that among the army of highwaymen, in and about London, was a barrister, several attornies, a graduate of the University of Cambridge, a stockbroker, and many keepers of apparently respectable taverns. These are but the salient points, below which, there existed an undistinguished mass of ignorance, dishonesty, lewdness, and brutality; which there was no police to prevent, and the sanguinary laws of the period were totally unable to repress. One or two annually appointed constables in each parish, and a few decrepid night watchmen, constituted the only police of the metropolis. All the coaches plying between Hampstead and the city would be stopped, and the passengers robbed in the open daylight; and, by the same mounted desperadoes, – day after day, – for a week together. The same on the roads from Islington, and from Hackney, and other suburban towns and villages. The apprehension of any of these villains was of no avail; their places were immediately filled by others, and the supply of highwaymen seemed inexhaustible. No private carriage could travel safely without an escort of armed servants; the mails were constantly robbed of their valuable contents, – that between Bristol and London being plundered about five times in as many weeks. In hopes of safety, plate and jewels were frequently sent in stage-waggons, and several of these were stopped successively between Notting-hill and Tyburn-gate, the harness cut, the waggons unloaded, and the boxes and packages opened and rifled, on the public road, during the space of several hours; after which, the thieves rode off unmolested with their spoil. Footpads plied their profitable trades on pedestrians, and the occupants of chairs, in such places as Charing Cross, Holborn, Fleet Street, and St. Paul's Churchyard, not unfrequently, if resisted, adding murder to robbery. The weekly hanging-day at Tyburn was the market of all the lower class of male pickpockets; the fallen of the other sex infesting the streets, taverns, and places of amusement; while the more aristocratic of both sexes filched pocket-books, papers, and purses, in the city, and on the Exchange. Truly, the period between 1720 and 1730 may be called, by way of climax, the Age of Crime, and Jonathan Wild, the creature of circumstances. The newspapers from 1721 to 1725 frequently contained a string of paragraphs more than a column in length, of robberies committed, without any of the thieves having been apprehended; and another column of short advertisements, in small type, as to pocket-books, bills, notes, and securities, &c., all of which were said to be – 'Lost'. Rewards were offered to those who would bring the property to Mr Jonathan Wild, at the King's Head in the Old Bailey, 'and no questions asked'. I counted fifty-seven acts of criminality related in one journal of that period; and, in another, thirty-three cases of pockets picked, of an aggregate sum of more than 22,000*l*. What was there to counteract this flood of iniquity? The Societies for the Reformation of Manners attempted it, and I have before me a printed List containing the Christian and surnames of about one hundred and twenty keepers of 'Bawdy Houses' *fined*; – of forty who were *carted*; and of one hundred and sixty prostitutes who were whipped in Bridewell, within a short period, through the exertions of these Societies. All the culprits, doubtless, immediately returned to their vile avocations. The Gallows could not contain all that were condemned to die, although sometimes from ten to twenty were hung together; and therefore, the greater number of the condemned were offered the alternative, – which they always accepted, – of being transported to the Plantations in America, with the certainty that, if they should ever return to England, identification would be the only step between them and death. Ships were continually dispatched to the American Colonies, with cargoes of these condemned wretches, varying from one hundred to three hundred, according to the size of the vessels; and on their arrival the prisoners were sold as Slaves to the Planters. They had no religious instruction; and, with such servants, the strong hand of the planter contained the power of life and death. Many committed additional crimes in the colonies, and perished miserably, others found their way back to England, hoping by disguise to conceal themselves; in this some succeeded, but many were executed, either 'for returning from transportation', or for the crimes into which they again relapsed. What could be done with such an army of tens of thousands of men and women, whose 'hands were against every man, and every man's hands against them?' The moral efforts of the Reformation Societies were as futile, to the use of the language of Defoe, 'as preaching the Gospel to a Kettle-Drum'. The punitive exertions of the same Society added no shame to the shameless, fining and exposure no remorse, and whipping no amendment. The Gallows at Tyburn, certainly rid the world of those who were actually suspended there; but it had lost its terrors for the masses who crowded the long line of march from Newgate, and swelled the procession of sympathising admirers of the condemned. As a specific deterrent against crime, it was an utter failure; – in an age when every serious offence was punishable with death. The multitude of criminals at large who attended these *levées*, to see their friends and companions 'turned off', looked upon the gallows as their own final destination, and determined that 'their lives, if short, should be merry'.

Mr *John Applebee*, the proprietor of *The Original Journal*, carried on the general business of a printer in Water Lane, Whitefriars. He might also with propriety be designated the official printer of Newgate, and from his office were issued the printed Papers of the Ordinary, – as to the conduct of the condemned felons under his spiritual care, – and their confessions, if any. The last dying speeches of criminals were known to be correct, if Mr Applebee's name was printed on the papers; and, in any extraordinary case, with the consent of the condemned, the narrative of his life was taken from his own lips, or any paper he had written was given to Mr Applebee, and embodied in a pamphlet, often printed before, but published immediately after, the execution. For these purposes, Mr Applebee, or any one authorised to represent him, had access to the prisoners in Newgate, during all the six years that Daniel Defoe was connected with the management of *The Original Journal*.

A short experience would suffice to convince our author that the largest proportion of these papers and books circulated among the criminal population, and were read with great avidity. An examination of the lowest class of thieves' literature of the time printed in other offices, shows that successful highwaymen and burglars were exalted into heroes, whose great deeds were more held up as examples for imitation, than as warnings to be avoided; and even those who had expiated their crimes upon the scaffold were objects of highest admiration when they 'died game'. If any such became penitents, they were execrated as sneaks and cowards. No point of morality was ever touched upon in these stories, any more than in the lewd literature provided for the same readers in the lives of Mother Needham, Sally Salisbury, Mother Wisebourne, Elizabeth Mann, commonly called the Royal Sovereign, or Mary Parramore. Subsequent productions by Defoe, to be noticed in their place, show that, as connected with *Applebee's Journal*, he availed himself of the official privilege of visiting these abandoned and apparently lost criminals; and that he studied how, if possible, they might be benefited. True, they appeared inaccessible to the direct teachings of religion, and the precepts of pure morality; but facts proved that histories of the lives of criminals like themselves could engage their attention; and, without further possible degradation, might not the offences related, be shown to bring misery to the offender? Some moral reflections could be carefully interspersed in the narrative, and the whole story lead its readers, imperceptibly perhaps, to the conclusion, that virtue alone secures happiness; and that, while life remains, it is never too late to mend.

Besides, multitudes of these hopeless wretches were constantly being expatriated, as the only condition upon which they were permitted to live. They had before them a voyage of some months, during which. they were kept, for safety, under the strictest seclusion and discipline. Might not a ray of hope find its way into their darkened minds, during this tedious journey, if – allured by a glaring titlepage, – they could be induced to read of men and women who had been quite as bad as themselves, yet had in the new world – whither they were going, – begun to lead honest lives, had ultimately obtained freedom, and even riches, and some degree of higher pleasures never enjoyed before? Any convict, thus reconciled to banishment, and prevented from returning to England, would be one human life saved from the inevitable penalty of human justice; and, continued longer within reach of that Higher Mercy that extends to the 'uttermost'. These were the circumstances, and such, doubtless, among the motives, that induced Defoe to write books, never intended for the drawing-room tables of the nineteenth century; but admirably suited to improve the condition of the poor outcasts, with whom he had been so remarkably brought into contact. (vol. i, pp. 338–44.)

(e) On the *Journal of the Plague Year:*

Our author knew by experience the importance of bringing forward some person who was trustworthy, a substantial man, of good moral and religious character, and allowing him to relate, the occurrences in which he had taken part, and the things he had seen with his own eyes. Hence the fiction of the worthy Saddler, who says he 'lived without Aldgate about mid-way between Aldgate Church and Whitechapel-Bars, on the left Hand, or North side of the Street'. It is now impossible clearly to distinguish what is authentic from that supplied by the imagination of our Author; but if we could separate what is only personal to the narrator, his establishment and family, – from all that relates to the developement and progress of the disease; I believe we should find that the latter is much more an authentic history than has been credited.

Without a knowledge of the book itself, it would be difficult to understand, that a subject, so uninviting as the Plague, could have been treated in a manner interesting to all readers. But we turn over the titlepage, and without even the formality of any Introduction or Preface, we meet with a man who tells us what he knows. Occasionally he wanders in his story, and sometimes mentions very trivial things, but they only prevent monotony, and every little incident helps to increase the conviction that the whole is a reality. In his *Journal of the Plague Year*, Defoe has carried his peculiar art of circumstantial fidelity to the greatest perfection; and it is no wonder that so grave a work should have deceived the celebrated Dr Mead, the head of his profession, and at that time directed by the Government to report on the precautionary means for *preventing the Plague*. The plain matter-of-fact stile of our author in this Journal, – the artful manner in which he has throughout concealed all art under a truthful simplicity, – his well-timed lectures upon the uncertainty of life, and the tone of sincere, but not obtrusive piety, that pervades the narrative, eminently fitted it to be a seasonable and useful book when it first appeared. It cannot now be read without the deepest interest; and it will continue to be read as long as the memory of the Great Plague shall stand on the records of history. (vol. i, pp. 359–60.)

(f) On *Roxana:*

There are many incidents in the story, very distasteful to a pure and virtuous mind, and the book is even less presentable, according to our modern views of delicacy, than either of its predecessors; yet no reader can possibly mistake the lessons designed to be taught, namely, that prosperous wickedness has a worm at the root, that turns all its fruits to rottenness; and that sin ensures its own effectual punishment. In addition to this general conclusion, every separate sinful action is made the subject of reprehension; there are frequent flashes of conscience which make Roxana tremble, and pause in her guilty courses; and the moral and religious reflections that run through the work, could not fail to benefit readers who having fallen themselves, were incapable of being injured by the relation of Roxana's crimes. This, it should always be remembered, was the class for whom Defoe wrote the book. He was the last man to add fuel to a flame he was endeavouring to extinguish. With him the prosperity of the wicked always comes to an end, even in this life. He did not tell the story for the sake of amusement; but that he might infuse with it moral instruction and good principles, as an essential part of the narrative. The characters and manners are those of the time, – his portraits are natural, – and I cannot but hope that many poor degraded women would be brought, by the perusal, to think seriously; and through repentance, seek to lead new and better lives. (vol. i, p. 374.)

(g) On *A Narrative of all the Robberies . . . of Jack Sheppard:*

I cannot quit the above pamphlet, without a few remarks on the natural and simple manner in which the whole story is related. There is such an air of candour and truthfulness, pervading all the details of the most minute circumstances, as only Defoe could impart to any narrative, whether real or imaginary. This is especially the case in the description of the last Escape from Newgate; in relating which, his mind seems to linger with a feeling of gratitude towards the Iron Bar 'of about two feet and a half in length, and an inch square', which did him so good service; and he pronounces it 'a most notable Implement'. The relation of this part is told with the same spirit as the ingenious and successful contrivances of Crusoe; and the attention of the reader is so concentrated, as to lose sight of the Criminal, and to think only of the Man, struggling for liberty and life. Throughout the story there is perceptible, continuous alternations of mind, between expressions of sincere penitence dictated by conscience; and the irrepressible vanity of his exploits, which was a predominant feature of his character. (vol. i, p. 388.)

(h) On *A New Voyage Round the World:*

The great object of Defoe seems to have been, to avoid the dry details of most of the accounts then existing, by marking out a new course; and thus, combining amusement, with an accurate geographical account of the Pacific Ocean, and part of the Continent of South America. These important ends he has admirably accomplished. When ready to depart from Manilla the idea occurred, to the commander of the expedition, of steering away North, and endeavouring to find a north-eastern passage to England. He debates the matter with himself, in a most able manner; considering the various directions in which the attempt might be made, and *naively* says, – as if foreseeing and ridiculing future expeditions to the polar regions, – 'It is true that these Northern Discoveries might be inimitably fine, and most glorious Things to the British Nation'. Common sense prevails, and he sails southward, and turns eastward, through then almost unknown islands of the Pacific Ocean, to South America. All this part of the work is filled with the character and productions of the places at which the ship touched, and the habits and appearance of the people; and is made intensely interesting by the charming manner in which the scenes are related. The most original and finest part of the book however, is the latter half, containing, first his own excursion, with a Spanish Gentleman and attendants, from Baldivia in Chili through the defiles of the Andes; and, the subsequent journey of a detachment of fifty sailors, overland, from the same point, across Chili and Patagonia; the ships meanwhile sailing from Baldivia round Cape Horn, and meeting the enterprising Travellers at the mouth of the River Camarones, on the Atlantic Coast. Through all this, the genius of the writer lavishes his inexhaustible power of word-painting; equal, in the exercise of his art, – whether it be an individual portrait; – the picture of a domestic interior, with all its Chilian surroundings; – the patient winding, through dark ravines, and up fearful ascents, of men, and mules, and baggage; – the lurid midnight light of volcanoes, in the midst of lofty mountains, and deep vallies; – or, the illimitable outspread space, to the east, of desert and lake, seen, far as the eye can stretch, – from the summit, whence flow the great Rivers of the Continent. All this is enlivened with variety of incident, and with entertaining dialogue, that completes the charm of the journey. (vol. i, pp. 395–6.)

(i) On *Conjugal Lewdness:*

There has probably been no practical improvement whatever, as to the ill circumstances too frequently leading to, or arising out of, the Marriage Union, since the days of Defoe; yet, what is called modern refinement, and delicacy of expression, makes it difficult for his biographer to do justice to a treatise on the subject by him, inculcating the highest morality, and written with great seriousness and force of argument. Not a word in his book is intended to pander to impurity; but on the contrary, his standard of matrimonial delicacy of conduct is placed so high, as to be rather aimed at, than attained. Defoe was a sincere advocate for the state of matrimony; and considered that when rightly entered into, it was the highest condition of human felicity. To reason against the institution from the numerous unhappy matches, he says, 'is only arguing the Ignorance and Corruption of Mankind; which, as they are the Cause, so they are discovered in the unhappy Consequences. Did men expect Happiness in a married Condition, they would begin it and end it after another manner, and take greater thought before they engaged in it.' The matter of the work is excellent; the illustrative stories and dialogues, entertaining and instructive – the satire is free from any admixture of levity, – and the moral so pure and convincing, that the reader is constrained to do justice to the piety and benevolence of the author. But the difficulty of the biographer is not removed by these admirable qualities; – the diction is that of more than a century ago, and many words were then commonly used that are now rarely heard among those who call themselves polite; nor was it possible, exercising all the caution and delicacy of which he was capable, that the author could do justice to his subject, without relating circumstances, from which the viciously disposed might stir up the impurities already existing in their own minds. I am of opinion that while virtuous and pious readers, of both sexes, who have attained mature years, may read this book with great profit; yet the advantage of its *general* circulation among adults is questionable; and it is, I think, by no means a book to be placed in the hands of young unmarried persons of the present age. (vol. i, pp. 423–4.)

(j) Concluding summary:

Thus have I completed my task of re-writing the Life of one who combines in himself the remarkable qualities of being the most voluminous and versatile of English authors, – Daniel Defoe. A man whose large intellect gave to the world a library of his own writings: – consisting of poetry, satire, irony, humour, and pathos; of treatises and pamphlets on peace and war, party conflicts in Church and State, and on civil and religious liberty; of trade and commerce, at home and abroad, its freedom and extension; of morals and instruction, as applicable to children, to the relations of the sexes, in courtship, and in marriage; to the duties and obligations of servants and masters, trades-men, merchants, and gentlemen; of works on municipal and social institutions, including hospitals, colleges, asylums, and police; of romances, more intensely real and natural than those of any other author, of history, and of real and imaginary voyages and travels, including the geography, and the natural and artificial productions of every part of the globe; of books on the marvellous and supernatural, comprising, dæmons, apparitions, dreams, and magic. In every department of this vast range of literary labour, he was an able writer, – in many he excelled all who had preceded him, – and in some, is still, – and will probably ever remain, – unequalled. Throughout these ubiquitous manifestations of his genius, we have found in him, inflexibility of purpose, indomitable courage, and unwearied perseverance, combined with devoted loyalty to the constitutional government of his country, and an earnest faith in the revelation of God. From infancy he had known the Bible; and to the end of life it continued to be with him the supreme test of all human action. His conviction of a constantly watchful and overruling Providence was so strong as to verge on superstition. In an age of political and religious strife he took a prominent part; but he lived and died a true Protestant and a Catholic Christian. (vol. i, p. 473.)

30. The legacy of Defoe

1869

From an article, 'The Later Life of De Foe', in the *British Quarterly Review*, l (October 1869), 483–519. This was a review of Lee's biography, critical in some respects of his findings, but moving on to wider issues also – as in the passages quoted.

(a) Defoe's place in literary history:

When the burden of public controversy was removed, a great weight seems to have dropped from him. His mind had, as it were, been harnessed to the service of the State; his imagination had been held in captivity to his work. Released from this thraldom, it sprang forward with all the lightness of youth and all the energy of manhood. With ordinary men, the imagination is most active in early life, and often exhausts itself before the powers of the mind are matured. While De Foe cannot be placed in the same rank with Shakespeare or Milton, he had this in common with them, that he wrote only after having had a large experience of mankind. Hence the fulness and the variety of all his works of imagination, and the astonishing amount of accurate information which they display. He had the accumulated resources of a whole lifetime upon which to draw. If his works are read carefully, and from the point of view of his own age, the objections to the subjects which he occasionally chose will utterly disappear. None of them are coarse, although they deal with coarse persons. There is not in the whole number any indication of grossness of mind in the author, such as we find in Swift's *Tale of a Tub*, or the *Letters to Stella*. They are written with a consistent unity of purpose, and a high moral intention. While the adventures of the heroes and heroines are sufficiently novel and exciting, vice is never made to be other than detestable, or the end of a vicious life other than bad. This is the case, not merely with *Colonel Jack* and *Captain Singleton*, but with *Roxana* and *Moll Flanders*. What the author says in the preface to the first of these works, holds good of all, and it shows with what practical purpose he invariably wrote. 'Here', he remarks, 'is room for just and copious observations on the blessings and advantages of a sober and well-governed education, and the ruin of so many thousands of all ranks for the want of it; here, also, we may see how much public schools and charities might be improved, to prevent the destruction of so many unhappy children, as in this town are every year bred up for the executioner. Every vicious reader will here be encouraged to change, and it will appear that the best and only good end of an impious, mis-spent life, is repentance.' These works were written within four years, between 1719 and 1722. The world gave its verdict as to their merits, long before the critics spoke. Far greater works have since been written, but none of the same character. In that minute detail of narrative which cheats the dullest imagination, De Foe had only one predecessor. This was Chaucer. There, however, the resemblance stops, for De Foe, although he wrote much verse, was no poet. But, as Chaucer was the father of English poetry, so De Foe was the father of English novel-writing. With what surprise and avidity his works of fiction were received may be judged from the fact, that *Robinson Crusoe* went through four editions in as many months, *Moll Flanders* was printed three times within a year, and *Colonel Jack* twice within four weeks. How the rich vein which the author of these works opened was soon afterwards worked by Richardson, Fielding, and Smollett, need not be told. (pp. 505–6.)

(b) On Defoe's domestic manuals:

Scarcely less popular than these were the various works of political and social economy produced at the same period of life. Upon such subjects, De Foe brought to bear that singular penetrative sagacity of intellect which distinguished him, as a writer, from all his contemporaries. The most useful and most widely circulated of these works is the *Family Instructor*, which is still being reprinted and may be met with in many families, but more often in the United States than in England. As a popular exposition and enforcement of religious duty, it is of high practical value; as regards De Foe himself, it is pleasant to know that it was one of the first which he published after the cessation of his more public political life. Hard, constant, and bitter as that life had been, it had neither crushed nor weakened his religious sensibilities. The influence of his early education, the memory of his pious home, the force of religious conviction, all were as fresh as ever. Added to these were now the experience and judgment of manhood, and the literary art which enabled him to put truth and duty in attractive form. Of the same class is *Religious Courtship*, where the obligations of religious marriages are enforced with grave and serious earnestness. Having said what he had to say for childhood and youth, De Foe next addressed himself to the heads of families in respect to the employment and government of servants, where, in addition to amusing anecdote, there is, as there is in all De Foe's works, a fund of practical suggestion. This subject was pursued in *Everybody's Business is Nobody's Business*, into which *Punch*, when his humour refuses to flow with its old and ordinary ease, might dip for many an instance of Jeames's aristocratic pride and Sarah's 'servantgalism'. For practical wisdom, however, no work of this class equals the *Compleat English Tradesman*. There is scarcely a page of this work which may not now be read with as much advantage by all persons connected with business as when it was first written. De Foe had been a tradesman himself, and could look back, in most respects, upon an unfortunate experience. Sound common sense and shrewd observation, dressed in a lively and fascinating style, are the characteristics of this work. Human nature always repeats itself, but seldom with more exactness than in the experiences of trade. (p. 508.)

(c) Defoe's achievement:

The service rendered by De Foe to his generation can never be correctly estimated. We should require to live in his own time to know the extent of his influence. As we judge him, with all his life before us, he seems to us to have been, next to Milton, the first Englishman who had an adequate sense of the power of PUBLIC OPINION, and of the use to which that opinion might be put. Milton saw the necessity of making as well as of guiding it, and of fortifying the strength of even Cromwell's Government, by a *Defence of the People of England*, before the opinion of civilized Europe. De Foe arose at a different crisis of the nation's history, when all was confusion and turmoil, but when, as he saw, the safety of the State rested as much upon the power of the pen as upon the power of the sword. The weapon that he could use, with more permanent effect than kings and parliaments could bring to bear, he used with unequalled persistency and success. It was in 1687, when the liberties of England hung by little more than a spider's thread, that he first took up his pen to protest against the acceptance of James II's 'Declaration of Liberty of Conscience'. He was one of the most prominent defenders of William's policy of a standing army. By his *True Born Englishman* he effectually turned the tide of public opinion against the Tories and Jacobites. When boroughs were bought and sold in a manner that might bring a blush of shame even into a Bridgewater elector's cheek, he exposed the iniquity of elections, and advocated an uninfluenced expression of the people's convictions. In his *Shortest Way with the Dissenters*, he made ecclesiastical tyranny appear as ridiculous as it was odious, and made even the High Church party of Queen Anne's time, with its Souths and Sacheverells, abjure their principles and recall their purposes. His *Hymn to the Pillory* stopped for ever the most disgraceful mode of punishing the exercise of liberty of thought that was known to his generation. If his exhortations to Dissenters, to be more consistent and courageous, even, as he suggested, to the forming of a Liberation League in defence of their liberties, and for the achievement of all their rights fell, or appear to have fallen, to the ground, they took seed, and in their proper time brought forth fruit, as all true work will do. What he did when the House of Hanover was in its greatest jeopardy, we have already seen: he took effectual measures to prevent any danger arising from the excitement of public opinion. The Constitution being secured, he next addressed himself to the education of the people in affairs of commercial interest, social morality, and domestic piety. He was the first to discover the necessity of a system of national instruction; the first to advocate the superior education of women; the first to see the advantages of the systematic teaching of the arts and sciences; the first to advocate an open university, and the first to proclaim and defend the principles of free trade. He was the first who thought of commenting upon current news in the manner of a 'leading article', and the first English writer of prose fiction. We might almost add, that he was the first 'Political Dissenter'; but the shades of Hooper, Latimer, Robinson, Roger Williams, Bunyan, and Milton, rise before us, and we can only say that, in this respect, he ranks with his predecessors. He was the most conspicuous political Dissenter of his time.

Such a man as De Foe was, must necessarily have led the solitary inner life that we know he lived. His deepest thoughts were not of his own age. He threw himself into the arena of contemporary politics, because he saw the necessity of informing an ignorant and guiding a purposeless people, as well as of removing prejudices and cooling passions. But the principles that laid beneath his opinions were shared in by very few, certainly not by the statesmen with whom he was brought into most intimate contact, excepting, perhaps, such statesmen as William III and Somers. They lived for their day, as such men do, and have earned, in consequence, the comparative indifference of posterity. De Foe must have known that his various suggestions would never be adopted by the people or the Parliament that was contemporary with himself, and that they would turn, as they did turn, a deaf ear to his lofty appeals to their patriotic feeling. What he had to say, however, he said, and left the result. It is the doom of nearly all such men to live within themselves. Nor often is it that such a doom is an unhappy one. Allied to it there is, nearly always, a strong and sure confidence in the future, and always the rest that comes, some time or other, to the man who knows his own integrity, and knows that he has found the truth. Yet, even De Foe, sagacious, far-sighted, and imaginative as he was, could not have dreamed of the extent of his future influence and fame. Better, perhaps, that he did not dream of it; for nothing, we may be sure, would so soon demoralise a man – acting as palsy upon his mind – as the certainty that what he had already done would give him at least an earthly immortality.

When De Foe's writings were first collected, their variety and versatility, the moral courage and personal sufferings of their author, attracted the deepest attention. Sir Walter Scott was the first critic who attempted an analysis of his style; paying to it that generous tribute which one man of genius and simplicity of mind will always be glad to pay to another, in whom he recognises the qualities which he most admires. Sir Walter enlarged upon its inimitable naturalness. This is its principal characteristic. De Foe was destitute of the art of polish; and, indeed, he often wrote – as a man who wrote so much must do – with at least occasional looseness and slovenliness. But he was a master of words; and when he was moved by deep feeling, as at the time that he wrote the *Appeal*, he wrote with great emphasis and conciseness, with not a word too much or too little. The most conspicuous characteristic of his intellect was inventiveness; but he had allied to it two other qualities which are seldom found in its connection, namely, breadth and persistency of purpose. Satire and pathos are often found combined, as in Hood and Thackeray; but in De Foe they were combined in very unequal proportions, the power of satire considerably predominating over the softer quality. He often moves to smiles, but seldom or never to tears. He thought more than he felt, and imagined more than he had experienced, although his experience had been bitter and sharp, beyond that of any of his contemporaries. It may be supposed that the people of his own time, seeing how generally unpopular he was, and how frequently punishment visited him, had a sort of contempt for him; and this is his own testimony. But the contempt was not as for a small man, for it was always mixed with hatred and malice. His enemies knew his power, and feared it. (pp. 517–19.)

31. Victorian orthodoxy: style and narrative method

1869

From an article, 'A Great Whig Journalist', in *Blackwood's Edinburgh Magazine*, cvi (October 1869), 457–87. The quotation is from 458–9. Although rather a biographic excursion than a review, the piece derives largely from Lee's account. In the Wellesley index it is attributed to Charles Mackay (1814–89), a writer principally on American affairs.

It has been the custom, mainly influenced by the minute, painstaking, lifelike descriptions in *Robinson Crusoe* and the *Journal of the Plague Year*, to represent Defoe as a consummate master of the English language. Yet he scarcely deserves such high praise. With all his merits as a writer of simple colloquial English – as plain, easy, and unadorned as the speeches of Mr Cobden or Mr Bright,[1] and quite as telling and effective – Defoe's style was somewhat of the driest. He lacked the poetic touch, and neither in his prose nor in his verse had any of the divine afflatus which warms the blood of the reader. His verses are as poor as common-sense and a stiff manner can make them; and his prose is uniformly as plain and logical, though not so wordy, as a lawyer's brief. He had the merits of precision and concision, and scarcely ever used a word that would not have been plain to the least educated; but he was utterly deficient in enthusiasm, and had none of the fine frenzy which in some writers stirs the heart 'as with the sound of a trumpet'. His great characteristic was the singular power which he possessed of putting himself so thoroughly in the place of the fictitious personages whom he invented, as to make fiction look more like truth than the barest and most positive truth itself when narrated by an inferior pen. His *Robinson Crusoe* and his *Journal of the Plague of London* are in this respect unrivalled. Upon these two books his fame will

---

[1] John Bright (1811–89), radical orator and politician. For Cobden see p. 121 above.

always rest; so lifelike, so minute in the smallest details, so full of inventions that no other writer would have thought of inventing, so microscopic in the little side touches and side lights, that the reader is so continually impressed with the simple naturalness of all he is told that he completely loses sight of the consummate art which has produced the result, and accepts the fiction as authentic history. It was this peculiar talent applied to political disquisition that more than anything else brought Defoe into the troubles that embittered his life. He put himself so completely into the place of others, and exercised such fine banter, and such delicate, all but imperceptible, irony, that he deceived both friend and foe – very often to his own great tribulation when his foes discovered the hoax. He cut blocks with a razor, and the razor, as was natural, got the worst of the encounter, as will be seen from the story of his life and career.

32. The *Edinburgh Review* on Defoe

1870

Extracts from a review of Lord Stanhope's *History of England 1701–1713* in the *Edinburgh Review*, cxxxv (October 1870), 548–50. The Wellesley index attributes this to Herman Merivale (1806–74), writer on political economy.

There was, however, one eminent writer of the period who might serve as the prototype of the prolific, versatile, indefatigable class of slaves to the press whom modern facilities of production have created. This was De Foe, whose extraordinary fertility of composition and powers of labour, combined with a genius so exceptional and solitary as his, render his life a riddle in his literary, as it assuredly is in his political character. Lord Stanhope does him scant justice when he rates him 'far indeed above' such writers as 'Oldmixon, full of party zeal, but little distinguished by ability, and not at all by truth;' but below, if we understand him rightly, the rank of Steele and Prior. In mere effectiveness, and the art of telling home-truths, or what were wished to pass as such, we should place him very far above either of those showy gladiators. But his careless, desultory, as well as inaccurate style, the result of constant writing against time and for daily bread, no doubt placed him at a great disadvantage in the eyes of the polished world, and permitted Swift – the only contemporary whose original genius equalled or surpassed his own – to call him a 'stupid illiterate scribbler,' 'the fellow that was pilloried, I have forgotten his name,' without animadversion from his readers. 'About this time,' says Sir Walter Scott – namely, in 1710 – he, 'De Foe, had written down his own reputation'. . . . Such was the birth of the most thoroughly English work of genius, perhaps, which the English language has engendered; the fruit of occasional and doubtless much-enjoyed intervals, snatched from the daily demand of the printer's devil for newspaper copy. And *Robinson Crusoe* was followed in rapid succession by those other well-known works of fiction which, even by themselves, would have secured for the old and used-up scribbler, as his enemies termed him, a very high place in the library of English romance. Rétif de la Bretonne,[1] a man of very inferior powers to De Foe, but with something of his faculty of evoking homely interest by lifelike incident, was called the 'Rousseau of the gutter', 'le Rousseau du ruisseau'; and some at least of De Foe's productions of this period – not the least popular – might entitle him to the distinction of a similar title. But *Robinson Crusoe* stands alone.

[1] French novelist (1734–1806), author of numerous books including *Monsieur Nicolas* (1794–97).

33. The supremacy of *Crusoe*

1871

From a review article, based on Lee's biography, in the *Cornhill Magazine*, xxiii (March 1871), 310–20. It is unsigned, but subsequently found its way into *Studies in English Literature* (1876), by the man of letters John Dennis, author of *The Age of Pope* (1894).

Daniel Defoe, one of the most popular of English authors, and probably the most voluminous writer in the language, is to many readers little better than a name. They are familiar with *Robinson Crusoe*, with the *History of the Plague*, and with *Mrs Veal's Apparition*; they know, because Pope has told them, that Defoe stood in the pillory; and they know also, because Hume has told them, that he was a party-writer; doubtless they know, too, that he was a Dissenter, in an age when Dissent was unpopular; and that, after a laborious and troubled life, he was buried in the famous burial-ground consecrated to dissenting dust in Bunhill Fields. These facts, with, perhaps, half-a-dozen more, comprise, we venture to say, the popular knowledge of Defoe. Compared with Robinson Crusoe and his man Friday, he is but the shadow of a shade. The author's immortal tale, translated into all languages that can boast a literature, is a household book throughout the world: but the author himself is for the most part neglected and unknown. The more we consider this anomaly the stranger does it appear. . . .

It was an old man – for a man so buffeted with the storms of fortune may be reckoned old at fifty-nine – and it was, as we have said, after a fit of apoplexy, that Defoe produced his unrivalled story. Like Richardson, he won his fame at a period when, in most men, the imaginative faculty becomes dormant. Defoe was in his staid Dutch fashion a consummate literary artist. There have been greater novelists, but not one, we think, who has shown more skill in the management of his materials, or produced so fine an effect from the accumulation of prosaic details. *Robinson Crusoe* became famous immediately, has been famous ever since, and is likely to continue popular so long as literature endures. In this tale Defoe exhibits an intense imagination which at times leads him to the verge of poetry. All his fictions display an infinite amount of invention, and of practical experience; but the first and best of them is perhaps the only one in which the supreme faculty comes into play, the only one that awakens strong emotion in the reader and carries him, despite the homely, colloquial style of narrative, into a region of high romance. 'Crusoe's lonely isle' has a more familiar hold upon our boys than any historic site with which they are acquainted. Few spots distinguished in geography have a greater interest than this. It is something to discover an island, but it is better to create one, and Defoe's freehold is more precious, and bids fair to be more permanent than any possessed by duke or marquis. 'This man could have founded a colony as well as governed it', said a statesman after reading Defoe's great novel. . . .

One more remark suggested by *Robinson Crusoe* will not be inappropriate. When a man produces an incomparable work, we are content to solve all difficulties regarding it, by saying that it is a work of genius. That Defoe's novel merits this distinction none will question, although it may not rank with the noblest creations of literature; for the story is not, like Shakespeare's *Tempest*, a splendid effort of the imagination, but is rather the fruit of a life's experience, and of accumulated stores of knowledge. We cannot accept Mr Henry Kingsley's theory, that 'this wondrous romance of *Robinson Crusoe* is no romance at all, but a merely allegorical account of Defoe's own life for twenty-eight years';[1] and when he says there is no doubt at all that by the cannibal Caribbees, Defoe meant the Tories, and that the name of the first savage he killed with his gun was called Sacheverell, we can but smile at the ingenious discovery. It is evident, no doubt, that in this his wisest and most beautiful work, the author records much that he himself had learnt and suffered during a troubled life. In all his fictions, indeed, he identifies himself with his characters; and even his villains – women as well as men – bear a family likeness to their literary father. It seems hard to say this of such characters as Moll Flanders, Roxana, and Colonel Jack; but while committing hateful sins and crimes, and relating what they have done, they moralize upon their evil deeds with the seriousness and sobriety of a sedate old gentleman whose one object in life is the benefit of his fellow-creatures. Yet the descent from the light and purity of the great romance to the oppressive and noxious atmosphere of the minor

[1] Henry Kingsley (1830–76), novelist and brother of the better-known Charles, had written an introduction to the Globe edition of *Robinson Crusoe* (1868).

novels is great indeed. *Robinson Crusoe* stands out from its companions like a noble mountain amidst a range of stunted hillocks; it is a book so manly in tone, so feminine in sweetness, so Christian in feeling, that it deserves a place on the same shelf with the *Faery Queene* and the *Pilgrim's Progress*. But on what shelf, and with what companions, shall we place *Roxana* and *Moll Flanders*, *Colonel Jack*, and *Captain Singleton*? Not certainly with books in which splendid powers are perverted to evil, and vice is tricked out to wear the semblance of virtue; but among books that display, with the fidelity of a photograph, human nature at its worst, vice in all its grossness, and the low aims of low people in all their vulgarity. Love, in the highest meaning of the word, was unknown to Defoe, and is not, therefore, portrayed in his novels. He wrote only of what he knew, and of this he knew nothing. His women are without grace, without purity, without dignity, they are even without passion; and when led astray, are not influenced by their affections, but by a love of greed. Their aims are mercenary, their manners loose, their language commonplace; they are wholly destitute of sentiment and of the charm of poetry. But they act and speak like living beings, instead of moving like puppets. The truth of the likenesses reconciles us to their coarseness. They interest us, because of the one touch of nature, and as specimens of our common humanity.

Defoe professes to write always with a moral, and even with a religious purpose. He was an honest and severe Presbyterian, who regarded actors as the 'sons of hell', and was so thorough a Sabbatarian that he considered the licensing of a certain number of hackney-coaches to ply on Sundays as the worst blemish of King William's reign, and we suppose, therefore, a greater slur upon his memory than the massacre of Glencoe. He had from his youth belonged to a strait sect, and had shown himself willing to suffer persecution for his creed. When his minor fictions were published Defoe was more than sixty years of age, and had just produced one of the wholesomest and most beautiful tales we possess in the language. Is it possible that these far inferior books were written years before, when he was immured in Newgate, and when, doubtless, he acquired much of the special knowledge they exhibit, and that the extraordinary popularity of *Robinson Crusoe*, which gained its high position at a bound, induced him to give them also to the world? It would be a satisfaction to think that such novels as *Moll Flanders* and *Roxana* were not among the last works of an old man. His aim, it may be admitted, was to portray the ugliness of vice and the divine beauty of virtue, and certainly he displays vice after a very undraped fashion. If people don't dislike it, he says it is their own fault; and their fault, too, if they do not gain instruction from the inevitable moral which follows the representation. But the first object of fiction is amusement; and this, in the novels we are speaking of, can only be gathered from the vicious or criminal adventures of the characters described. Books such as these are not taken up for the sake of instruction. It is impossible, therefore, to accept Defoe's asseverations that his sole object in writing his fictions was didactic, and we agree with Mr Wilson and Mr Lee, that they cannot be recommended for indiscriminate perusal. . . .

How clear-sighted this man was, what abundant energy he possessed, how willingly he sacrificed private emolument for the public good, with what cheerfulness he turned the most adverse circumstances to practical account, how strong he was in the invincible ardour of an heroic soul – all this is duly set forth in Mr Lee's biography. Forget the six fatal letters,[1] and you will acknowledge that a braver and nobler specimen of English manhood never walked this island; remembering them sorrowfully, as you needs must, and while perplexed at the unrighteous conduct of a righteous man, you are content to confess you do not understand the inconsistency, and to accept, as compensation, the virtues of a life.

[1] i.e. the six letters to Charles Delafaye, first printed by Lee, establishing Defoe's connection with Mist's *Weekly Journal*.

34. William Minto on Defoe

1879

Extracts from chapter IX, 'The Place of Defoe's Fictions in his Life', in William Minto's *Daniel Defoe*, a volume in the important English Men of Letters series, edited by John Morley. The book first appeared in 1879: the text is that of the uniform edition (1895), pp. 140–57 (with omissions). Minto (1845–93), Scottish critic and journalist, was Professor of Logic and Literature at Aberdeen University from 1880.

In writing for the entertainment of his own time, Defoe took the surest way of writing for the entertainment of all time. Yet if he had never chanced to write *Robinson Crusoe*, he would now have a very obscure place in English literature. His 'natural infirmity of homely plain writing', as he humorously described it, might have drawn students to his works, but they ran considerable risk of lying in utter oblivion. He was at war with the whole guild of respectable writers who have become classics; they despised him as an illiterate fellow, a vulgar huckster, and never alluded to him except in terms of contempt. He was not slow to retort their civilities; but the retorts might very easily have sunk beneath the waters, while the assaults were preserved by their mutual support. The vast mass of Defoe's writings received no kindly aid from distinguished contemporaries to float them down the stream; everything was done that bitter dislike and supercilious indifference could do to submerge them. *Robinson Crusoe* was their sole life buoy.

It would be a mistake to suppose that the vitality of *Robinson Crusoe* is a happy accident, and that others of Defoe's tales have as much claim in point of merit to permanence. *Robinson Crusoe* has lived longest, because it lives most, because it was detached as it were from its own time and organized for separate existence. It is the only one of Defoe's tales that shows what he could do as an artist. We might have seen from the others that he had the genius of a great artist; here we have the possibility realized, the convincing proof of accomplished work. *Moll Flanders* is in some respects superior as a novel. Moll is a much more complicated character than the simple, open minded, manly mariner of York; a strangely mixed compound of craft and impulse, selfishness and generosity – in short, a thoroughly bad woman, made bad by circumstances. In tracing the vigilant resolution with which she plays upon human weakness, the spasms of compunction which shoot across her wily designs, the selfish afterthoughts which paralyse her generous impulses, her fits of dare-devil courage and uncontrollable panic, and the steady current of good-humoured satisfaction with herself which makes her chuckle equally over mishaps and successes, Defoe has gone much more deeply into the springs of action, and sketched a much richer page in the natural history of his species than in *Robinson Crusoe*. True, it is a more repulsive page, but that is not the only reason why it has fallen into comparative oblivion, and exists now only as a parasite upon the more popular work. It is not equally well constructed for the struggle of existence among books. No book can live for ever which is not firmly organized round some central principle of life, and that principle in itself imperishable. It must have a heart and members; the members must be soundly compacted and the heart superior to decay. Compared with *Robinson Crusoe*, *Moll Flanders* is only a string of diverting incidents, the lowest type of book organism, very brilliant while it is fresh and new, but not qualified to survive competitors for the world's interest. There is no unique creative purpose in it to bind the whole together; it might be cut into pieces, each capable of wriggling amusingly by itself. The gradual corruption of the heroine's virtue, which is the encompassing scheme of the tale, is too thin as well as too common an artistic envelope; the incidents burst through it at so many points that it becomes a shapeless mass. But in *Robinson Crusoe* we have real growth from a vigorous germ. The central idea round which the tale is organized, the position of a man cast ashore on a desert island, abandoned to his own resources, suddenly shot beyond help or counsel from his fellow-creatures, is one that must live as long as the uncertainty of human life.

The germ of *Robinson Crusoe*, the actual experience of Alexander Selkirk, went floating about for several years, and more than one artist dallied with it, till it finally settled and took root in the mind of the one man of his generation most capable of giving it a home and working out its artistic possibilities. Defoe was the only man of letters in his time who might have been thrown on a desert island without finding himself at a loss what to do. The art required for developing the position in imagination was not of a complicated kind, and yet it is one of the rarest of gifts. Something more was wanted than simply conceiving what a man in such a situation would probably feel and probably do. Above all, it was necessary that his perplexities should be unexpected, and his expedients for meeting them unexpected; yet both perplexities and expedients so real and life-like that, when we were told them, we should wonder we had not thought of them before. One gift was indispensable for this, however many might be accessory, the genius of circumstantial invention – not a very exalted order of genius, perhaps, but quite as rare as any other intellectual prodigy.* . . .

But whatever it was that made the germ idea of *Robinson Crusoe* take root in Defoe's mind, he worked it out as an artist. Artists of a more emotional type might have drawn much more elaborate and affecting word-pictures of the mariner's feelings in various trying situations, gone much deeper into his changing moods, and shaken our souls with pity and terror over the solitary castaway's alarms and fits of despair. Defoe's aims lay another way. His Crusoe is not a man given to the luxury of grieving. If he had begun to pity himself, he would have been undone. Perhaps Defoe's imaginative force was not of a kind that could have done justice to the agonies of a shipwrecked sentimentalist; he has left no proof that it was; but if he had represented Crusoe bemoaning his misfortunes, brooding over his fears, or sighing with Ossianic sorrow over his lost companions and friends, he would have spoiled the consistency of the character. The lonely man had his moments of panic and his days of dejection, but they did not dwell in his memory. Defoe no doubt followed his own natural bent, but he also showed true art in confining Crusoe's recollections as closely as he does to his efforts to extricate himself from difficulties that would have overwhelmed a man of softer temperament. The subject had fascinated him, and he found enough in it to engross his powers without travelling beyond its limits for diverting episodes, as he does more or less in all the rest of his tales. The diverting episodes in *Robinson Crusoe* all help the verisimilitude of the story.

When, however, the ingenious inventor had completed the story artistically, carried us through all the outcast's anxieties and efforts, and shown him triumphant over all difficulties, prosperous, and again in communication with the outer world, the spirit of the literary trader

* Mr Leslie Stephen seems to me to underrate the rarity of this peculiar gift in his brilliant essay on Defoe's Novels in *Hours in a Library*. [Minto's note.]

would not let the finished work alone. The story, as a work of art, ends
with Crusoe's departure from the island, or at any rate with his return
to England. Its unity is then complete. But Robinson Crusoe at once
became a popular hero, and Defoe was too keen a man of business to
miss the chance of further profit from so lucrative a vein. He did not
mind the sneers of hostile critics. They made merry over the trifling
inconsistencies in the tale. How, for example, they asked, could
Crusoe have stuffed his pockets with biscuits when he had taken off all
his clothes before swimming to the wreck? How could he have been at
such a loss for clothes after those he had put off were washed away by
the rising tide, when he had the ship's stores to choose from? How
could he have seen the goat's eyes in the cave when it was pitch dark?
How could the Spaniards give Friday's father an agreement in writing,
when they had neither paper nor ink? How did Friday come to know
so intimately the habits of bears, the bear not being a denizen of the
West Indian islands? On the ground of these and such-like trifles, one
critic declared that the book seems calculated for the mob, and will
not bear the eye of a rational reader, and that 'all but the very canaille
are satisfied of the worthlessness of the performance'. Defoe, we may
suppose, was not much moved by these strictures, as edition after
edition of the work was demanded. He corrected one or two little
inaccuracies, and at once set about writing a Second Part, and a volume
of *Serious Reflections* which had occurred to Crusoe amidst his adventures. These were purely commercial excrescences upon the original
work. They were popular enough at the time, but those who are
tempted now to accompany Crusoe in his second visit to his island and
his enterprising travels in the East, agree that the Second Part is of
inferior interest to the first, and very few now read the *Serious Reflections*.

Colonel Jack, Moll Flanders, Roxana are not criminals from malice;
they do not commit crimes for the mere pleasure of the fact. They all
believe that but for the force of circumstances they might have been
orderly, contented, virtuous members of society. The Colonel, a
London Arab, a child of the criminal regiment, began to steal before
he knew that it was not the approved way of making a livelihood. Moll
and Roxana were overreached by acts against which they were too
weak to cope. Even after they were tempted into taking the wrong
turning, they did not pursue the downward road without compunction.
Many good people might say of them, 'There, but for the grace of
God, goes myself'. But it was not from the point of view of a Baxter[1]

---

[1] Richard Baxter (1615–91), Puritan writer and preacher.

or a Bunyan that Defoe regarded them, though he credited them with many edifying reflections. He was careful to say that he would never have written the stories of their lives, if he had not thought that they would be useful as awful examples of the effects of bad education and the indulgence of restlessness and vanity; but he enters into their ingenious shifts and successes with a joyous sympathy that would have been impossible if their reckless adventurous living by their wits had not had a strong charm for him. We often find peeping out in Defoe's writings that roguish cynicism which we should expect in a man whose own life was so far from being straightforward. He was too much dependent upon the public acceptance of honest professions to be eager in depreciating the value of the article, but when he found other people protesting disinterested motives, he could not always resist reminding them that they were no more disinterested than the Jack-pudding who avowed that he cured diseases from mere love of his kind. Having yielded to circumstances himself, and finding life enjoyable in dubious paths, he had a certain animosity against those who had maintained their integrity and kept to the highroad, and a corresponding pleasure in showing that the motives of the sinner were not after all so very different from the motives of the saint.

The aims in life of Defoe's thieves and pirates are at bottom very little different from the ambition which he undertakes to direct in the *Complete English Tradesman*, and their maxims of conduct have much in common with this ideal. Self-interest is on the look-out, and Self-reliance at the helm.

A tradesman behind his counter must have no flesh and blood about him, no passions, no resentment; he must never be angry – no, not so much as seem to be so, if a customer tumbles him five hundred pounds worth of goods, and scarce bids money for anything; nay, though they really come to his shop with no intent to buy, as many do, only to see what is to be sold, and though he knows they cannot be better pleased than they are at some other shop where they intend to buy, 'tis all one; the tradesman must take it, he must place it to the account of his calling, that 'tis his business to be ill-used, and resent nothing; and so must answer as obligingly to those who give him an hour or two's trouble, and buy nothing, as he does to those who, in half the time, lay out ten or twenty pounds. The case is plain; and if some do give him trouble, and do not buy, others make amends, and do buy; and as for the trouble, 'tis the business of the shop.

All Defoe's heroes and heroines are animated by this practical spirit, this thoroughgoing subordination of means to ends. When they have an end in view, the plunder of a house, the capture of a ship, the ensnaring of a dupe, they allow neither passion, nor resentment, nor sentiment in any shape or form to stand in their way. Every other consideration is put on one side when the business of the shop has to be attended to. They are all tradesmen who have strayed into unlawful courses. They have nothing about them of the heroism of sin; their crimes are not the result of ungovernable passion, or even of antipathy to conventional restraints; circumstances and not any law-defying bias of disposition have made them criminals. How is it that the novelist contrives to make them so interesting? Is it because we are a nation of shopkeepers, and enjoy following lines of business which are a little out of our ordinary routine? Or is it simply that he makes us enjoy their courage and cleverness without thinking of the purposes with which these qualities are displayed? Defoe takes such delight in tracing their bold expedients, their dexterous intriguing and manoeuvring, that he seldom allows us to think of anything but the success or failure of their enterprises. Our attention is concentrated on the game, and we pay no heed for the moment to the players or the stakes.

Appendix I

This is not an exhaustive bibliography of all comments made on Defoe in his lifetime. Professor W. L. Payne is preparing a full list of items about Defoe. Here I have restricted myself to materials embodying a substantial response to Defoe's work. *Obiter dicta* and casual thrusts at Defoe (which can be found in at least ten of John Oldmixon's books, for instance) are therefore omitted. I have also excluded (1) material published in newspapers and periodicals such as the *Rehearsal*, the *Observator*, Read's *Weekly Journal*, in the original issue or reprinted in volume form; (2) replies to pamphlets once attributed to Defoe, where these are now expunged from the canon, *unless* Defoe is mentioned by name in the text of the reply; (3) dubious items where Defoe may or may not be the object. I have not on principle left out commendatory references, but the overwhelming majority of cases involve deprecatory treatment of Defoe and his work.

The list incorporates: first, a key number to which references in the Introduction are cued; second, the Morgan index number (see Bibliography, section III); third, the author, where known; fourth, short title; fifth, publisher(s); sixth, the principal work(s) by Defoe under scrutiny. Bracketed names in the author column represent the known authors of works published anonymously; a question mark means that the identification is not certain. A dash in the last column means that the publication is a general attack, personal criticism or a reply to unspecified works.

Key no.	Morgan no.	Author	Short title	Publisher	Works by Defoe
			1701		
011	C114	—	Remarks upon the Two Great Questions Consider'd	—	The Two Great Questions Consider'd (Moore, no. 24)[1]
012	D111	—	The Ballad Answered, with the Memorial, alias Legion, Reply'd to Paragraph by Paragraph	Booksellers of London and Westminster (pirate?) Printed by D. Edwards	The Ballad (Moore, no. 36)
012A	E151	—	The Memorial Answered (another version of no. 12)	—	The Ballad
013	D114	—	England's Enemies Expos'd	—	Legion (Moore, no. 35)
014	D124	[W. Pittis]	The True Englishman Answer'd Paragraph by Paragraph	—	The True-Born Englishman (Moore, no. 28)
015	D144	—	The English Gentleman Justified. A Poem	J. Nutt	The True-Born Englishman
016	D212	J. Howe	Some Considerations of a Preface to an Enquiry	T. Parkhurst	An Enquiry into Occasional Conformity (Moore, no. 17)
017	—	—	Englishmen no Bastards	A. Baldwin	The True-Born Englishman
018	—	—	The History of the Kentish Petition, Answer'd Paragraph by Paragraph	—	The History of the Kentish Petition (Moore, no. 37)

[1] For an explanation of Moore numbers, see headnote to Appendix II, on p. 220.

019	—	—	Animadversions upon the Succession to the Crown of England Considered	—	The Succession Considered (Moore, no. 29)
0110	—	—	The Fable of the Cuckoo	—	The True-Born Englishman
0111	—	—	The Female Critick	E. Rumball	The True-Born Englishman
			1702		
021	E166	[J. Drake?]	Some Necessary Considerations relating to all future Elections	—	A New Test of the Church of England's Loyalty (Moore, no. 44)
022	E412	—	Reasons Prov'd to be Unreasonable	—	Reasons against a War with France (Moore, no. 39)
			1703		
031	E157	—	The True-Born Hugonot	—	Shortest Way, etc.
032	F150	—	The Fox with his Fire-brand	—	Shortest Way (Moore, no. 50)
033	F156	—	The Scribler's Doom; or, the Pillory in Fashion	J. Sharp	Shortest Way
034	F328	—	Reflections upon a late Scandalous and Malicious Pamphlet	—	Shortest Way
035	F340	—	The Safest Way with the Dissenters	—	Shortest Way
036	F354	—	The Shortest Way with the Dissenters ... Considered (text of Shortest Way appended in some edns)	—	Shortest Way
037	F398	[Defoe?]	A Dialogue between a Dissenter and the Observator (attributed by Moore, no. 52, to Defoe himself)	—	Shortest Way

Key no.	Morgan no.	Author	Short title	Publisher	Works by Defoe
038	—	Leslie	The New Association. Part II	—	Shortest Way
039	—	—	The Shortest Way with Whores and Rogues	—	Shortest Way
0310	—	—	Remarks on the Author of the Hymn to the Pillory	—	Hymn to the Pillory (Moore, no. 59)
0311	—	—	The Reformer Reformed or the Shortest Way with Daniel de Fooe	[Not seen]	—
0312	—	—	A Hymn to Tyburn	—	Hymn to the Pillory
0313	—	Dibben	Verses on Defoe in the Pillory (see J. R. Moore, Defoe in the Pillory, p. 1)	—	
			1704		
041	G36	Mary Astell	A Fair Way with the Dissenters	R. Wilkin	Shortest Way
042	G145	Defoe	An Elegy on the Author of the True-Born Englishman	—	The True-Born Englishman
043	G405	—	Peace and Union	—	Peace without Union (Moore, no. 66)
044	G491	Ned Ward	The Dissenting Hypocrite	—	Peace without Union
045	—	—	Reflections upon a Passage in a Pamphlet	—	Peace without Union

No.	Code	Author	Title	Publisher	Reference
046	—	—	Legion's Humble Address Answer'd Paragraph by Paragraph	—	Legion
047	—	—	Visits from the Shades	—	[Not seen]

1705

No.	Code	Author	Title	Publisher	Reference
051	H125	—	Daniel the Prophet no Conjuror	—	Review, etc.
052	H135	—	The Republican Bullies	J. Nutt	Review (Moore, no. 522)
053	H201-2	[Lord Haversham]	The Lord Haversham's Speech / The Lord Haversham's Vindication	H. Hills	Review / Review
054	H460	Ned Ward	Hudibras Redivivus	B. Bragg	The True-Born Englishman, etc.
055	—	J. Dunton	Life and Errors	B. Bragge	Various
056	—	—	The Diet of Poland	—	The Dyet of Poland (Moore, no. 100)
057	—	J. Browne	Considered Paragraph by Paragraph / A Vindication of the Specimen for a Translation of Horace	B. Bragge	Review
058	H66	J. Browne	The Mooncalf	[Not seen]	[Not seen]
059	—	J. Browne	The Review Review'd	[Not seen]	[Not seen]

1706

No.	Code	Author	Title	Publisher	Reference
061	I1	P. Abercromby	The Advantages of the Act of Security	—	The Advantages of Scotland (Moore, no. 138)
062	I63	Francis Bugg	A Quaker Catechism	[Not seen]	[Not seen]
063	I118	[John Hamilton, Lord Belhaven?]	The Scots Answer to the British Vision	—	The Vision (Moore, no. 123)

Key no.	Morgan no.	Author	Short title	Publisher	Works by Defoe
063A	—	[John Hamilton, Lord Belhaven?]	A Second Defence of the Scotish Vision	—	The Vision
064	I288	—	The Moderation, Justice and Manners of the Review	B. Brag	Review
065	I341	—	Remarks on the Review, no. 74	—	Review
066	I363	[J. Sharp?]	An Appeal of the Clergy of the Church of England	R. Wilkin	Review
067	—	W. Black	A Letter concerning the Remarks	—	A Fourth Essay (Moore, no. 124)
067A	—	W. Black	The Preface to the Fifth Essay Considered	—	A Fifth Essay (Moore, no. 138)
068	—	—	The Source of our Present Fears	[Not seen]	
069	—	—	Jure Divino toss'd in a Blanket	[Not seen]	
0610	—	—	Observations on the Bankrupts Bill	B. Bragg	Remarks on the Bill (Moore, no. 112)
0611	—	—	An Equivalent for De Foe	—	An Enquiry (Moore, no. 136)
0612	—	J. Browne	The Review and Observator Review'd	J. Nutt	Review
			1707		
071	J258	[Hugh James?]	An Answer to the Experiment	J. Morphew	Experiment (Moore, no. 94)
072	J476	[James Webster]	The Author of the Lawful Prejudices Defended	—	Dissenters in England Vindicated (Moore, no. 140)
073	—	[W. Black]	A Reply to the Author of the Advantages to Scotland . . .	—	The Advantages of Scotland (Moore, nos 134, 138)

APPENDIX I

074	—	—	Answer to a letter concerning Trade	—	A Letter concerning Trade (Moore, no. 135)
075	—	[J. Browne]	'The Country Parson's Advice' in Poems on Affairs of State	—	
076	—	—	The Character of a Turncoat	[Not seen]	
1708					
081	K123	[J. Clark?]	A paper concerning Daniel De Foe	Printed by J. Watson	History of the Union (Moore, no. 161)
082	—	—	A Dialogue between Louis le petit and Harlequin	[Not seen]	
083	—	—	The Welsh Monster	—	Review, Legion, Shortest Way
1709					
091	L77	[J. Clark]	A Just Reprimand to Daniel de Foe	A. Henderson, J. Wardlaw, J. Stewart	Review, etc.
1710					
101	M173	'Q.T.'	An Anagram on Daniel de Foe, author of . . . the Review	[Not seen]	
102	M180	—	An Epigram on Daniel de Foe	[Not seen]	
103	M188	—	A Reproof to Mr. Clark, and a brief Vindication of Mr. De Foe	J. Moncur	(reply to no. 091)

Key no.	Morgan no.	Author	Short title	Publisher	Works by Defoe
104	M551	W. Robertson	*Dissenters Self-Condemn'd*	J. Morphew	Preface to De Laune, *Plea for the Non-Conformists* (Moore, no. 118)
105	M768	—	*Wonder upon Wonders*	[Not seen]	
106	—	—	*An Impartial Survey of Mr. De Foe's Singular Modesty and Veracity*	J. Morphew	*Experiment* (Moore, no. 94)
107	—	—	*A Letter to Mr. Daniel Foe*	—	*Review*, Preface to De Laune
108	—	Ned Ward	*Vulgus Britannicus*	J. Woodward, J. Morphew	
109	—	—	*The Tale of a Cock-Match*	[Not seen]	
			1711		
111	N150	—	*A Hue and Cry after Daniel Foe*	Booksellers of London and Westminster	—
112	N360	[A. Maynwaring]	*A Letter to a High-Churchman*	A. Baldwin	*Reasons why this Nation* (Moore, no. 216)
113	N456	—	*The Observator's Letter to his Counsel*	—	
114	—	'Robin-Hog'	*A Hue and Cry after Daniel de Foe*	—	*Review*, etc.
115	—	—	*The three False Brethren*	[Not seen]	
116	N635	—	*A Caveat to the Treaters*	S. Popping	Various

1713

No.	Cat.	Author	Title	Publisher	Related
131	P181	—	Judas Discover'd	E. Curl?	
132	P502	[J. Oldmixon]	Remarks on a Scandalous Libel	A. Baldwin	A Letter from a Member of the House of Commons (Moore, no. 265) *Mercator*
133	—	[J. Addison]	The Late Tryal and Conviction of Count Tariff	A. Baldwin	—

1714

No.	Cat.	Author	Title	Publisher	Related
141	Q48	[W. Pittis]	The History of the Mitre and the Purse, part i	J. Morphew	—
141A	Q49	[W. Pittis]	Ibid., part ii	J. Morphew	—
142	Q81	[Lord Bolingbroke?]	Considerations upon The Secret History of the White Staff	A. Moore	Secret History of the White Staff (Moore, no. 280) (Reply to no. 141)
143	Q166	[J. Oldmixon]	Considerations on the History of the Mitre and Purse	J. Roberts	
144	Q180	[J. Oldmixon]	The Secret History of the White Staff ...(another version of no. 146 part i)	R. Mathard	Secret History of the White Staff
145	Q185	—	The White Staff's Speech	J. Roberts	Secret History of the White Staff
146	Q190	[J. Oldmixon]	A Detection of the Sophistry and Falsities, parts i-iii	J. Roberts	Secret History of the White Staff
146A, B					
147	Q385	—	A Letter to the People of England	J. Oldisworth	Letter to the Dissenters (Moore, no. 269)

Key no.	Morgan no.	Author	Short title	Publisher	Works by Defoe
148	Q539	[J. Oldmixon]	Remarks on the Letter to the Dissenters	J. Roberts, T. Harrison, A. Dodd, R. Bond	Letter to the Dissenters
149	—	—	A Vindication of the Earl of Nottingham	J. Roberts	—
1410	—	J. Dunton	The Impeachment	—	—
			1715		
151	Q29	[W. Pittis]	Queen Anne Vindicated	J. Baker	Secret History of the White Staff
152	R89	—	Mr. Burnet's Defence	J. Roberts	A Letter to a Merry Young Gentleman (Moore, no. 301)
153	R174	[J. Oldmixon]	Remarks on a Late Libel	J. Roberts	(Attacks Francis Atterbury's Advice to the Freeholders; Defoe assailed in passing)
			1717		
171	—	—	An Answer to the Character and Conduct of R- W-, Esq.	J. Roberts	The Conduct of Robert Walpole (Moore, no. 370)
172	—	—	A Presbyterian Getting on Horse-back	D. Richmond	The Question Fairly Stated (Moore, no. 365)

1719

No.	Title			
191	A Brief Answer to a Brief State of the Question	J. Roberts	—	A Brief State of the Question (Moore, no. 420)
192	A Further Examination of the Weavers Pretences	J. Roberts	—	The Just Complaint (Moore, no. 416)

1720

No.	Title			
201	The Turkey Merchants and their Trade Vindicated	—	'A Merchant'	The Case Fairly Stated (Moore, no. 418)

1725

No.	Title			
251	The Comb-Brush	[Not seen]	—	
252	Every-body's Business is No-body's Business Answered	[Not seen]	—	

1729

No.	Title			
291	Servitude: a Poem	T. Worrall	R. Dodsley	Every-body's Business (Moore, no. 472)

ADDENDUM: 1713

No.	Title			
134	A Letter to a West-Country Clothier	J. Baker	—	Mercator, etc.

Appendix II

Books and pamphlets mentioned in the text are listed by the year, according to the reference number in J. R. Moore, *A Checklist of the Writings of Daniel Defoe* (Bloomington, 1960). Periodicals to which Defoe contributed are listed separately at the end, as in Moore. Defoe's approximate age is given following the year.

Year	Age	Moore no.	Short Title
1692	32	10	*To the Athenian Society*
1697	37	14	*Character of the late Dr. Annesley*
		16	*An Essay upon Projects*
1701	41	28	*The True-Born Englishman*
1702	42	50	*The Shortest Way with the Dissenters*
1703	43	58	*A True Collection of the Writings*
		59	*A Hymn to the Pillory*
1704	44	83	*An Essay on the Late Storm*
		88	*Giving Alms no Charity*
1705	45	107	*A True Relation of the Apparition of one Mrs. Veal*
1706	46	115	*Jure Divino*
		129	*Caledonia*
1709	49	161	*The History of the Union*
1713	53	251	*And What if the Pretender Should Come?*
		265	*A Letter from a Member of the House of Commons*
1714	54	280	*The Secret History of the White Staff*, Part I
1715	55	307	*An Appeal to Honour and Justice*
		309, 403	*The Family Instructor* (1715–18)
1717	57	368	*Memoirs of the Church of Scotland*
1719	59	412, 417, 436	*Robinson Crusoe* and sequels (1719–20)
1720	60	432	*Life and Adventures of Mr. Duncan Campbell*
		434	*Memoirs of a Cavalier*
		435	*Captain Singleton*

Year	Age	Moore no.	Short Title
1722	62	446	*Moll Flanders*
		448	*Religious Courtship*
		449	*A Journal of the Plague Year*
		452	*Colonel Jack*
1724	64	456	*The Fortunate Mistress* [*Roxana*]
		459–461	*A Tour thro' Great Britain* (1724–6)
		468	*The History of the Remarkable Life of Jack Sheppard*
		469	*A New Voyage Round the World*
1725	65	472	*Every-body's Business, is No-body's Business*
		475	*The Complete English Tradesman* (1725–7)
1726	66	480	*The Political History of the Devil*
		487	*A System of Magick*
1727	67	489	*Conjugal Lewdness*
		494	*An Essay on the History and Reality of Apparitions*
1728	68	499	*A Plan of the English Commerce*
		500	*The Memoirs of an English Officer*
1704–13	—	522	*The Review*
1720–6	—	542	*Applebee's Weekly Journal*

Bibliography

Materials are arranged under three headings. The first section comprises the few studies undertaken on the British reception of Defoe. The second contains items on translations and adaptations, *Robinsonades*, foreign influence, etc. Finally I have listed ancillary aids of various kinds.

I

Burch, C. E., 'British Criticism of Defoe as a Novelist 1719–1860', *Englische Studien*, lxvii (1932), 178–98: very useful in assembling references, though sometimes confused and imperceptive in the linking commentary.

'Defoe's British Reputation 1869–94', *Englische Studien*, lxviii (1934), 410–23.

'Notes on the Contemporary Popularity of Defoe's *Review*', *Philological Quarterly*, xvi (1937), 210–13: argues that there is clear evidence that the *Review* had wide influence, although circulation figures are lacking.

Watt, I., 'The Recent Critical Fortunes of *Moll Flanders*', *Eighteenth Century Studies*, i (1967), 109–26.

II

Deneke, O., *Robinson Crusoe in Deutschland 1720–80* (Göttingen, 1934).

Gove, P. B., *The Imaginary Voyage in Prose Fiction* (1961). A new edition of a work first published in 1941; pp. 122–54 supply the fullest modern account of the vogue for voyages on the model of *Crusoe*.

Hettner, Hermann J. T., *Robinson und die Robinsonaden* (Berlin, 1854). A short pioneering monograph.

Kippenberg, August, *Robinson in Deutschland 1731–43* (Hanover, 1892). Lists the early German editions.

Mann, W. E., *Robinson Crusoé en France* (Paris, 1916). A workmanlike survey.

Nourrisson, Paul, *Jean-Jacques Rousseau et Robinson Crusoé* (Paris, 1931). Chiefly a study of the idea of solitude in Rousseau's life and work.

Staverman, W. H., *Robinson Crusoe in Nederland* (Groningen, 1907). Lists early Dutch editions.

Ulrich, Hermann, *Robinson und Robinsonaden* (Weimar, 1898). Remains the most extensive bibliography of the subject.

III

Foxon, D. F., 'Defoe: A Specimen of a Catalogue of English Verse, 1701–1750', *The Library*, xx (1965), 277–97. Invaluable for its listing of early editions of Defoe's poems.

Moore, J. R., *A Checklist of the Writings of Daniel Defoe* (Bloomington, 1960). Not impeccable but a remarkable compilation, and an indispensable guide through the tangled thicket of Defoe's writings.

Morgan, W. T., *A Bibliography of British History 1700–15* (Bloomington, 1934–42). Useful in the identification of contemporary attacks.

Nangle, B. C., *The Monthly Review: 1st Series* (Oxford, 1934).

The Monthly Review: 2nd Series (Oxford, 1955). Provides an index of articles and contributors.

Index

Materials are listed as follows: I. Books and pamphlets by Defoe (for a chronological list, see pp. 220–1); II. Reviewers and critics cited; III. Journals cited; IV. Names (a selective list, including writers used as a comparison or touchstone in assessing Defoe).

I. BOOKS AND PAMPHLETS BY DEFOE

II. REVIEWERS AND CRITICS

III. JOURNALS